SOCRATES IN THE *APOLOGY*

SOCRATES IN THE *APOLOGY*

AN
ESSAY
ON PLATO'S
APOLOGY
OF SOCRATES

———

C. D. C. REEVE

HACKETT PUBLISHING COMPANY
INDIANAPOLIS/CAMBRIDGE

7466

For further information, please address
Hackett Publishing Company
P.O. Box 44937
Indianapolis, Indiana 46204

The paper used in this publication
meets the minimum requirements of
American National Standard for Information Sciences—
Permanence of Paper for Printed Library Materials,
ANSI Z39.48-1984.

∞

95 94 93 92 91 90   1 2 3 4 5 6 7 8 9 10

Library of Congress Cataloging-in-Publication Data
Reeve, C. D. C., 1948–
Socrates in the Apology :
an essay on Plato's Apology of Socrates /
C. D. C. Reeve.   p.   cm.
Bibliography: p.   Includes indexes.
ISBN 0-87220-089-2 (Alk. paper)

1. Plato.   Apology.
2. Socrates—Trials, litigation, etc.
I. Title.
B365.R44 1989   89-33069   184—dc20   CIP

The interior and cover design
of this book
adapted by Dan Kirklin
from the original designs
by Meg Davis
for the interior and cover of
Philosopher-Kings
The Argument of Plato's
Republic
by C. D. C. Reeve

The quotation on page vi is from *A Bend in the River*, by V. S. Naipaul, reprinted by permission of Alfred A. Knopf, Inc., New York.

The quotation on page 108 is from *The Autobiography of William Butler Yeats*, reprinted by permission of The Macmillan Company, New York.

For
Alison, Catherine, and John

The world is what it is; men who are nothing, who allow themselves to become nothing, have no place in it.

V. S. NAIPAUL

CONTENTS

CONTENTS

INTRODUCTION

No one can conceive fairly the character of Sokratēs who does not enter into the spirit of that impressive discourse [the *Apology*].   —GROTE

The first aim of this essay is to give a detailed interpretation of Plato's *Apology*, available to readers with different backgrounds and interests, which confronts and attempts to solve the multitude of problems, both analytical and historical, this deceptively simple text raises. The second aim, parasitic on the first, is to reach an understanding of Socrates himself as he appears in the *Apology*.

While it is unnecessary to dilate on the first aim, it does merit brief elaboration. Like the Gospels, the *Apology* is part of our common culture. Like the Gospels, it suffers—if that is the right word—from having as its chief protagonist a world-historical figure about whom almost everyone has views and feelings. Like the Gospels, it is part of a larger whole—Plato's Socratic dialogues[1]—in relation to which it is inevitably seen and understood. Like the Gospels, it is an interdisciplinary text studied, sometimes in proprietary fashion, by classicists, philosophers, historians, literary scholars, and students of law, politics, and religion. A writer on the *Apology* is necessarily involved, as a result, in a complex dialectic with the *Apology* itself, with the Socratic dialogues, and with their many and various interpreters.

To keep this dialectic within manageable limits, I have tried as far as possible to treat the *Apology* as a self-contained work, drawing on the other dialogues and other ancient writings about Socrates for the ancillary purposes of corroborating an interpretation, filling out the details of a doctrine, or solving a puzzle otherwise intractable. In developing my own argument, I have necessarily confronted a representative sample of the most compelling variant interpretations. But I have not attempted

---

1. The roster of Socratic dialogues—or dialogues thought to reflect the views of the historical Socrates—currently accepted by most authorities is (in alphabetical order) as follows: *Apology, Charmides, Crito, Euthydemus, Euthyphro, Gorgias, Hippias Major, Hippias Minor, Ion, Laches, Lysis, Menexenus, Protagoras,* and *Republic 1*. Guthrie (1975, 39-66) is a sensible and succinct review of the issues.

to survey the immense and often frustrating secondary literature on Socrates or on the *Apology* proper. To have done so would have resulted in a longer book but not, I am persuaded, a better or more useful one.

I turn now to my second aim.

Six problems in particular vex the student of Plato's Socrates: the problem of the elenchus (Socrates' characteristic method of inquiry and refutation), the problem of Socratic ignorance (or Socratic knowledge), the problem of Socratic virtue (*aretē*),[2] the problem of Socratic teaching, the problem of Socratic politics, and the problem of Socratic irony. Accounts of Socrates can often be categorized and individuated by reference to these problems and their putative solutions.

Socrates presents himself in the *Apology* as someone who questions others about virtue and who examines or refutes them by means of an elenchus when they have answered inadequately. He also presents himself, however, as the servant of Apollo, as someone whose divinely inspired mission is not simply to refute people but to get them to care about virtue and their psyches—their souls—above everything else. The problem is to reconcile the mission with the means of executing it. Why does Socrates think that showing someone that he cannot defend his views about virtue against the elenchus is a way of getting him to care for his psyche? Why does he think that a gadfly can be an apostle of Delphi? This is the problem of the elenchus.

In addition to presenting himself as the elenchus-wielding servant of Apollo, Socrates also makes the disclaimer traditionally captured in the slogan "Socrates knows only that he knows nothing." He makes a number of other specific claims, however, which strongly suggest that he must indeed know what he claims not to know. Prominent among these—though more so in the other Socratic dialogues than in the *Apology* itself—are the infamous paradoxes of Socratic ethics: virtue is knowledge; akrasia (weakness of will) is impossible; no one is voluntarily vicious. What is it that Socrates does not know, then? What is it

2. If something is a knife (say) or a man, its *aretē* as a knife or a man is that state or property of it that makes it a good knife or a good man. See *Chrm.* 161a8-9; *Euthphr.* 6d9-e1; *Grg.* 506d2-4; *Prt.* 332b4-6; *R.* 353d9-354a2. The *aretē* of a knife might include having a sharp blade; the *aretē* of a man might include being intelligent, well-born, just, or courageous. *Aretē* is thus broader than our notion of moral virtue. It applies to things (such as knives) which are not moral agents. And it applies to aspects of moral agents (such as intelligence or family status) which are not normally considered to be moral aspects of them. For these reasons it is sometimes more appropriate to render *aretē* as 'excellence'. But 'virtue' remains the most favoured translation. And once these few facts are borne in mind it should seldom mislead.

that he does know? This is the two-sided problem of Socratic ignorance.

The problem of ignorance is sharpened by the Socratic paradoxes. For if Socrates' disclaimer of knowledge is sincere and if knowledge is even necessary for virtue, Socrates must lack both knowledge and virtue. Yet he seems to be virtuous and to present himself as such. This is the problem of Socratic virtue.

Socrates is often characterized as one of the greatest teachers the world has seen. Yet he denies that he is a teacher, and he makes that denial part of his defense against the charge that he has corrupted the youth. The resultant dilemma is the problem of Socratic teaching.

If knowledge of the sort that enables someone to withstand elenctic examination is necessary for virtue, it seems that virtue will be the prerogative of the few. If only the virtuous rule or govern well, it seems that government ought to be in the hands of the knowledgeable few, rather than in those of the ignorant many. This sounds antidemocratic. But it is antidemocratic only if possession of that knowledge is envisaged as a real possibility—as, of course, it would be if Socrates himself possessed and taught it. The problems of Socratic knowledge, virtue, and teaching are central, then, to the problem of Socratic politics. But they are also central to the assessment of Socrates' defense against Meletus' charges; for many believe that the latter resulted from suspicion of Socrates as the teacher of the notorious enemies of Athenian democracy, Alcibiades and Critias.

The final element in the constellation of problems surrounding Socrates is Socratic irony. Many have argued that, if Socrates' disclaimers of knowledge and teaching are to be consistent with his possession of the knowledge he disclaims and with his elenctic activities, they must be ironical. The problem is to find a plausible role for irony in Socrates' elenctic, psyche-improving mission. That is difficult enough. But the difficulties do not end there; for these Socratic disclaimers are not restricted to the elenctic situation; they are also key components of his defense against Meletus. If we resort to irony to solve the problems of Socratic ignorance and teaching, we must, therefore, find a plausible role for irony in that defense.

The *Apology* raises all of these problems, and many others as well. But because of its peculiar nature it also suggests ways in which they might be profitably tackled, and—or so I shall argue—persuasively solved.

In most of the other Socratic dialogues, it is Socrates' interlocutors who are caught in the harsh light of the elenchus. Their beliefs, especially their ethical beliefs, are submitted to scrutiny; the level of their understanding of them, and of their self-understanding, is plumbed, while about himself and his own beliefs Socrates is mostly silent. In the

Apology, by contrast, Socrates is trying to characterize himself, to explain the distinctive nature of his brand of wisdom, and to justify his *modus operandi*. This is how he understands himself and his activities. This is his self-interpretation—the richest single self-portrait that we have. Moreover, the *Apology* presents Socrates in a social and historical context about which we have considerable independent knowledge. And that knowledge—whether about Athenian law, or the Delphic oracle, or Greek religion, or the political situation in Athens in 399—gives us a kind of handle on him which we would otherwise lack. It is this potent combination of detailed self-portrait and historical context which makes the *Apology* such a fertile source of insight into Socrates.

Let me briefly indicate what we shall discover. The goal of elenctic examination is to persuade people to care for virtue more than for wealth and other conventional goods, in part by showing them that they already believe that virtue is more valuable than any of these things. Even if virtue is not, in fact, more valuable, however, elenctic examination nonetheless improves the psyches of those repeatedly subjected to it by saving them from the hubris—the "most blameworthy ignorance"—of thinking they have expert craft-knowledge of virtue when they do not. Elenctic examination constitutes service to Apollo because, in disabusing people of their hubris, it brings about something he particularly values, namely, human recognition of human limitations.

Socrates knows—or claims to know—many things, including things about the virtues, including what they are, and some of the things he claims to know are established by arguments he uses in elenctic examination. But his disclaimer of knowledge applies only to the expert craft-knowledge of virtue, which is identical to the craft of politics, and this he genuinely lacks. Indeed, he thinks that such knowledge is almost certainly beyond the reach of anyone except the gods.

Socrates thinks that this expert knowledge is identical to virtue. It follows that he is not virtuous. But he never claims he is virtuous. Instead he claims that, having tried as far as he can to avoid the blameworthy ignorance of thinking he knows when he does not, he is not voluntarily (or culpably) vicious. Given the prevalence of hubris, this makes Socrates one of the most virtuous (or most nearly virtuous) of people.

The beliefs drawn upon by Socrates in elenctic examination are those of his interlocutor. The beliefs he draws out are already (implicitly) there. He imparts nothing of his own. This is what renders his disclaimer of teaching credible. Moreover, what he draws upon is not something technical or intellectually outré, but rather something widely acceptable. That, in essence, is why Socrates is willing to question almost anyone, not just the intellectually gifted few. That is why he thinks that the examined life is for all human beings. Socrates' elenctic mission to Athens, his elenctic philosophizing, is in one important sense, then, profoundly and fundamentally democratic.

Because Socrates' disclaimers of knowledge are true, because his virtue (or absence of voluntary vice) is compatible with his nonpossession of the knowledge necessary for virtue, because his disclaimer of teaching is credible, there is no fundamental irony in his disclaimers. Conventional wisdom notwithstanding, Socrates mostly means just what he says.

What is true of Socrates in these matters is equally true of him when he is on trial for his life. His defense is reasonable, intelligibly motivated, nonevasive, and seriously or nonironically tendered. It establishes that he is innocent of the legal charges brought against him. It is a defense appropriate to a man whose most basic characterization of himself is as a philosopher servant of Apollo; a man whose devotion to the gods is founded not in unquestioning religious faith, but in elenctic philosophy, in human wisdom.

Students of Socrates will recognize some familiar themes in this brief thumbnail sketch, but also some new ones and a new way of orchestrating them.

Socrates is a historical figure. His trial is a historical event. But is the *Apology* a historical document? Did the historical Socrates really say what it presents him as saying at his trial in 399? I know of no fully satisfactory answer, and I offer none (although much of what I argue is certainly relevant to the issue). My interest is in Plato's Socrates and in the things he says, whether they are fact, fiction, or—as is perhaps most likely—something in between. I have often found it convenient, nonetheless, to treat what Socrates says as history rather than fiction and to raise the kinds of questions about it more appropriate to the former than the latter. I doubt that this will cause confusion or that it will seriously compromise what amounts on my part to agnosticism rather than skepticism on the so-called Socratic problem.[3]

In keeping with my aim of reaching a fairly wide audience, I have not presupposed any knowledge of Greek. But interpretative questions sometimes—not often in this case—depend on issues of translation, so

---

3. The Socratic problem is discussed in Guthrie (1971a, 3-57); Lacey (1971); Vogel (1955). The historicity of the *Apology* is defended in Brickhouse and Smith (1988, 2-10).

that I have occasionally had to discuss the Greek text. A patient Greek-less reader should have little difficulty following these infrequent discussions.

For references to Plato's works, I have used the standard system of Stephanus page numbers and letters together with the line numbers of Burnet, *Platonis Opera* (for example, 18c1-3, 6d9-e6). Readers using a translation equipped with Stephanus page numbers will easily locate the appropriate passage. Abbreviated references to other ancient works, which are (with few exceptions) those adopted in the *Oxford Classical Dictionary*, are usually self-explanatory. Other references (for example, 1.8, 3.3) are internal.

I have drawn freely on the available translations of the ancient works I quote—West's *Apology* was particularly useful—emending and adapting them to suit my purposes.

I am grateful to Gregory Vlastos for helpful and encouraging comments and suggestions and for letting me see some of his unpublished papers (one of which in particular led me to rethink and substantially modify my views on Socratic religion); to the publisher's reader, Richard Kraut, whose sensitive queries provoked many improvements; to Walter Englert for help with Greek; to Don Rutherford and Peter Steinberger for useful written comments; to Carrie Swanson for assisting with proofreading and the Index Locorum; and, especially, to Neil Thomason, who has been helping me clarify my views on the *Apology* since I first committed them to paper in 1982. Recent work on Socrates by Terry Irwin, Richard Kraut, and Alexander Nehamas has often been the stimulus to fruitful thought, no less when I ended up disagreeing with it than when I found it congenial.

As I was putting the finishing touches to this essay, Thomas Brick-house and Nicholas Smith were kind enough to send me in page proof a copy of their own forthcoming book on the *Apology*. Many of their views were already familiar from earlier publications. But I was glad to have the chance to respond to their latest thoughts and to discover that, though our conceptions of Socrates were very different, we were, none-theless, sometimes allied on novel points of interpretation.

A Vollum Fellowship in 1986, generously supplemented by C. N. and M. R. Reeve, provided the leisure necessary for writing; the loving companionship of Alison provided the no less necessary peace of mind.

To all at Hackett, but especially to my editor Dan Kirklin, I offer my warmest thanks for their unfailing courtesy, efficiency, and solicitude.

Portland, Oregon
December, 1988

Abbreviations of Plato's Works

Ap.	*Apology*
Chrm.	*Charmides*
Crat.	*Cratylus*
Cri.	*Crito*
Euthd.	*Euthydemus*
Euthphr.	*Euthyphro*
Grg.	*Gorgias*
Hp. Ma.	*Hippias Major*
Hp. Mi.	*Hippias Minor*
La.	*Laches*
Lg.	*Laws*
Ly.	*Lysis*
Mx.	*Menexenus*
Men.	*Meno*
Phd.	*Phaedo*
Phdr.	*Phaedrus*
Plt.	*Politicus (Statesman)*
Prt.	*Protagoras*
R.	*Republic*
Smp.	*Symposium*
Tht.	*Theaetetus*

Disputed or Spurious Works

Alc. 1	*Alcibiades 1*
Alc. 2	*Alcibiades 2*
Amat.	*Amatores*
Cleit.	*Cleitophon*
Def.	*Definitions*
Hipparch.	*Hipparchus*
Thg.	*Theages*

SOCRATES IN THE *APOLOGY*

ONE

THE
FALSE
SOCRATES

What Socrates said meant something completely different.   —KIERKEGAARD

He always knew the way out; knew it yet would not tell it.   —EMERSON

The *Apology* is usually divided up in the following way: the *opening address* (17a1–18a6), in which Socrates distinguishes the kind of speech he plans to make from the one made by the prosecution; the *prothesis* (18a7–19a7), in which he outlines the plan of the defense; the *defense proper*, which consists of the defense against the popular caricature (19a8–24b2) and the defense against the formal charges brought by Meletus (24b3–28a1);[1] the *digression* (28a2–34b5), in which Socrates describes his divinely enjoined, philosophical mission to Athens; the *epilogue* (34b6–35d8), in which he returns to the rhetorical themes of the opening address; the *counterpenalty* (35e1–38b9), in which he proposes an alternative to the death penalty demanded by the prosecution; and, finally, the death penalty having been chosen by the jury, a *closing address* (38c1–42a5).

This standard division, though solidly based in the text, somewhat conceals a broader tripartite structure which needs emphasis. From the beginning of the opening address through the defense against the ancient caricature (17a1–24b2), Socrates' characterization of himself is largely negative: he is not what the ancient caricature makes him out to be, but something else. That is the first movement in his speech. The second movement, the defense against Meletus (24b3–28a1), is also negative. But, because it takes the form of an elenchus, it has a strong positive component as well. What it says is, "I am not guilty." But what it shows—and shows for the only time in the *Apology*—is Socrates as he normally is, engaged in rather than describing the activities which are his philosophical life, his service to Apollo. Then, in the digression, and continuing through the counterpenalty to the end of the closing address (28b3–42a5), Socrates' characterization itself becomes more positive: this is what he is really like; this is what the jurors should have in mind

---

1. Meletus and his fellow accuser, Anytus, are discussed in 2.3. About Lycon, the third accuser, nothing significant is known.

as they decide his guilt or innocence. The broader structure is reflected in my own discussion. The present chapter deals with the false Socrates of the prosecution and ancient caricature; the next with Meletus' charges; the third with the true Socrates. But positive and negative, true and false, being what they are, the false Socrates will, of course, tell us much about the true.

1.1 THE OPENING ADDRESS

Socrates introduces himself and his speech of defense with the following address to the jurors:

I do not know, men of Athens, how you have been affected by my accusers; for my part, I was almost carried away in spite of myself, they spoke so persuasively. Yet hardly anything they said is true. Of the many falsehoods they told, one most surprised me, when they said that you should take care not to be deceived by a clever [*deinou*] speaker like me. That they are not ashamed that they will immediately be refuted by what I do, when I show myself not to be a clever speaker at all, that I think is most shameless on their part—unless, of course, by a clever speaker they mean the one who speaks the truth. If this is what they are saying, then I would agree that I am an orator, but not one of their sort. These men, then, as I say, have said little or nothing that is true, while from me you will hear the whole truth, but not, by god, men of Athens, expressed in fine language embellished with choice phrases and words, like theirs, nor carefully arranged, but things spoken as I please in the words that come to me—for I put my trust in the justice of what I say— and let none of you expect anything else. Surely, it would not be fitting, men, for someone of my age to come before you making up stories like a youth. And, men of Athens, I do beg and beseech you: if you hear me making my defense in the same words that I am accustomed to use in the marketplace by the banker's tables, where many of you have heard me, and elsewhere, do not be surprised and create a disturbance [*thorubein*] because of this. For this is how it is: now, for the first time, I have come before a law court [*nun egō prōton epi dikastērion anabebēka*], at the age of seventy; the manner of speaking here is simply foreign to me [*atechnōs oun zenōs echō tēs enthade lexeōs*]. So just as if I were really a foreigner, you would certainly excuse me if I spoke in that dialect and manner to which I was accustomed, so too my present request seems a just one, that you pay no attention to my manner of speaking—whether it is better or worse—but concentrate your attention on whether what I say is just. For this is the excellence [*aretē*] of a judge, while that of an orator is to speak the truth. (17a1−18a6)

Is it an ironical address? Has Socrates come before the court clothed in the trope to which he has given his name—Socratic irony?[2] Is "something contrary to what is said to be understood?" (Quintilian, *Inst.* 9.22.44).

Two reasons have been given for returning an affirmative answer. First, Socrates denies that he is a clever speaker, but he is clearly a clever speaker: "The first level of irony in the *Apology* presents the apparent falsehood: Socrates disclaims ability to make a speech, and proceeds to make so able a speech that it is a masterpiece of rhetoric" (Allen 1980, 5−6). Second, Socrates disclaims "all knowledge of forensic diction" (Burnet 1924, 67). Yet the opening address itself suggests that he was familiar with the writings of the forensic orators. The topics it covers— the counteraccusation that the prosecutors are lying, the denial of being a clever speaker, the asking pardon for speaking in ordinary fashion, the plea of unfamiliarity with the law courts, the request for an impartial hearing, the deprecation of disturbance, the disclaiming of a style unsuited to an old man— "may be completely paralleled" from the speeches of the orators Lysias, Isocrates, and Aeschines (Riddell 1877, xx−xxi). The disclaimer of oratory, it is concluded, is "a piece of Socratic *eirōneia* [irony], and, like most disclaimers made by Socrates, to be taken *cum grano salis*" (Burnet 1924, 67).

Initially somewhat compelling, this reasoning trades on serious misperception. Socrates does not deny that "he has any skill in speaking," or that "he cannot make a speech." He does not deny that he is, in all senses of the word, a clever speaker. He is not the kind of "clever" (*deinon*) speaker his accusers have made him out to be, one who will use his quasi-magical rhetorical powers in order to make the weaker argument appear the stronger.[3] But if a clever speaker is one who speaks the

---

2. 'Irony' is defined in the *OED* as "dissimulation, pretence; especially in reference to the ignorance feigned by Socrates as a means of confuting an adversary." Unlike what we call irony, its Greek ancestor, *eirōneia*, involves an intention to deceive. When Thrasymachus says, "This is Socrates' habitual *eirōneia*" (*R.* 337a4−5), he is charging Socrates with lying, not with meaning the contrary of what he says. Vlastos (1987b) argues that Socratic irony is "complex" irony in which "what is said both is and isn't what is meant." Kierkegaard (1965) is a famous but idiosyncratic and unreliable discussion of Socratic irony.

3. *Deinon*, which has no exact English equivalent, often carries this connotation of trickery or magic. See Liddell and Scott (1966, s.v. *deinos*). The connection between rhetoric and magic is explored in Romilly (1975).

truth, he is quite willing to be called an excellent orator (17b4–6, 18a5–6). Socrates does not say either that he knows nothing about rhetoric or that he is unfamiliar with forensic diction:

> When he [Socrates] says *atechnōs oun zenōs echō tēs enthade lexeōs*, he is not being 'ironical', he merely means that he has never had occasion to speak in a law-court before, since he has never been a party to a case (this is clearly the meaning of *nun egō prōton epi dikastērion anabebēka* . . .): he does not mean that he has never been present at a trial, and knows nothing of the methods of courts and forensic oratory. (Hackforth 1933, 56)

Later, indeed, Socrates is explicit that he has "often [*pollakis*]" been present at the trials of others (35a4–7). The fact, therefore, that his opening address is similar in structure to speeches of the orators is insufficient to establish that it is ironical.

What Socrates actually says is that he will not make a speech like that of his accusers, "carefully arranged" and "embellished with choice phrases and words." Instead, he will extemporize, speaking as he pleases in the words that come to him and putting his trust in the truth and justice of what he says rather than in rhetorical niceties. This does not imply that Socrates will eschew rhetoric altogether (whatever that would mean) but only that the rhetoric he employs will be keyed to truth, justice, and rational persuasion rather than to gaining acquittal by swaying the emotions of the jurors in his favour. It does not imply either, and should not lead us to expect, that Socrates will deliver a haphazard or disorganized speech. He has had "experience of many arguments" (*Grg.* 457c4–5), after all, and is so used to defending himself in elenctic tussles, that there is a sense in which, as he puts it, he has spent his "whole life" preparing his legal defense (Xenophon, *Ap.* 3).

Does Socrates live up to what is in essence a promise that he will subordinate a rhetoric of nonrational persuasion to a rhetoric of truth-telling? Most writers are agreed that he does. Indeed, many argue that he goes so far in this direction that he purposely antagonizes and alienates the jury.[4] Three examples, in particular, are commonly cited. First, in his cross-examination of Meletus, Socrates seems to imply that he

---

4. Xenophon traces the *megalēgoria*, the antagonizing big talk or boastfulness, which in his view characterized Socrates' defense, to a desire for death as a release from old age (*Ap.* 1–2). Epictetus (*Discourses*, ii.2.18) advises a defendant not to assert that he will abstain from begging for mercy "unless like Socrates he intends to provoke the judges." Cf. Grote (1888, 7: 157–163). Brickhouse and Smith (1988, 37–47, 210–214) are among the few dissenters.

alone makes the youth better while "the many [*hoi de polloi*] . . . corrupt them" (25a12−b7). This implication seems to combine insult and arrogance in a way likely to alienate. Second, Socrates seems to insult the jury again by telling them that "no one will preserve his life if he genuinely opposes you or any other multitude and prevents the occurrence in the polis of many unjust and illegal things" (31e2−4). Finally, having been found guilty, Socrates seems to offer what many take to be his most serious provocation to the jury, first, by proposing that he deserves a great civic honour, namely, free meals in the prytaneum, and then by proposing a ridiculous fine. When we examine these examples more carefully, we shall see that they provide little support for the view that Socrates is arrogant, boastful, or intentionally alienating—a view Socrates himself explicitly warns against (37a2−5). The fact that they are so frequently cited to support it, however, is compelling evidence of just how successful Socrates has been in fulfilling his promise to subordinate persuasion to telling the truth. His speech is "a masterpiece of rhetoric." But it is not a masterpiece of the rhetoric he disclaims.

Also important in this regard and serving to moderate the extreme view that Socrates engages in alienation or counterpersuasion are the striking parallels, down to specific similarities of phrase, between the *Apology* and Gorgias' *Defense of Palamedes*.[5] Socrates and Palamedes both cite their modest means as proof of their sincerity (*Ap.* 31c2−3; *Pal.* 15). Both argue that the charges they face are not only false but contradictory (*Ap.* 27a1−7; *Pal.* 25−26). Both raise the question of what advantage they would have gained by committing the crime alleged against them (*Ap.* 25d8−26a6; *Pal.* 13). Both reject appeals to pity and claim to rest their case on truth and justice (*Ap.* 34b6−35d8; *Pal.* 33). Both claim to be the benefactors of their judges (*Ap.* 30c2−31a7; *Pal.* 30). Both claim to find death preferable to dishonour (*Ap.* 28b3−9; *Pal.* 35). Both urge the jury not to hurry what old age will soon accomplish (*Ap.* 38c5−8; *Pal.* 34−35). Both contrast actions with words (*Ap.* 32a4−5; *Pal.* 34). Both mention that the jury will be guilty of condemning an innocent man and will be themselves condemned eventually (*Ap.* 38c1−4; *Pal.*

5. Diels and Krantz (1952, 2: B11a); Freeman (1977, 134−138). The suggestion of Brickhouse and Smith (1988, 50 n. 7) that these parallels are due simply to the fact that Socrates is "a highly intelligent and educated man . . . seriously seeking acquittal" and that *Pal.* is a collection of stock rhetorical devices for achieving that goal does not survive confrontation with the evidence which follows. See Coulter (1964). Guthrie (1975, 76−77) provides some necessary correctives to Coulter's conclusions. Gorgias' views are discussed in Guthrie (1971b) and Kerferd (1981).

36). Socrates says that "the unexamined life is not worth living for a human being" (*Ap.* 38a5−6); Palamades says that "a life without trust is not worth living" (*Pal.* 21). Towards the end of his speech (41a8−b5), Socrates explicitly compares himself to Palamades, as he does, indeed, in Xenophon's *Apology* (26).

The precise purpose of these seemingly intentional parallels is difficult, if not now impossible, to judge. Perhaps, as some have argued, Socrates (or Plato) is borrowing from Gorgias in order to set up an implicit contrast between Gorgianic rhetoric, which aims "to stir passions, and thereby to deceive," with Socratic rhetoric, which aims primarily at truth (Romilly 1975, 25). But, whether intentional or not, these parallels with a speech whose entire purpose is persuasion are good evidence that the subordination of persuasion to truth-telling in Socrates' speech is subordination only and not the abandonment of persuasion altogether. Socrates aims to persuade the jury of his innocence, as we shall see, but he is not willing to do so at the expense of truth, justice, or his own deepest convictions.

In addition to saying that he will subordinate a rhetoric of persuasion to a rhetoric of truth, Socrates also says that he will speak "in the same words that I am accustomed to use in the marketplace by the banker's tables, where many of you have heard me," and he requests the jurors not to create a disturbance at this. Now, if he were here predicting demotic, or marketplace, Greek, we might conceivably convict him of some very minor ironical dissimulation. For his diction is, to some degree at least, "periodic and marked by the neatly balanced antitheses of Greek rhetorical style" (Allen 1980, 5). But this is not what he means. What Socrates is referring to, while it may well include other aspects of his normal way of talking, is primarily elenctic examination and the characteristic and provocative doctrines which are part and parcel of it.[6] He makes this clear by his explicit references back to his initial request. The first of these occurs just as he is about to use the elenchus to catch Meletus in a contradiction:

> I think he contradicts himself in his writ, as if he said, "Socrates does injustice by not believing in the gods and believing in the gods." . . . Examine with me, men, how he seems to me to say

6. Noticed by Grube (1975, 28 n. 6). Another feature of Socrates' accustomed manner of speaking is the use of craft analogies (20a6−b6, 25a12−c4): "But you see, Socrates, explained Critias, you will have to avoid your favourite topic—the cobblers, builders, and metal-workers; for it is already worn to rags by you in my opinion" (Xenophon, *Mem.* I.ii.37). As Irwin (1977, 71−77) shows, however, these analogies, too, are elenctic baggage.

8

this. But you others, as I begged of you from the beginning, remember not to make a disturbance [*thorubein*] if I speak in the manner to which I am accustomed. (27a4−b2)

The second prefaces an appeal to his characteristic doctrine—his paradigm "unacceptable proposition" (1.8)—that it is better to suffer injustice than to do it:

Do not make a disturbance, men of Athens, but abide by what I begged of you, not to create a disturbance at the things I say [*mē thorubein eph' hois an legō*], but to listen. For I think you will be benefited by listening. I am going to tell you other things at which you will perhaps cry out. By no means do this. (30c2−6)

And, indeed, elenctic examination *is* Socrates' accustomed way of speaking. It is the way they have all heard him speak in the agora. Unlike demotic, which must have sounded often in an Athenian court, it was sufficiently unusual in court proceedings to merit special advance mention: "The nearest approach to cross-examination [in Athenian law] was the questions addressed by a litigant to his opponent, but here again the extant orations furnish no such examples as Socrates' examination of Meletus" (Bonner and Smith 1938, 2: 297). Socrates is not ironically promising demotic, then; he is nonironically promising that he will use the elenchus and express the views which are a characteristic part of it.

There is no doubt some innocent irony in Socrates' remark that he was almost swept away by the eloquence of his accusers. But there is no fundamental irony in his opening speech, no reason to think that from the very outset an ironical tone has been established. There may, of course, be some fundamental irony later. But nothing in Socrates' opening remarks should lead us to expect it at every turn.

1.2 THE DEFENSE AGAINST THE POPULAR CARICATURE

In the Prothesis (18a7−19a7), Socrates outlines the plan of his defense. He distinguishes Meletus' new formal charges from a long-lived popular caricature of himself which is likely to have prejudiced the jury. He thinks that Meletus has relied on the existence of this prejudicial caricature in bringing his charges (19b1−2) and that without it the charges would not be difficult to refute (28a2−4). Consequently, he makes the caricature his first target. He knows it will not be easy to undermine. Its originators, unlike Meletus, are not there to be "examined [*elegxai*]" (18d2−7); prejudice long ingrained is not easily overcome (18e5−19a7, 24a1−4, 28a6−8). But if he is right in thinking that prejudice is the major obstacle to acquittal—and that is something we shall investigate in 2.3—his strategy is a sound and reasonable one.

The popular caricature portrays Socrates as a generic intellectual (23d4−7), a heady mixture of natural scientist and forensic orator, "who thinks about things in the sky, who has investigated everything concerning what is beneath the earth, who makes the weaker speech the stronger" (19b4−c1). This reputation is prejudicial because such advanced thinkers are widely believed to be atheists: "Those, men of Athens, who have spread this report are my dangerous accusers; for their hearers believe that investigators of these things do not believe in gods [*oude theous nomizein*]" (18c1−3).[7] And atheism, as we shall see in 2.1, is precisely the burden of Meletus' indictment. Atheism is the thread, therefore, which links the new formal charges Socrates faces to the ancient slanders against him.

Socrates treats this ancient caricature as consisting of essentially two separate charges, that he is a professor and teacher of oratory and natural science and that he is a fee-earning sophist teacher of virtue (19d8−20c3).[8] And he responds to these charges in quite different ways. He dismisses the first in under twenty lines (19a8−d7). The Socrates presented in Aristophanes' *Clouds* professes science and oratory. But Socrates himself has "no share" in such activities. And the majority of the five hundred jurors[9] who have listened to him regularly in the agora—perhaps for as long as thirty years (1.4)—can witness on his behalf that they have never heard him "discoursing [*dialegomenou*] on such things either much or little" (19c7−d7; 1.3). Clearly, then, Socrates does not believe that the jury will, on reflection, find it credible that he is an orator and a scientist. The second charge, on the other hand, requires extended treatment (19d8−24b2); for though Socrates never discourses on natural science or oratory, he talks about virtue every day of his life (29d2−30b4, 38a1−6). This gives at least superficial plausibility to the charge that he is a sophist teacher of virtue (19d8−20c3). Consequently, he tries to explain how his wisdom differs from that of Gorgias and the other sophists and how, despite the fact that he knows nothing

7. In Aristophanes, *Clouds*, 1506−1509, Strepsiades urges that Socrates and Chaerephon should be burned to death "mostly because they have blasphemed the gods."

8. Guthrie (1971b) and Kerferd (1981) are sensible contemporary treatments of the sophists. Grote (1888, 7: 1−80) is a celebrated account still very much worth reading.

9. See Burnet (1924, 150−151).

of the things they claim to know (20c1−3), his wisdom got confused with theirs (20c4−24b2).[10]

Socrates attributes the popular misperception of him as a sophist teacher of virtue to his possession of "a certain kind of wisdom" (20d6−7), which he calls "human wisdom [anthōpinē sophia]" (20d8). And he claims that Apollo no less will testify on his behalf to its "existence and nature" (20e6−8). Apollo's testimony is the famous Delphic oracle to Chaerephon, discussed in 1.4−5 and 1.10.

As a result of this oracle, Socrates began a search for someone wiser than himself. And because politicians have "the best reputations for wisdom" (22a5−6), his first candidate was drawn from their ranks:

> So I thoroughly examined this man—there is no need for me to name him, but he was one of our politicians—and when I examined him, men of Athens, and engaged him in conversation, my experience was something like this: I came to believe that this man seemed to be wise to many people and most of all to himself, but that he was not. And then I tried to show him that though he supposed himself wise, he was not. On account of this he came to hate me, as did many of those present. So I went away and thought to myself: "I am wiser than this person. It looks as though neither of us knows anything fine and good [kalon kagathon], but he thinks he knows something when he does not know it, while I, just as I do not know, do not think that I know. So it is likely that in just this one little thing I am wiser than he is, that what I do not know, I do not suppose that I know." (21c3−d7)

Thus began a systematic examination of all those with a reputation as wise men (21e3−4).

Having examined the politicians, Socrates turned to the poets, the traditional teachers of ethical values,[11] and questioned them about their poems:

10. Part of Socrates' explanation is that people listening to him thought that "I myself am wise in the things about which I refute someone else" (23a1−5). But these things consist exclusively in beliefs about the virtues (21b7−22e5, 29d2−30b4, 38a1−6), never in beliefs about oratory or science (19c7−d7). This is further proof that Socrates' account of the aetiology of his reputation as a sophist teacher of virtue is not intended to apply to his reputation as a natural scientist and orator. At 23d1−9, Socrates describes the route by which his accusers (and the groups they represent) brought science and oratory back into the picture.

11. See Beck (1964, 72−141).

I took up those poems of theirs which it seemed to me they had worked on most, and I examined them on what they said [*ti legoien*], so that I might also learn something from them at the same time. (22b2—5)

But they were no better able to answer his questions than their non-specialist audience: "They say many fine things, but they know nothing of what they speak" (22c2—3). Because of their poetic abilities, however, the poets supposed that "they were the wisest of people in the other things also, in which they were not wise" (22c5—6).

Finally, Socrates went to the craftsmen, whose reputation for wisdom is inferior to that of the poets and politicians. And among them he at last found some genuine knowledge and wisdom:

Finally, I went to the craftsmen, for I was aware that I knew practically nothing, and I knew that I would find that they knew many fine things. In this I was not mistaken; they knew things that I did not know, and in that way they were wiser than I. But, men of Athens, the good craftsmen also seemed to me to make the same mistake as the poets: each of them, because he performed his craft well, thought himself wisest in the other things, the most important things [*talla ta megista*], and this error of theirs seemed to overshadow the wisdom they had. So I asked myself, on behalf of the oracle, whether I would prefer to be as I am, being in no way wise in their wisdom nor ignorant in their ignorance. I answered myself and the oracle that it profits me to be as I am. (22c9—e5)

The craftsmen possess more of one kind of wisdom than Socrates does. But he is wiser than they are, because he possesses more of another more important kind of wisdom (22e4—5).[12]

In each case, then, the same pattern emerges. On the one hand, there is a kind of knowledge or wisdom that the politicians, poets, and craftsmen falsely believe they possess and that Socrates is aware he lacks—knowledge that is fine and good, knowledge that would make its possessor the wisest of men, knowledge of the most important things. On the other hand, there is the human wisdom Socrates possesses and the others lack precisely because of that awareness. The natures of these two kinds of knowledge will occupy us in 1.6—8, 3.4, and 3.9.

12. The fact that Socrates says that the craftsmen were wiser than him in regard to their crafts suggests that he was not, as some scholars believe, trained in the craft of stonecarving by his father. See Zeller (1885, 55—56 n. 1). Cf. Burnet (1924, 50—51).

It is in this distinction between significant knowledge of the most important things and human wisdom that Socrates finds the key to the oracle's message and the explanation of the false caricature of him as a generic intellectual:

> It looks as though, gentlemen, it is really the god who is wise, and in this oracle he is saying that human wisdom [hē anthrōpinē sophia] is worth little or nothing. In speaking of Socrates here before you and in making use of my name, he appears to be taking me as an example, as if to say, "That one of you, humans, is wisest who, like Socrates, knows that in truth he is worth nothing in regard to wisdom." (23a5–b4; cf. Hp. Ma. 289b3–7)

Socrates now sees that the import of the oracle is quite general, that he is simply an example used by Delphi to illustrate a general deflationary view of the wisdom of which human beings are capable. Real human wisdom involves seeing that one does not possess any significant knowledge of the most important things, that in all probability such knowledge belongs only to the god. Because Socrates sees this and is innocent of the hubris of the politicians, poets, and craftsmen, he is wisest. We shall discover why in 1.7.

The distinction between human wisdom and significant knowledge of the most important things was lost on the majority of people, however, who, seeing Socrates refute the views of others on these things, concluded that he possessed the knowledge he showed others to lack (23a1–5). Hence he came to have a reputation for knowing precisely the things that the god had attested he was wise for recognizing he did not know at all.

Having reached this conclusion about the probable meaning of the oracle (21e4–22a1) through his examination of the politicians, poets, and craftsmen, Socrates came to see in it a divine injunction to extend his examinations beyond the initial group of those traditionally thought to be wise:

> So even now I still go around investigating according to the god, searching out anyone, citizen or stranger, I think wise. And whenever someone does not seem so to me, I come to the god's aid and show that he is not wise. And because of this occupation, I have had no leisure worth speaking of to do any of the things concerning the polis or any of my own private things; instead I live in great poverty because of my service to the god. (23b4–c1)

This is clearly a distinct phase in Socrates' elenctic activities.

13

Both phases, however, had unhappy consequences. Examining those with a reputation for wisdom made Socrates a hated and unpopular man (22e6–23a3). For the men he himself showed to lack knowledge came to hate him, as did many of the bystanders (21d1). More catholic examination led to his being on trial for his life:

> The young men who follow me of their own accord—those who have most leisure, the sons of the wealthiest—enjoy hearing people being examined; they themselves often imitate me and try to examine others. I think they find plenty of people who think they know something, but in fact know little or nothing. The result is that those whom they question are angry, not with them but with me. They say, this Socrates is a most polluted fellow [*miarotatos*][13] who corrupts the youth. If one asks them, however, what he does or what he teaches to corrupt them, they are silent, because they do not know, but, so as not to appear at a loss, they mention those things that are available against all philosophers, about "astronomy and things beneath the earth," and "not believing in the gods," and "making the weaker argument the stronger." For I do not think that they would be willing to tell the truth, that it is clear that they pretend to know, but know nothing. (23c2–d9)

Meletus, Anytus, and Lycon represent people of this sort, "Meletus being angry on behalf of the poets, Anytus on behalf of the politicians and craftsmen, and Lycon on behalf of the orators" (23e4–24a1).

Thus, as Socrates represents the matter—and this will be of some importance in 2.3—it is anger at the humiliation inflicted by his young imitators that motivated Meletus, Anytus, and Lycon to prosecute him for corruption, and it is their inability to specify the precise nature of the corruption that has led them to the charge, available against all philosophers, of "not believing in the gods."

1.3 SOCRATES' DISCLAIMER OF SCIENCE AND ORATORY

As part of his defense against the prejudicial caricature of himself as a generic intellectual, Socrates disclaims any share in the kind of knowledge of science and forensic oratory attributed to him in *Clouds*. We must now try to determine what this disclaimer amounts to and whether or not it is credible.

---

13. The significance of this characterization is discussed in 2.2 n. 35.

Despite the claims of some scholars to the contrary,[14] Socrates cannot be denying, whether ironically or otherwise, that he is acquainted with the advanced scientific views of others. For later in the *Apology* he shows himself familiar with the views of Anaxagoras and suggests that they are common knowledge:

> My dear Meletus, do you think that you are prosecuting Anaxagoras? And do you so much despise these men here and think that they are so ignorant of letters, that they do not know that the books of Anaxagoras are full of such theories ["that the sun is a stone and the moon earth"], and that the young men learn from me what they can sometimes buy for at most a drachma in the orchestra, and that they won't ridicule Socrates if he claims such views to be his own, especially as they are so strange? (26d6–e2)

Nor is there any reason to think that Socrates is denying that he knows the kinds of astronomical facts, of the sort familiar to mariners, farmers, or laymen, in which no one sees any harm. The point at issue—as the phrase "if he claims such views to be his own" (26e1–2) makes clear—is whether he is himself a scientist and teacher of science, whether he claims personal authority in scientific matters and professes the sorts of arcane views about things in the sky and beneath the earth that earn one the reputation of being an advanced atheistical thinker. And what is true of science is also true of oratory. Socrates is well acquainted with the work of the orators and never denies that he is. But, unlike his namesake in *Clouds*, he is not a self-proclaimed professor of oratory.

Is there any reason to think that Socrates' disclaimer of science and oratory, understood in *this* way, is insincere or knowingly false? Three pieces of evidence are particularly relevant here: the so-called "autobiographical" section of the *Phaedo*,[15] which bears specifically on science; Xenophon's *Memorabilia*; and *Clouds*, which bears on both science and oratory.

In the *Phaedo* (96a6–99d2), Socrates claims that when he was young "he was remarkably keen on the kind of wisdom known as natural

14. See Burnet (1924, 82). Hackforth (1933, 146–154) is critical.

15. Few scholars would now include the *Phaedo* among the Socratic dialogues or would expect to find consistency of doctrine between it and the *Apology*. But the section in question, like the famous death scene (117a4–118a17), is sometimes thought to have a better claim to being about the historical Socrates than the rest of the dialogue. See Guthrie (1971a, 101–105); Lacey (1971, 43–44). Gill (1973) is an important discussion of the historicity of the death scene.

science" (96a6−8). Far from leading him to develop *outré* physical theories of his own, however, that interest led him to skepticism:

> I finally judged myself to have absolutely no gift for this kind of inquiry. I'll tell you a good enough sign of this: there had been things that I previously did know for sure, at least I and others thought we knew them; yet I was then so utterly blinded by this kind of inquiry, that I unlearned even those things that I formerly supposed I knew. (96c1−6)

Eventually, he abandoned the study of nature altogether (99d4−5). Socrates does not say that he discussed physical questions with anyone—his interest in natural science may have been entirely a private matter. And, in any case, the outcome of his study was agnosticism about astronomy and things beneath the earth, not strange or advanced doctrines.[16]

All in all, then, there is nothing in the *Phaedo* to give us pause. It raises problems only if we adopt the completely unjustified view that in the *Apology* Socrates denies any familiarity with natural science or with common beliefs about nature. But, then, that view causes problems internal to the *Apology* itself, since, as we have seen, Socrates there exhibits familiarity with Anaxagoras' views.

The account given by Xenophon is, broadly speaking, along the same lines as the *Phaedo*. Socrates was "not unfamiliar" with the more complicated parts of geometry (*Mem.* IV.vii.3) and "attended lectures" on astronomy (*Mem.* IV.vii.5). But these topics were not what he talked about himself, "his own conversation was ever of human things" (*Mem.* I.i.16). Somewhat inconsistently, however, Xenophon also represents Socrates as teaching a teleological theory of the natural world, according to which god designed the world to satisfy man's needs (*Mem.* I.iv.2−19, IV.iii.2−17).[17] The inconsistency is perhaps reduced by the pertinent suggestion that this doctrine originated in ethical theory rather than in natural science: "Not aware himself that he [Socrates] was engaged on natural science, he only studied the relation of means to ends in the world in the moral interest of piety" (Zeller 1885, 175). Such doctrine as this could hardly, in any case, lead anyone who heard it to believe that Socrates was an atheist.

We turn, now, necessarily at considerably greater length, to *Clouds*. The picture here is obviously quite different. For Aristophanes presents

16. See Dover (1971, 67−68); Guthrie (1971a, 103−104).

17. See Furley (1987, 1: 14).

16

Socrates as being, in regard to science and oratory, exactly what Socrates himself says he is not, namely, an adept and a teacher. So our question is one of whom to believe—Aristophanes or Socrates.

In the early verses of *Clouds* (112−118), Socrates appears in two different, but related, roles: first, as the head of the *phrontistērion*, or "thinkery," a school where, for a small fee, usually in kind (856−858, 1146−1149), one can learn the just logic, which represents traditional aristocratic values (961−1023), and also the unjust logic, which represents the new values of the sophists (1036−1104); second, as the ascetic high priest (833−839) of a mystery religion, with initiation rites (140), oaths of secrecy (143), and monastic seclusion (198−199), who teaches a variety of sciences, including a mechanistic theory of the cosmos (94−99, 331−407), on the basis of which he denies the existence of Zeus (367) and the other gods of tradition (423), worshipping in their place the various forms of Air (264), including the eponymous Clouds, as the only gods (364).

Each of these roles is important in the play. But it is clear that the first is more central to the plot than the second; for Strepsiades is not interested in mystery religion or in living in monastic seclusion for the rest of his life. He is not, for that matter, interested in science. He comes to the *phrontistērion* solely for the purpose of learning the unjust logic, so that he can escape the debts incurred by his extravagant son, Pheidippides:

> I wish to learn to speak. But teach me your second [unjust] logic, the one that enables someone to escape his debts. Name your own price; by all the gods I'll pay it. (239−246)

When Strepsiades proves unteachable himself, he prevails upon Pheidippides to attend the *phrontistērion* in his place, introducing him to Socrates with the following words:

> Teach him each of your logics, the stronger, as you call it, and the weaker, the unjust one which can defeat the stronger. Or if not both, then, at all events, the unjust one. (882−885)

Again, Strepsiades' eye is solely on the unjust logic. Pheidippides proves more tractable than his father. He learns both logics and can "argue down justice" (887−888, 1339) with either one (1336−1337). Indeed, he can argue down even those traditional values, such as honouring parents, which his father, naturally enough, would like him to retain. The result is that Strepsiades blames Socrates for the corruption of his son (1464−1466) and burns the *phrontistērion* to the ground (1472−1510).

17

Clearly, then, it is Socrates, the teacher of sophistic oratory, of the unjust logic, who drives the main action of the play.[18]

But the first role is central for another reason which has not always been sufficiently emphasized. The vast majority of the specific scientific and related religious views propounded by Socrates have to do with *air* in some shape or form. And air plays an integrative symbolic role in the play strongly at odds with its having an origin in anything other than the poet's structural imagination. Air is the medium of speech. Therefore, clouds, a form of air (330) both visible and stageable, make a dramatically compelling object of worship for those who put their trust in oratory rather than in Zeus:

> To them we owe our judgement and skill in debate and intelligence and marvels of rhetoric and longwindedness and the power to crush an opponent and quickness of grasp. (316–318)

Moreover, air and clouds have elaborate conventional metaphorical associations with intellectuals. The latter have their heads in the clouds (331–334); they are up in the air, as Socrates is when we first encounter him (219–234), rather than down to earth; and so on. Consequently, they offer the poet a rich comic vein to mine.

We have good reason to think, then, that the majority of the specific scientific views attributed to Socrates in *Clouds* are not the adventitious product of Aristophanes' knowledge of Socrates himself, but a dramatic invention largely dictated by his primary role as a teacher of unjust logic.[19]

To this reason, based primarily on considerations internal to *Clouds*, we may add another of a different sort, namely, the total absence of any evidence that corroborates this part of Aristophanes' portrait:

> The doxographical tradition contains not the slightest trace of any scientific theory attributable to Socrates, and it seems equally unlikely that a man of his presumed ability should have made no contribution to the subject had he persisted in it so far as to become head of a school, or that any contribution he did make should have sunk without a trace. (Lacey 1971, 27)

That no such evidence was available to Aristotle, who would surely have known about it, is established by his characterization of Socrates as

---

18. "Aristophanes attacked him [Socrates] in his plays for making the weaker argument appear the stronger" (Diogenes Laertius, 2.20).

19. Cf. Montuori (1981, 102–108).

having concerned himself "with ethics and not at all with nature in general" (*Metaph.* 987b1−2).

What, then, of oratory? Socrates makes no secret in the *Apology* of the fact that the young men who follow him around learn how to refute others through seeing him do it (23c2−5). But whether rightly or wrongly (and that is an issue to which we shall have to return in 3.8) he clearly does not think that he is on that account their teacher (33a5−6), or that what they learn is specifically a technique, whether original with him or not, to enable them to make the weaker argument the stronger (19a8−d7). Consequently, Socrates' disclaimer of oratory should not be taken to extend to the elenchus or its unintended inculcation through practice. It follows that the attack on the elenchus which some critics have discerned in *Clouds*—specifically in the exchange between the just and unjust logics—while it *may*, perhaps, be a genuine feature of the play (and this itself is a controversial matter to which we shall also have to return in 3.8), cannot be relevant to the question of whether Socrates is being sincere in making that disclaimer.

The elenchus aside, then, the real issue is whether *Clouds* gives us any reason to believe that Socrates claimed to know and to be able to teach oratory. And surely it does not. For Socrates is not represented in *Clouds* as the purveyor of any credible strategies of forensic oratory. He claims, to be sure, that students can learn the unjust logic in the *phrontistērion* (1147−1150). But what exactly they learn in learning this, if it is not the elenchus, is left in the comic dark of jokes about the gender of nouns (658−694).

And, as in the case of science, the silence of history underwrites this view. For if Socrates had made any contribution to oratory, we would expect it to "have come through to Aristotle and to have been mentioned by him in his work *The Sophist*, lost to us but used by late ancient writers interested in the history of philosophy" (Dover 1972, 117 n. 12).

Clouds gives us little or no reason, then, to attribute either specific scientific doctrines or—the elenchus aside—specific strategies of forensic oratory to Socrates. To that extent it is lacking in the detail which lends credibility to otherwise uncorroborated historical evidence. There is a general reason, nonetheless, to believe that the portrait the play presents of Socrates cannot be wholly wide of the mark. It is this. To achieve its comic purpose, *Clouds*, like all successful satire, had to be based on something. If the Socrates it presented was sufficiently unlike the Socrates the audience knew, it would fail. Surely, then, we can infer that Socrates must have been a teacher of science and oratory of some sort.

There are essentially two reasons not to accept this argument. The first is that an earlier version of *Clouds*—the only one that we know to have been staged—did fail, being judged third out of three contenders.[20] Perhaps it failed because the audience did not find the portrait of Socrates as an orator-scientist sufficiently credible. Perhaps the present version of the play would have failed for the same reason. We do not know. The point remains that we cannot be sure that our version of *Clouds* is successful satire, and so we cannot argue from its success to the verisimilitude of its portrayal of Socrates. The second reason to reject the present argument has to do with satire in general. While it is true that successful satire must be based on something, what it must be based on is not fact, but its audience's—possibly false—beliefs and prejudices. Hence, if we can find a plausible basis for Aristophanes' satirical portrait of Socrates in such beliefs, we can block the inference from the demands on successful satire to truth or fact. And Socrates himself suggests a basis of just this sort. He tells us that his young followers imitate his elenctic techniques on others, who, as a result, charge him with their corruption. Here—provided this was already true when *Clouds* was first produced in 423—is a basis for his representation as a teacher of the unjust logic. Socrates tells us, too, that certain charges were available in Athens against all philosophers, among them the charge of teaching about "astronomy and things beneath the earth" (23d2–9). Here is a basis for his representation as a scientist.

We can explain away the evidence in *Clouds*, then, at least to some extent. But why should we explain it away? The most straightforward answer is this. Socrates not only makes the disclaimers about science and oratory we have been discussing, he appeals to the jury—who have had over twenty more years to observe him about his elenctic business in the public agora than the original audience of *Clouds*—as witness to the truth of what he says. He asks them to confront their prejudicial beliefs about advanced thinkers with their actual knowledge of him. And this appeal is simply not intelligible, whether as irony or anything else short of madness, unless he believed its outcome to be certainly favourable: "It was customary to ask the diecasts who knew to inform their neighbors. Naturally the diecasts could be called upon as confirmatory witnesses only in matters of public knowledge" (Bonner and Smith 1938, 2: 125). The fact that Socrates makes his appeal with such confidence, therefore, and spends such little time on this part of the prejudicial caricature, gives us a powerful reason to treat *Clouds* as something other than the truth.

Much more needs to be said about *Clouds*, of course, before any of these conclusions can be taken as certainly established. But perhaps enough has been said to show that to try to use *Clouds* as evidence of the

20. See Dover (1972, 101–105).

ironical nature of Socrates' disclaimer of science and oratory is a deeply problematic undertaking.

1.4 THE RELIGIOUS ORIGINS OF SOCRATES' MISSION

Socrates began his elenctic mission sometime after the oracle to Chaerephon (23b4–c1). The following passage from the *Laches* suggests that he was then in early adulthood:

> Lysimachus, it truly seems to me that you only know Socrates from what you know of his father and that you haven't had anything to do with him personally except, perhaps, when he was a boy, when you might have met him with his father in his own district at the temple or at some local gathering. But it is certain that you haven't had to do with him since he has become older [*presbuteros*].—What makes you say that, Nicias?—It seems to me you do not know that anyone who comes face to face with Socrates and converses with him, although they may have started on a completely different topic, is inevitably turned around by the argument until he is led to give an account of himself and of his way of life, past and present. And once he has been led into that, Socrates will never let him go until he has well and truly examined all of his ways. (187d6–188a3)

This would date the oracle in the 430s, or some thirty years prior to Socrates' trial in 399. And most scholars now accept that rough date.[21]

The account which Socrates gives of the oracle is as follows:

> You know Chaerephon. He was my companion from youth as well as the companion of most of you, sharing in your recent exile and return. You know what sort of man Chaerephon was, how impulsive in everything he did. He went to Delphi and dared to consult the oracle about this—as I say, do not create a disturbance, gentlemen—he asked if there is anyone wiser than I. The Pythia replied that no one is wiser. Chaerephon is dead, but his brother here will testify to these things. (20e8–21a8)[22]

21. See Guthrie (1971a, 85–86); Parke and Wormell (1956, 1: 401–403); Strycker (1975, 40–41).

22. During the brief rule of the Thirty Tyrants (404/403), the supporters of democracy were driven into exile from Athens. After the defeat of the Thirty, they returned to Athens (2.3). Chaerephon's brother, Chaerecrates, is mentioned in Xenophon, *Mem.* II.iii.1–19. Montuori (1981, 65) suggests that Xenophon's portrayal of the brothers as quarrelling raises a question about whether

21

The Pythia—the Delphic priestess through whom Apollo spoke—said that "no one is wis*er* [*sophōteron*]" than Socrates. A few lines later, however, Socrates represents Apollo as making the apparently stronger claim that he is wis*est*: "What does he [Apollo] mean by saying that I am wisest [*sophōtaton*]" (21b5–6). There seems to be a problem, therefore, about just what Apollo really said. But the problem is more apparent than real. Socrates' final account of what the oracle means is this: "That one of you, humans, is wisest [*sophōtatos*] who, like Socrates, knows that in truth he is worth nothing in regard to wisdom" (23b1–4). And this makes it clear that, as Socrates understands the matter, anyone as wise as himself would also be wisest of men. To be wisest is not to be wiser than anyone else; it is to be included in a class of equally wise people who are wiser than those not in that class. Hence the two earlier inter-pretations Socrates gives of the oracle differ only verbally from one another. No one is wiser than Socrates just in case Socrates is wisest of men.

Socrates' initial response to this oracular characterization of him was one of puzzlement and perplexity: "What is the god saying, what riddle is he uttering [*ti pote ainittetai*]?" (21b3–4).[23] For, on the one hand, he knew that he was "wise in neither a great nor a small way" (21b4–5), on the other, he knew that the god could not be speaking falsely (21b6–7).

After a long period of simply being at a loss, Socrates attempted to solve the riddle as follows: "I went to one of those reputed wise, think-ing that there, if anywhere, I could refute the oracle [*elegxōn to manteion*] and say to it, 'This man is wiser than I, but you said that I was wisest' " (21b9–c2). This was the beginning of his questioning of the politicians, poets, and craftsmen described in 1.2.

Socrates' remark about "refuting" the oracle has led many writers to accuse him of impiety: "The fact that Socrates eventually becomes the

Chaerephon would have "revealed the secret" of the Delphic oracle to Chaere-crates. But this is farfetched. Socrates does not suggest that the Delphic oracle was a secret or that no one knew about it except Chaerephon and his brother. As Chaerephon's next of kin and as a democrat known to the jurors, Chaerecrates was simply an obvious choice as witness. See Bonner and Smith (1938, 2: 130).

23. Fontenrose (1981, 236) claims that the Delphic oracle's reputation for am-biguity "is wholly modern: Delphi had no such reputation in antiquity." He overlooks this text, however, which provides clear evidence that Delphi spoke in riddles. Moreover, his claim that the oracle delivered to Chaerephon is "not ambiguous" does not accord with Socrates' view of it; for Socrates argues that the oracle trades on a hitherto-unnoticed ambiguity in the notion of wisdom. See 1.6.

pious champion of the god's veracity draws attention away from his original impious intention and expectation: to show up the Delphic Apollo as a liar or a fool" (West 1979, 106).[24] But the accusation is misplaced. For Socrates clearly does not mean that he intended to refute the oracle outright. His plan, on discovering someone wiser than himself, was not to dismiss the oracle as false, but to return to Delphi in puzzlement (21c2). He believed from the beginning that, properly interpreted, the oracle had to be true. Apollo "cannot be speaking falsely; for that is not lawful [*themis*] for him" (21b6−7). Hence his strategy of refutation is interpretative only (21c6−22a1). By showing that one proposition the oracle might be taken to have expressed is false, he can get closer—in part by reapplication to Delphi itself—to the true proposition that is its real meaning.

Even this purely interpretative attitude, however, has been taken to show that Socrates does not treat the oracle seriously and that his interpretation of it is ironical:

His procedure of testing the oracle is incompatible with a serious acceptance of its authority; and . . . is itself evidence that he did not receive it in such a spirit as could make it possible for him to regard it as the voice of God, determining and ordering all his future activity. His interpretation of the oracle is a typical example of his accustomed irony. (Hackforth 1933, 94)

This view of the matter presupposes that Socrates could not both take the oracle seriously and inquire into its meaning. And this presupposition is false.[25] When Croesus reproached the oracle with having deceived him about his chances of defeating the Persians, he received the following reply:

As to the oracle, Croesus had no right to find fault with it: the god had declared that if he attacked the Persians he would bring down a mighty empire. After an answer like that, the wise thing would have been to send again to inquire which empire was meant, Cyrus' or his own. But as he misinterpreted what was said and made no second inquiry, he must admit the fault to have been his own. (Herodotus 1.91−92)

Not even Delphi itself, then, would have seen Socrates' attitude to its pronouncement as in some way ironical or impious.

24. Cf. Burnet (1924, 92); Hackforth (1933, 88−104); Ryle (1966, 177); Teloh (1986, 111).

25. See Guthrie (1971a, 86−87); Parke (1967, 113).

We turn, now, to Socrates' interpretation of the oracle. Socrates makes it quite clear that on numerous occasions he received definite orders from the god to examine his fellows:

> But why then do certain people enjoy spending considerable time with me? You have heard it, men of Athens, I have told you the whole truth. It is because they enjoy hearing men being examined who think they are wise but are not. For this is not unpleasant. I have been ordered [*prostetaktai*] to practice this, as I say, by the god through oracles and through dreams [*ek manteiōn kai ex enupniōn*] and in every other way that divine providence ever ordered [*prosetaxe*] a human being to practice anything at all. (33b9–c7)

There is no doubt, therefore, that Socrates believed he had ample evidence, quite apart from the original Delphic pronouncement, that his elenctic activities were divinely commanded.

At 28e4–6, however, long before he mentions these more explicit dreams and oracles, Socrates says: "The god stationed [*tattontos*] me [in Athens] . . . obliging [*dein*] me to live philosophizing and examining myself and others." A few lines later, referring back to this characterization, he says, "I will obey [*peisomai*] the god" (29d3–4). Finally, there is the following account of his activities, which forms part of the oracle story itself:

> After that, I kept going to one after another, perceiving with pain and fear that I was becoming hated, but thinking, nevertheless, that it was necessary to treat what pertained to the god as most important, so that I had to go, in seeking what the oracle was saying, to all those with a reputation for wisdom. And, by the dog, men of Athens—for I must speak the truth—I experienced something like this: in my investigation according to the god [*kata ton theon*], I found that those with the best reputations [the politicians] seemed to me nearly the most deficient, while those who were thought to be inferior [the craftsmen] seemed to me to have more wisdom. Indeed, I must display my wanderings to you as if they were labours I had undertaken to prove the god irrefutable. (21e3–22a8)

Here Socrates characterizes his investigation as being *kata ton theon*—a phrase to which he recurs at 23b5. It seems clear, therefore, that by the time he had completed his examination of the politicians, poets, and craftsman, Socrates took the oracle's pronouncement itself either as an explicit injunction to elenctically examine his fellows or, at the very least, as strongly commending, approving, and underwriting that activity.

The question is, what possible justification can Socrates have to think any of this? First, the oracle, even as he finally interprets it, is not an explicit command or imperative. Second, it does not mention elenctic examination. By the same token, and this is the third problem, it does not mention elenctic examination on ethical issues.

Faced with these three problems, which have not always been sufficiently distinguished from one another, interpreters have, by different routes, reached rather pessimistic conclusions about the cogency of the oracle story. Some have argued that the problems are the result of Plato's having inconsistently combined fact and fancy:

> What solution then can be offered for these difficulties? . . . I believe that Plato has caused them himself . . . by attempting to find in the oracle the source of Socrates' consciousness that his life's work—of exposing men's vain conceit of wisdom (his 'elenchtic' activity) on the one hand, and of urging them to care for their souls or their moral welfare (his 'protreptic' activity) on the other hand—was prescribed and inspired by a divine Master. (Hackforth 1933, 91–92)

Some deny that we are supposed to find in the oracle—or elsewhere in the *Apology* indeed—any explanation of why Socrates examined his fellows: "He nowhere explains just how the oracle was responsible for his undertaking his mission" (Brickhouse and Smith 1988, 98). Still others entertain the idea that the god in accordance with whom Socrates examines is not Apollo at all, but some other, non-Olympian deity: "How could the attempted refutation of the oracle be in accordance with the god? Perhaps 'the god' is not the Delphic god (Socrates never speaks of Apollo by name)" (West 1979, 125).[26] But are these responses justified? Has Socrates left the jury in ignorance about the bearing of the oracle on his philosophical life? He has not. A plausible explanation is implicit in what he tells them.

It is clear, first of all, that Socrates was already sufficiently religious and devoted to Apollo when he heard the news of the oracle to treat it very seriously; for who but a religious person already devoted to Apollo would puzzle over one of his oracles, set about a time-consuming activity to determine its meaning, and persist in that activity even when it

---

26. Other writers, too, have tried to make sinister capital out of Socrates' failure to name Apollo as the god he serves. Burnyeat (1988, 18) is a recent example. But this is unjustified; for Socrates does refer to the god he serves by means of a definite description— "the god, the one in Delphi [*ton theon ton en Delphois*]" (20e8)—which could have no denotation other than Apollo.

made him both poor and unpopular (21b2–22a1, 23b9–c1)?[27] Second, what the oracle said is that no one is wiser than Socrates. And the reason that Socrates found this puzzling was that he knew himself "to be wise in neither a great nor a small way" (21b4–6). The obvious people for him to go to, therefore, in search of an interpretation-aiding counterexample were those with a reputation for wisdom, and the obvious topics for him to discuss with them were those about which he believed himself not to be wise and they were believed to be wise. Third, in most cases, these topics were almost certainly ethical at the outset. But since we know that Socrates discussed poetry with the poets (22b2–8) and that, as a result of examining the craftsmen, he discovered that they "knew many fine things" about their crafts (22c9–e5), it is possible that in other cases his questioning originally ranged beyond ethics, coming to be exclusively ethical only as he began to see in his interlocutors' false presumptions in regard to ethics in particular a possible solution to the puzzle set by the oracle.

Putting these three facts together, we have an explanation, available to the jurors, of why Socrates began examining his fellows and why the topic of his examination was, or very soon became, ethics and the virtues.[28] What we do not have yet is an explanation of why this activity, thus begun, seemed to him to be *kata ton theon*.

If Socrates is right about the meaning of the oracle, the god Apollo has said that no human being possesses any real wisdom, any knowledge of the most important things, and that the person is wisest who, like Socrates, recognizes that this is so. According to Apollo, therefore, that is how things are. There is a sense in which Socrates is acting according

---

27. Montuori (1981, 125) overlooks this fact: "There is no evidence, at least in the *Apology*, that before the pronouncement of the oracle, Socrates had any great devotion to Apollo which would have earned him the favor of the god." 31c8–d4, 40a4–6, and 40b1 make it clear, indeed, that Socrates enjoyed Apollo's favour from childhood.

28. We need not suppose that Socrates' examination of the supposedly wise— or the self-examination which we shall see reason to think preceded it—initially took the form of a "standard elenchus" (1.7–8). Socrates may have found his best weapon, as he found its best target, only over the course of time. What ended up as a standard elenchus may have begun life as a much more generic kind of examination and refutation. Hence we should not expect to find an explanation of the precise form of examination Socrates' employed in the Delphic oracle. Neither should we suppose that the jury would have looked to it for such an explanation; for they are not likely to have been aware of the precise nature of a standard elenchus.

to Apollo, therefore, by refuting those who claim that they do have knowledge of the most important things, since he will be demonstrating that—appearances to the contrary—things really are in accord with what Apollo has said. By the same token, there is a clear sense in which he will be coming to the aid of Apollo and be engaged in service to him (23b4–c1), by demonstrating, in the face of apparent counterexample, that what the god has said is indeed true. Socrates' characterization of his activities at 22a6–8 strongly suggests that this is part at least of what he has in mind: "Indeed, I must display my wanderings to you as if they were labours I had undertaken to prove the god irrefutable."

If we suppose, however, that this is all that he has in mind, we face the following objection:

> How can his lifelong continuance of his activity on the same lines, after he had substantiated it [the truth of the oracle], be still explained as obedience? It may be replied that though he had substantiated it to his own satisfaction, it was still incumbent on him to substantiate it before others; but who will believe that Socrates really conceived his life's work to have consisted in substantiating an oracle before men who had most of them never heard of it? What a pitiable and absurd thing the sense of a divine mission would then become! (Hackforth 1933, 90–91)

As Socrates came to interpret the oracle, however, it contains not only the factual claim that no human being possesses any knowledge of the most important things but also the *value judgement* that the person is *wisest* who recognizes this fact. Consequently, the oracle has, in what we shall see to be characteristic Delphian fashion, commended antihubristic awareness of human limitations in wisdom. And value judgements and commendations, even if they are not, as some recent philosophers have claimed, disguised imperatives, certainly have—especially when uttered by a god to a religious person already devoted to him—strong action-guiding force.

It follows that by refuting those who claim to have knowledge of the most important things and, more especially, by getting them to see that they do not know what they claim to know, Socrates is helping to bring about something that Apollo especially commends and values. But if this is so, his elenctic activities do not become senseless once it has been sufficiently established that the oracle is true. They go on being important as long as he believes that they continue to bring about something Apollo values. Moreover, it becomes much more intelligible that Socrates should think of his activities as he does. For to help bring about something Apollo values is to aid and serve him and in that much more full-blooded sense to act in accordance with him—notice that Socrates speaks of himself as coming "to the aid of the god" only at the stage at which he tries to get the interlocutor to recognize his own lack of wisdom (23b3−6). We can also see in this antihubristic aspect of the elenchus the beginning of an explanation of the religio-ethical significance Socrates attributes to it (30a7−b4, 36d9−e1); for anything that helps one to avoid something so repugnant to Apollo and so inimical to human well-being as hubris is of enormous significance to ethics and religion.[29]

The Delphic oracle can be seen, then, as underwriting and initiating Socrates' elenctic mission. His interpretation of it is, therefore, reasonable and intelligible. But why does he do what the oracle commends? Why does he obey the orders that later dreams and oracles more explicitly contained? So far we have settled for the answer that Socrates was a religious man, disposed to heed the word of the god. But in 1.10, equipped with a better understanding of Socrates' human wisdom, we shall have to return to that answer to determine whether it is really the last word on the matter or whether Socratic religion is itself based on something else.

1.5 WHY DELPHI PRAISED SOCRATES' WISDOM

The majority of interpreters of Socrates' account of the Delphic oracle have urged the following argument on us: Chaerephon must have had some reason to think that Socrates was wise before asking his question of the oracle, and, more important, the oracle must have had some reason for returning the answer it did; therefore, Socrates must have done something sufficiently remarkable to earn himself a considerable reputation for wisdom—news of it travelled to Delphi, after all—before the oracle delivered its fateful response.[30]

This argument seems unexceptionable. But in fact it is quite controversial; for it presupposes that the Delphic oracle did indeed rely on evidence in making its pronouncements. Some historians believe this to have been the case:

29. The Greek concept of *hubris*, which differs significantly from our own much narrower concept, is examined in Dover (1974, 54−55, 110−111); MacDowell (1978, 129−132); Nilsson (1948, 52−59).

30. See Brickhouse and Smith (1988, 94−95); Burnet (1924, 74−75, 90−91); Kraut (1984, 271 n. 43); Taylor (1952, 78−79); Vlastos (1985, 26−29).

The Pythia entered into a mantic frenzy or state of trance, in which she uttered unintelligible sounds . . . the attendant priests interpreted these sounds, giving the inquirer a coherent, more or less ambiguous reply usually expressed in dactylic-hexameter verse. The priests' interpretations . . . were slanted and colored by their devotion to Delphic interests and by the unexampled knowledge of Greek affairs and of Mediterranean lands which they picked up from the numerous visitors who came to Delphi from the whole Greek world.[31]

But others completely reject this idea. They argue that Delphi relied not on information but on banality and on telling people what they expected to hear.[32]

There were, moreover, two methods of consulting the oracle. One, involving the sacrifice of sheep and goats, was quite expensive but resulted in a written response. The other—the so-called method of "the two beans"—was substantially cheaper but resulted only in a response by lot. Since Chaerephon was notoriously poor, it seems probable that he consulted the oracle by the latter method. He asked, "Is anyone wiser than Socrates?" The Pythia responded by drawing forth a bean whose colour indicated a negative answer. Hence, even if Delphi sometimes relied on evidence, the message to Chaerephon in particular may have been based on nothing more than the luck of the draw.[33] There is more than one reason, then, to be circumspect about using that message to argue backwards to the facts about Socrates' previous life on which it was allegedly based.

31. This succinct summary of a view he himself rejects is due to Fontenrose (1981, 6). The view is defended by Parke and Wormell (1956, 1: 30–41) and to some extent by Guthrie (1968, 262).

32. See Fontenrose (1981, 7–8, 11–57, 233–239).

33. Xenophon gives a somewhat different account of what the oracle communicated to Chaerephon: "When Chaerephon inquired at the Delphic oracle about me, in the presence of many people [pollōn parontōn], Apollo answered that no man was more free than I, or more just, or more moderate" (Ap. 14). This is additional evidence that Chaerephon consulted the lot oracle. First, the significance of the outcome of a lot might be variously characterized. And, second, the phrase pollōn parontōn suggests that the lot oracle was involved; for few people were admitted into the presence of the Pythia during a verbal consultation. See Parke (1961, 249–250; 1967, 72–88, 112–113); Parke and Wormell (1956, 1: 17–45). Clouds (103–104) attests to Chaerephon's poverty, as does his failure to appear in Davies (1971).

Nonetheless, because there is uncertainty about how Delphi operated, uncertainty about whether even the lot oracle was entirely a chance affair, and no more than reasonable probability that Chaerephon did, indeed, consult the lot, it is prudent to try to discover what, if anything, the oracle *might* have been relying on in responding to Chaerephon as it did.

A host of candidates have been proposed. Some argue, citing *Clouds* as corroborative evidence, that Socrates must have been an able natural scientist in his early life and that it was his scientific contributions that recommended him to Delphi.[34] Some claim that it was dialectical ability, not science, that played this role.[35] Some believe that it was Socrates' philosophical doctrines that Delphi found appealing.[36] Some completely reject the oracle story as Platonic invention, on the grounds that none of these candidates is unproblematic.[37] There is a candidate remaining, however, immune to the objections the others face, something the Delphic oracle would have found commendable and that Socrates himself believed it was actually commending (23a5−b4), namely, human wisdom or, at any rate, human wisdom appropriately understood.

The inscriptions on the walls of the temple at Delphi well convey the spirit the oracle stood for: Know thyself [*gnothi sauton*]; Nothing in excess [*meden agan*]; Curb thy spirit [*thumou kratei*]; Observe the limit [*peras epitelei*]; Hate hubris [*hubrim meisei*]; Bow before the divine [*proskunei to theion*]; Fear authority [*to kartoum phobou*]; Glory not in strength [*epi rōmēi mē kauchō*].[38] There is no record, absent the case in point, of the oracle ever having praised anyone for what we would think of as his significant or noteworthy positive achievements or abilities, whether ethical, dialectical, scientific, or otherwise: Delphi was not the ancient equivalent of the Nobel Prize Committee:

> We meet with even greater difficulties if we examine the Delphic pronouncement within the Delphic oracular tradition and bearing in mind the nature of the religion of Apollo. It then becomes impossible to believe that the Sanctuary of Delphi, which was the jealous and intransigent custodian which opposed to the insolence

34. See Burnet (1924, 74−75, 90−91); Taylor (1933, 37−88).

35. See Vlastos (1985, 26−29).

36. See Brickhouse and Smith (1988, 94−95).

37. See Montuori (1981, 140); Gomperz (1931, 2: 104−108).

38. See Guthrie (1955, 183−204); Parke and Wormell (1956, 1: 378−392).

of *hubris* the humility of measure and restraint, could confer on anyone a prize that praised his own wisdom. (Montuori 1981, 133)

On the other hand, there are many stories of the following kind. Someone powerful, grand, famous for his wisdom, or in some other way noteworthy for his accomplishments asks the oracle to say who is wisest, most pious, happiest, or what have you, expecting that he himself will be named. But the oracle names some unknown person living in humble and quiet obscurity. The person whose offerings are most pleasing to the god is not the wealthy Magnesian who brought Apollo a hecatomb of victims, but Clearachus of Methydrium, a poor and unknown farmer. The happiest man is not Gyges, the ruler of Lydia, but Aglaus of Psophis, an obscure Arcadian, who has never left his tiny plot of land. Chilon the Spartan and Anacharsis the Scythian are each famous for wisdom, but Myson of Oeta, a humble peasant living in a backward part of Greece, "is provided with sounder brains" than either of them.[39]

What we know about the oracle, then, makes it very unlikely that it was praising Socrates for his contributions to science, ethical theory, or dialectic, and very likely that it was using him, in the way that it used Clearachus, Aglaus, and Myson, as an example of someone who was wise because he made no hubristic claims to wisdom. And this is Socrates' own view of the matter; for he understands the oracle to be using him as an example to make a general deflationary point about human wisdom (23a5−b4). On this showing, it is as wrongheaded to ask after the nature of the significant positive achievements in knowledge which commended Socrates to Delphi as it would be to ask the parallel questions about Clearachus, Aglaus, or Myson.

Nonetheless, if, as we are supposing, Delphi was relying on evidence in making its response to Chaerephon, it must have had some reason to believe that Socrates was like Myson, not like Chilon or Anacharsis. What might that reason have been?

Socrates does not say that he began to examine people only after he heard what the oracle had said.[40] Instead, he implies that he began his examination of those with a reputation for wisdom at that point (21b9−23b4) and that, having completed it in a systematic fashion and having come to a conclusion about what the oracle meant, he then extended his examination to "anyone, citizen or alien, whom I think wise" (23b5−6). Hence there is nothing here to exclude the possibility

---

39. These stories are collected in Parke and Wormell (1956, 1: 378−392).

40. See Strycker (1975, 46).

that Socrates engaged in elenctic examination (or prototypical elenctic examination) prior to the oracle. To the contrary, there is good reason to believe that he did precisely that.

When Socrates heard Chaerephon's news, he already knew that he was "wise in neither a great nor a small way" (21b4–5). He already knew that he possessed none of the knowledge that the politicians, poets, and craftsmen claim. How did he know this? The most plausible explanation is that he knew it in precisely the way that he subsequently came to know the parallel fact about other people, namely, by means of the elenchus or its intellectual predecessors. For elenctic examination is always self-examination (*Ap.* 38a4–5; *Chrm.* 166c7–d2; *Grg.* 506a3–5). It is these pre-oracle activities, leading as they did not to hubristic claims to wisdom but to modest human wisdom, that offer us a credible basis, if one is needed, for the oracle's pronouncement.

But if this is right, what made Chaerephon believe that Socrates was wise? Surely, *he* cannot be supposed to have been a partisan of mere human wisdom any more than the friends of Myson are likely to have thought him to be the wisest of men. Are we not, then, forced to search once more for some Socratic wisdom which is not human wisdom? We are not. There is another explanation.

We have seen reason to believe that Socrates used the elenchus before he heard the oracle. Chaerephon, his "friend from youth" (20e8–21a1), must often have seen Socrates use it on people he thought wise and, perhaps, have been a victim of it himself. As a result, he could have come to believe, as so many of his fellow Athenians did (23a1–5), that Socrates was a very wise man indeed.[41] Then, in his enthusiasm, he went to Delphi to ask whether anyone was wiser than Socrates and received the response, typically Delphian in its power to mislead the overconfident, that no one is wiser.

Provided, therefore, that human wisdom really is just the antihubristic recognition of one's own limitations in wisdom, and that is something we are about to investigate, the oracle to Chaerephon is intelligible whether as the product of chance or as an estimate of Socrates based on actual knowledge of him. But if human wisdom turns out to be something different, then only the possibility that Chaerephon consulted the lot oracle saves the oracle story from the incoherences which scholars have repeatedly found in it.

41. A similar view is suggested by Kraut (1984, 271 n. 43). We need not suppose, however, that the people Socrates examined were "major figures" in order to explain Chaerephon's enthusiasm.

Having examined his first politician, Socrates concludes: "So it is likely that in just this one little thing [*smikrōi tini autōi toutōi*] I am wiser than he is, that what I do not know, I do not suppose that I know" (21d6−7). Then he identifies the thing in question with what makes him wiser than the poets: "So I went away from there too thinking that I was superior to them in the very same way that I was to the politicians [*enteuthen tōi autōi oiomenos perigegonenai hōiper kai tōn politikōn*]" (22c6−8). Finally, having examined the craftsmen, he identifies what makes him wiser than them with what makes him wiser than the poets:

> But, men of Athens, the good craftsmen also seemed to me to make the same mistake as the poets [*hamartēma hoper kai ho poiētai*]: each of them, because he performed his craft well, thought himself wisest in the other things, the most important things [*talla ta megista*], and this error of theirs seemed to overshadow the wisdom they had. (22d4−e1)

Working backwards through this chain of identities, we see that human wisdom has to do exclusively with "the most important things" and with Socrates' recognition of his lack of knowledge about them.

But what are the most important things? Socrates leaves us in no doubt about his answer:

> If one of you disputes this and says he does care [about wisdom, truth, and the best possible state of the psyche; 29e1−3], I will not immediately let him go, nor will I go away myself, but I will speak with him, examine him, and use the elenchus on him, and if he does not seem to me to possess virtue but only says that he does, I will reproach him, saying that he attaches least importance to the most important things [*ta pleistou*] and treats the less important things as more important. (29e3−30a2; cf. *Alc. 1* 118a7−12)

The virtues are the greatest and most important things. And the reason they are most important is that without them nothing else—not even other apparently good things such as wealth—is unequivocally good: "Wealth does not bring about virtue, but it is virtue that makes wealth and everything else, both public and private, good for a man" (30b2−4; 3.4).

Now we have seen already that Socrates is wiser than the poets and politicians in the very same way that he is wiser than the craftsmen who falsely believe they know about the most important things—the virtues.

It follows that the things the poets write about (22a8–c8) and the fine and good things the politicians think they know about (21d2–6) must be the virtues. And this makes good sense. For the poets are the traditional teachers of virtue, and the politicians are supposed to be its shepherds and guardians (*Euthphr.* 2c2–3a5; *Euthd.* 292b4–c1; *Grg.* 515b6–517c4; cf. *Lg.* 650b6–9).

But if human wisdom has to do exclusively with the virtues in this way, it cannot be an achievement of human wisdom on Socrates' part to recognize that he has none of the kind of knowledge of science and oratory attributed to him in *Clouds* (19a8–d7); for the latter is not knowledge of virtue.[42] And what is true of science and oratory is even more obviously true of the ordinary crafts. Socrates recognizes that he does not have knowledge of these. But this recognition does not make him wiser than the craftsmen. What makes him wiser is, as we have seen, one thing alone: they falsely believe that they have knowledge about the virtues, while he knows that he does not have it. Knowing that one is neither potter nor tanner is not an achievement of human wisdom either.[43] Again, this makes good sense: Athens must have been full of people who realized that they knew neither craft, nor oratory, nor science. But, if Socrates is right, it contained scarcely anyone, beyond himself, possessed of human wisdom.

Besides disclaiming the knowledge of virtue claimed by the politicians, poets, and craftsmen, Socrates also disclaims the knowledge of virtue claimed by professional sophist teachers of it—*expert knowledge* as we may call it:

> I, men of Athens, have acquired this name [of being a sophist teacher of virtue] through nothing but a sort of wisdom. What sort of wisdom? Just the sort which is, no doubt, human wisdom [*anthrōpinē sophia*]; for it looks as though in this I am really wise [*tō onti gar kinduneuō tautēn einai sophos*]. But those of whom I spoke just now [Gorgias, Prodicus, Hippias, and Evenus] are wise in a wisdom that is more than human—I do not know how else to speak of it; for I at least do not know it [*ou gar dē egōge autēn epistamai*], but whoever says that I do speaks to slander me. (20d6–e3; cf. 20c1–3)

---

42. This important fact is overlooked by Vlastos (1985, 27 n. 68). Burnet (1924, 88–89) gets it more or less right: "Socrates is not here speaking of natural science, but of the teaching of the great 'sophists' in the more restricted sense given to the word by Protagoras."

43. See Kraut (1984, 239–240 n. 83); Irwin (1977, 73, 296 n. 28).

Appearances to the contrary, this is not a disclaimer of something new; for the politicians, poets, and craftsmen do not think that they have just a little knowledge of virtue; they think that they have the kind of significant knowledge of it that makes them *wisest* of men (22c4−6, 22d6−8). Moreover, Socrates argues that he got the reputation for having the kind of knowledge about virtue that Gorgias, Prodicus, and the other sophists claim because people attributed to him the very wisdom he showed the politicians, poets, and craftsmen to lack (20c4−23a5). Hence the wisdom he showed them to lack must be more or less the same as the knowledge of virtue claimed by the sophists. When it comes to ethics and the virtues, we may infer, most people think they are something of an expert.

Human wisdom seems, then, to consist, at least in part, in recognizing that one does not possess any expert knowledge of virtue when one does not. But there must, surely, be more to it than that. Otherwise it seems that anyone who recognized that he lacked such knowledge would possess human wisdom and be as wise as Socrates, even if his recognition was a result of general skepticism or below-normal intelligence. What is the missing ingredient?

Socrates came to the recognition that he lacked expert knowledge of virtue through examining himself and others (28e4−6, 38a2−6). But, as we shall see in 1.8 and 3.4, an elenchus is not an entirely negative process. In many cases, it disabuses someone of the hubris of thinking that his confident beliefs constitute expert knowledge of virtue by convincing him of a proposition about virtue which conflicts with those beliefs. Successful elenctic examination removes ethical hubris by refuting the confident claims which embody it. But it refutes those claims by defending other ethical claims. The latter differ significantly from their predecessors, however, in two crucial respects. First, they are and are recognized as being not expert knowledge of virtue but at best *nonexpert knowledge* of it. Second, because they are entailed by propositions almost everyone believes, they themselves are implicitly believed by everyone.

It is this second fact that explains why Socrates is wiser than the politicians, poets, and craftsmen in just the "one little thing" we began this section by trying to identify. His positive convictions do not make him wiser than these men, because they are the common possession of all (normal) human beings. That is why Socrates denies that he teaches anything to those he examines (3.8). Nonetheless, these positive convictions surely do distinguish Socrates from people who recognize that they lack expert knowledge of virtue out of general skepticism or below-normal intelligence.

There are two sides to human wisdom, then, corresponding to the two sides, negative and positive, of an elenchus. Through having one's confident ethical convictions refuted, perhaps on a daily basis (*Grg.* 513c7–d1), one is disabused of the hubris of thinking that one has expert ethical knowledge and simultaneously convinced of other ethical propositions which one recognizes as having at best the status of nonexpert knowledge and which are implicitly believed by all (normal) human beings.

Socrates registers his initial response to the oracle as follows: "For I know myself to be wise in neither a great nor a small way [*egō gar dē oute mega oute smikron sunoida emautōi sophos ōn*]" (21b4–5). Even very careful writers think he is making the claim, popularly attributed to him, that he knows only that he has no wisdom whatsoever, that he knows "absolutely nothing" (Vlastos 1985, 6 n. 13). But this seems an implausible interpretation of what he says. For Socrates is hardly denying that he knows lots and lots of such humdrum facts as that he has two hands, that the sun is in the sky, that he lives in Athens, that he fought at Delium, that he is puzzled by the oracle, and so on. Indeed, within a page, he explicitly says that he had such knowledge: "I knew [*ēidē*] that I would find that they [the craftsmen] knew many fine things" (22d1–2). All he is denying, it seems certain, is that he is in any way noteworthy in wisdom, that he has any expert knowledge of virtue which the ordinary man in the street does not have, that he knows anything that could possibly justify Delphi in thinking him wiser than his fellows.

Having deciphered the oracle, moreover, Socrates decisively revises this self-assessment. One writer has charted the course of revision as follows:

> Having finally understood what the oracle means, Socrates presumably realizes that his initial reaction to it . . . is self-contradictory. You cannot know that you have no knowledge, and similarly you cannot know that you are not wise even in a small way; for to know something is to have a small amount of wisdom. By putting his initial reaction to the oracle into the form of a self-contradiction, Socrates is telling his audience that he should have realized from the start that he was wrong to disavow all claims to knowledge and wisdom. (Kraut 1984, 272 n. 44)

But this account now seems mistaken. What Socrates actually discovers is that he was right to believe that he had no expert knowledge or wisdom but that the god was also right in saying that he was the wisest of men. For he discovers that there is "one little thing" which distinguishes him from all other men and makes him wiser than them:

they hubristically believe that they possess expert knowledge of virtue, whereas he knows that he does not possess it. This "one little thing" is human wisdom, which we can now see is precisely the sort of non-hubristic or deflationary wisdom we would expect Apollo and Delphi to commend.[44]

1.7 EXPERT KNOWLEDGE

Piecing together the various remarks Socrates makes about expert knowledge of virtue in the course of disavowing any share in it, we arrive at the following partial portrait.

First, expert knowledge seems to be, or to be relevantly like, craft-knowledge (*technē*). The only thing Socrates found in the course of his examination of the reputedly wise that he treats as making its possessors to any extent noteworthy in wisdom or knowledge is the craft-knowledge possessed by the various craftsmen (22c9−d4). Moreover, he presents Evenus as allegedly possessing a craft (20c1) which would enable him to make men virtuous, just as those who have mastered the crafts of horse-training or farming are able to make horses or calves virtuous or excellent.

Second, expert knowledge of virtue enables someone to teach people to be virtuous. In Socrates' view, that is what the relevant sophists claimed to be able to do (*Grg.* 519c3−d1; *Hp. Ma.* 283c2−5; *La.* 186c2−5; *Prt.* 319a3−7). Gorgias, Prodicus, Hippias, and Evenus are mentioned precisely in regard to the question of who Callias should engage to teach his sons virtue (20a4−c3).

Third, expert knowledge is explanatory. Socrates argues that the poets do not compose by the kind of wisdom he is seeking, "but by some-

---

44. Misunderstandings of human wisdom have led some scholars to doubt that Socrates is a true Apollonian. Montuori (1981, 127−128) claims that human wisdom is skeptical "not only towards that wisdom of which the god is wise, but also towards the very existence of the divinity." Socrates has no share in expert knowledge of virtue, the wisdom which the god possesses. But he is not in the least skeptical about its nature or about whether or not there are gods who have it. See 1.10. Burkert (1985, 148) also goes wrong here. *Gnothi sauton*, know yourself, he argues, "is not intended in a psychological sense or in the existential-philosophical sense of Socrates, but in an anthropological sense: know that you are not a god. An ethics of the human emerges, but it is closer to pessimism than to a programme for human progress." Socrates' views about human wisdom are "anthropological," however, and do register something approaching pessimism about our capacity, as humans, to master our fates and to cease to be at the mercy of chance or luck.

thing in their nature and by inspiration," because they cannot adequately explain what it is their products, their poems, say or mean (22b2–c3).[45]

Fourth, if someone falsely believes that he has expert knowledge of virtue, it seems that, no matter what other wisdom he has, he will be less wise than someone who recognizes that he does not possess it. Socrates believes that his human wisdom makes him wiser than the craftsmen, on the grounds that their error in thinking they possessed expert knowledge of virtue "seemed to overshadow the wisdom they had" (22d8–e5).

Fifth, expert knowledge of virtue seems to be the sort of knowledge it is reasonable to suppose a god, and perhaps only a god, really possesses. Socrates refers to it as "a wisdom that is more than human" (20e1), never finds anyone who possesses it, even after years of searching, and claims that part of the message of the oracle is that "it is really the god who is wise and that in his oracle he is saying that human wisdom is worth little or nothing" (23a5–7).

Finally, Socrates presupposes throughout the *Apology* that those who cannot successfully defend themselves against the elenchus do not have expert knowledge of virtue. He never says in so many words, however, that what they cannot defend in particular is an account (*logos*) of what a virtue is. The famous "What is X (*ti esti*)?" question, so prominent a feature of many early Platonic dialogues, is not explicitly mentioned. Nonetheless, if, as is surely reasonable, we suppose that accounts of the virtues are among the targets of the elenchus in the *Apology* as well, then expert knowledge of virtue must enable someone to give an account of what a virtue is and to defend his account against the elenchus.

Although these facts about expert knowledge do not immediately tell us what it is, they point us in a fruitful direction; for the evidence we have concerning the roughly contemporary notion of a craft—stemming from such fifth-century Hippocratic treatises as *On Ancient Medicine* (*Med.*) and *On Craft* (*Cft.*), from Plato's other writings, and, of course, from Aristotle—strongly suggests that expert knowledge is precisely craft-knowledge.[46] And this, in fact, would make good sense: just as science is our paradigm of expertise, craft was the paradigm of expertise in Socrates' Greece. Fifth-century Greek physicians tried to prove that

---

45. See Irwin (1977, 296 n. 28).

46. The close relationship between ancient medicine and philosophy is discussed in Frede (1987, 225–260). Jaeger (1939, 3: 4) notices the analogies between "the ethical science of Socrates" and Greek medicine. The connections between *technē* and *epistēmē* in Plato are discussed in Lyons (1963, 139–228) and Schaerer (1930).

medicine is a craft, just as present-day psychiatrists try to prove that their discipline is a science.[47] It would be quite reasonable, therefore, for Socrates to suppose that those who claimed expertise or authority in ethics were claiming to have craft-knowledge of it.

What, then, is craft-knowledge? How did Socrates' intellectual contemporaries and near-contemporaries characterize it?

Craft-knowledge is, in the first place, *explanatory*. One must understand "the explanations [*ta aitia*]" of disease, if one is to give "proper care" (*Med.* 23). Knowledge of their explanations is necessary for both prevention and cure of diseases (*Cft.* 11). Flattery "has no rational account [*logon*] . . . and so it does not have the explanation [*aitian*] of each thing; and I do not call anything a craft which is without an account [*alogon*]" (Plato, *Grg.* 465a2−6). "Men of experience know that the thing is so but do not know why, while the others [who possess the relevant craft] know the 'why' and the explanation" (Aristotle, *Metaph.* 981a28−30).

Second, and perhaps as a consequence of being explanatory, crafts are *teachable*. "Anyone can be trained to be an expert who is lacking neither in education nor intelligence" (*Cft.* 9). Crafts are a form of knowledge, and all and only knowledge is teachable (Plato, *Prt.* 356e2−361b7). "Craftsmen can teach; men who rely on experience only cannot" (Aristotle, *Metaph.* 981b9−10).

Third, crafts have no need of luck or chance (*tuchē*); they are *luck-independent*. "They [the sick] did not want to look on barefaced luck, so they entrusted themselves to craft instead" (*Cft.* 4; 5−6; *Med.* 1, 12).[48] When wisdom, which is identified with the craft of politics, is present in someone, "the one in whom it is present is not still in need of good luck" (Plato, *Euthd.* 280b2−3; cf. *Grg.* 448c5−7). "Experience made craft, as Polus says, inexperience luck" (Aristotle, *Metaph.* 981a1−5; *EN.* 1140a16−20; *Po.* 1454a10−12).[49]

Crafts have other features, of course, some of which we shall examine below. But with just this much to hand, we can make considerable

47. Cf. Frede (1987, 233−234).

48. See Vlastos (1975, 406−407 n. 82).

49. Cf. Xenophon (*Mem.* III.ix.14): "When someone asked Socrates what he thought was the best pursuit for a man, he answered, Doing well [*eupraxia*]. Questioned further, as to whether he thought good luck [*eutuchian*] a pursuit, he said, On the contrary, I think that luck [*tuchēn*] and doing [*praxēn*] are opposites. To hit on something right by luck without search [*mē zētounta*] I call good luck; to do something well after study and practice I call doing well [*eupraxian*]; and those who pursue this I think do well [*eu prattein*]."

headway with expert knowledge. Crafts are explanatory and teachable. If expert knowledge of the virtues is craft-knowledge of them, then, we have an immediate explanation of why Socrates believes that it enables someone to teach virtue and to explain what he teaches. But, in addition, we have promising explanations of the other more mysterious features he attributes it.

Because "it is virtue that makes wealth and *everything else*, both public and private, good for a man" (30b3−4), virtue makes the knowledge of anything else, including the knowledge of the ordinary crafts, an unequivocally good thing for someone to have. Without virtue—or, worse, with a pretender in its stead—the possession of such knowledge, since it encourages false confidence, is a greater disaster than its nonpossession (*Euthd.* 279a1−281e5; *Men.* 87d11−89a3): not to know that one lacks craft-knowledge of virtue is culpable ignorance—the "most blameworthy ignorance of thinking that one knows when one does not know" (29b1−2). By leading the examined life, by submitting oneself to elenctic examination every day, one can avoid such ignorance and the vice to which it leads and "prepare oneself to be as good as possible" (39d7−8). That is why Socrates is really better off with just his human wisdom than all those craftsmen who, because they possess knowledge of their crafts, initially seem so much wiser.

Again, if virtue has the property of making life and its other components good and if craft is luck-independent, anyone who has craft-knowledge of virtue surely has a godlike power. For it does seem reasonable to suppose that only a godlike being could both reliably make himself virtuous and insulate the good he would thereby achieve from the threatening effects of bad luck (cf. *Men.* 100b2−4; *R.* 497b7−c3; 3.4).

One two-part feature of expert knowledge remains to be explained: Expert knowledge enables one to give accounts, and those accounts are elenchus-proof. It is hardly in doubt that, at least as far as Socrates is concerned, this is one of expert knowledge's most important features. But before we can decide whether craft-knowledge has it, we need to understand the feature itself somewhat better. We need to understand what it takes for a kind of knowledge to be elenchus-proof. And to do that we need to understand something about what it is supposed to be proof against.

A "standard elenchus" is an argument of the following form (Vlastos 1983b, 38−44; 1.8):

The candidate for the elenchus, C, produces a sincere belief, P, about a virtue (often a belief about what it is).

Under questioning, C accepts Q and R (or Q, R, S etc.).

Q and R entail not-P.

C's commitment to Q and R is sufficiently strong that, faced with the contradictory conclusion, he finds P to be problematic, not Q or R.

P is refuted.

What would it take for a belief to be proof against such an argument? The natural answer is that C's belief that P is elenchus-proof only if nothing in the universal set of his beliefs, to which his commitment is greater than it is to P itself, entails a proposition inconsistent with P.

The issue before us, then, seems to be twofold. Must some member of the set of beliefs which partly constitute someone's craft-knowledge of X be an account of what X is? Must that belief be elenchus-proof in the requisite sense?

In the Hippocratic treatises, form (*eidos*, *idea*), craft, and knowledge of what something is (*ti esti*) are found in close conceptual proximity. But the relations between them seem to be still largely implicit. *Med.* 22 distinguishes powers (*dunameis*) from structures (*schemata*). The former are "the intensity and strengths of the humours." The latter are anatomical properties of bones, organs, tissues, and the like. Both powers and structures seem to be included, however, in the wider class of forms: because hot things possess other *powers*, such as being insipid or astringent, it cannot be the case that they "participate in no other form [*eidei*]" than the hot (*Med.* 12); "there are many forms of structures [*eidea schematōn*] both inside and outside the body" (*Med.* 23). In *Med.* 20–24, we are told that part of the knowledge of "what man is [*ho ti estin anthrōpos*]," which a perfected medicine will provide, is knowledge of the powers of various diets and regimens and their effects on people whose bodies have different structures and powers. Medical knowledge of what man is seems, then, to involve knowing the form of a man and the forms of the various things which affect his health.[50]

In Plato's writings the equivalence between knowing the answer to Socrates' "What is X?" question and knowing the form of X is established from early on:[51]

50. For further discussion of the uses of *eidos* in the Hippocratic treatises see Baldry (1937); Gillespie (1912); Taylor (1911, 178–267).

51. This does not imply that the full-blooded "theory of forms," developed in such dialogues as the *Meno*, *Phaedo*, and *Republic*, is also present from the beginning. See Reeve (1988, 101–110).

Do you [Euthyphro] remember that I did not ask you to give me one or two examples of piety, but to explain that very form [*eidos*] which makes all pious things to be pious [*hōi panta ta hosia hosia estin*]? Do you not remember that you said that there was one form [*ideai*] which made impious acts to be impious, and pious things to be pious? . . . Tell me, then, what this form is [*tēn idean tis pote estin*], so that by looking to it and using it as a paradigm I may say that any act done by you or another which is of that sort is pious, and any act that isn't is impious. (6d9−e6)

The virtues, "even if they are many and various, all have one and the same form [*eidos*] which makes them virtues, and it is right to look to this when one is asked to make clear what virtue is" (*Men.* 72c6−d1). Craft and form are also related: the craftsman looks to the form in order to make particular things which have that form:

To what does the carpenter look in making the shuttle? Does he not look toward the thing it is the nature of a shuttle to be [*ho epephukei kerkizein*]? . . . And suppose the shuttle to be broken in the making, will he in making another look towards the broken one? Or will he look towards the form [*eidos*] he looked towards in making the other? . . . And might not that justly be called what the shuttle itself is [*auto ho estin kerkis*]? (*Crat.* 389a6−b6; cf. *R.* 596b5−8)

It seems, then, that someone who has craft-knowledge of X must know, in the requisite Socratic sense, what X is.

This same conceptual scheme also appears in Aristotle's writings:

From craft come the things whose form [*eidos*] is in the psyche of the producer—and by form I mean the essence [*to ti ēn einai*] of each thing and the primary substance [*ousian*]. . . . For example, health is the account in the psyche, the knowledge [of the form]. So the healthy thing comes to be when the physician reasons as follows: Since health is *this*, necessarily if the thing is to be healthy *this* must be present—for example, a uniform state—and if the latter is to be present, then there must be heat, and he goes on, always thinking like this, until he is led to a final this which he himself is able to make. Then the process from this point onward, toward health, is called production [*poiēsis*]. (*Metaph.* 1032a32−b10)

Indeed, the connections between craft, form, and knowing an account of what something essentially is, implicit in the Hippocratic treatises and explicit in Plato, have for Aristotle become literally definitive of craft.

The idea that someone who possesses craft-knowledge of X must know what X is is a persistent feature, then, of Greek thought about craft. The question is whether this knowledge must be elenchus-proof. Only Plato seems to claim explicitly that it must.[52] But his view is intelligible and might recommend itself to anyone. Craft-knowledge is explanatory. Someone who possesses it ought, therefore, to be able to express it (*Chrm.* 158e6–159a10; cf. Xenophon, *Mem.* IV.vi.1). Craft-knowledge, being knowledge, is consistent. A successful elenctic refutation could not, therefore, draw only on the interlocutor's craft-knowledge. But it seems certain that anyone who possessed craft-knowledge would be more committed to his craft beliefs than to any noncraft beliefs the elenchus showed to be inconsistent with them. An interlocutor who possessed craft-knowledge of virtue could answer Socrates' questions, then, and his answers would be elenchus-proof.

So far we have discovered that Socrates' near contemporaries are agreed that crafts are explanatory, teachable, and luck-independent. And in terms of these features we have been able to explain, at least in a provisional way, why Socrates says what he does about expert knowledge. This is strong evidence—which will be further strengthened in 3.4—that expert knowledge is indeed craft-knowledge. In the remainder of this section, we shall use this conclusion to determine whether expert knowledge has another feature thought to be definitive of the kind of knowledge Socrates disclaims.

The feature in question is *absolute certainty* or *infallibility*:

> When declaring that he [Socrates] knows absolutely nothing he is referring to that very strong sense in which philosophers had used them [the words for knowing] before and would go on using them long after—where one says one knows only when one is claiming certainty. (Vlastos 1985, 12; cf. 11-20).

The relevant notion of certainty or infallibility may be roughly characterized as follows. We have *fallible* knowledge that P if the evidence we have for P, though reasonable, does not entail P, does not preclude the possibility that P is false. We have *absolutely certain* or *infallible* knowledge that P if the evidence we have for P does entail P, does preclude the possibility that P is false. The question is, then, first, whether craft-knowledge is certain or infallible in this sense and, second, whether the knowledge Socrates claims is fallible.

52. Aristotle (*A. Po.* 72b3–4) does claim, however, that knowledge (*epistēmē*) must be elenchus-proof: "He who has unqualified knowledge [*epistamenon haplōs*] must be immovable by persuasion."

The starting points in medicine are "the observations made in the past" (*Med.* 2). The method is one of drawing on these to refine treatments, using "no other measure [*metron*] than bodily feeling" (*Med.* 9)—that is, how individual patients feel as a result of them—to determine their success. But because the relevant measure is bodily feeling, rather than something quantifiable, "exactness is difficult to achieve and small errors [*smikra hamartanein*] are bound to occur here and there" (*Med.* 9). Crafts strive for certainty, but "certainty [*atrekes*] is rarely seen" (*Med.* 9).

In Plato, the gap between crafts and certainty has widened and become more theoretical. Crafts (such as flute-playing) that use rather than produce can achieve certainty; for they yield knowledge, and knowledge is "infallible [*anamartēton*]." The productive crafts, however, cannot yield knowledge or certainty. The most we can hope for from them is true belief, and that only when their practitioners are guided by knowledgeable users (*R.* 477e4−478a1, 534b8−c5, 601d1−602a10).[53]

In Aristotle, this separation is all but complete. Full-blown knowledge is absolutely certain demonstrative knowledge of what is necessary or unalterable (*A. Po.* 71b9−72a14). Craft involves such knowledge and hence sometimes gets called *epistēmē* (*Metaph.* 981a5−7; cf. 981a10−12). But it also involves knowledge of particular things, which are neither necessary nor unalterable (*Metaph.* 981a16−17; *EN.* 1140a10−16, 1140a31−b4). Hence craft as a whole does not have the kind of demonstrative certainty required for full-blown knowledge (*EN.* 1140a31−b4; *MM.* 1197a33).

The story so far is one of increasing separation between craft and certainty. But we have omitted a crucial chapter. In Plato's Socratic dialogues, Socrates repeatedly makes the following four claims:

(1) Virtues are, or are closely analogous to, crafts (*Chrm.* 173a7−175a8; *Grg.* 460a5−461b2).

(2) Virtues must be always good, fine, and beneficial to their possessor, guaranteeing him happiness (*Euthd.* 278e5−279d6; *Men.* 88c2−5; 3.4).

(3) Only wisdom possesses these features, so that "wisdom is clearly virtue, either the whole of it or a part" (*Men.* 89a3; *Prt.* 351b4−362a4; 3.4).

(4) Wisdom would not be wisdom if it could make errors: "Wisdom everywhere makes men be of good fortune. For

53. See Reeve (1988, 58−95).

wisdom, I presume, could not make a mistake [*ou hamartanoi*] but must always do the right thing and achieve its end; for otherwise it would not be wisdom any longer" (*Euthd.* 280a6−8).

It seems clear, therefore, that Socrates is committed to the view that craft-knowledge is certain or infallible. That is why, when Thrasymachus claims that a craftsman "insofar as [*kath' hoson*] he is what we call him never makes errors [*oudepote hamartanei*]" (*R.* 340d7−e1), Socrates, unlike Thrasymachus' modern critics, accepts what he says without question.[54]

Socrates' near-contemporaries had doubts about the certainty of craft-knowledge. But Socrates himself seems to have had none. He did not disclaim craft-knowledge, however, simply and solely because it is certain; for he does not utterly disclaim certainty: "It is certain [*dēlon*]," he says at *Ap.* 41d3−6, "that it is now better for me to be dead and to leave my troubles behind" (3.11). And the expert craft-knowledge he does disclaim has other defining features besides certainty alone.

Expert knowledge seems to be craft-knowledge, then: that is to say, it is explanatory, teachable, luck-independent, elenchus-proof, certain knowledge.

1.8 NONEXPERT KNOWLEDGE

Thus far we have uncovered three distinct but related stages in Socrates' elenctic activities:

First Stage: Socrates examined himself and some others. This led him to the conclusion that he had no significant or noteworthy wisdom, and led Chaerephon to Delphi.

Second Stage: The Delphic oracle's response to Chaerephon— perplexing because of the negative outcome of the first stage—led Socrates to examine those with a reputation for wisdom, seeking to uncover in this way the true proposition which was the oracle's hidden meaning.

Third Stage: Having deciphered the oracle and found in it an Apollonian mandate to purge "himself and others" (38a4−5) of the hubris of thinking that they possessed expert knowledge of virtue, Socrates began his mission to Athens as servant to Apollo.

---

54. See Reeve (1985, 250−251).

We do not know the precise goal of first-stage examining, if it had one beyond intellectual exploration. But we know that its outcome was partly negative: "I know myself to be wise in neither a great nor a small way" (21b4–5). The goal of second-stage examining was to uncover the meaning of the oracle. The outcome was, again, partly negative (Socrates shows each reputedly wise person "that though he supposed himself wise, he was not"), but also partly positive (Socrates uncovered the meaning of the oracle and realized that he possessed human wisdom). The goal of third-stage examining was one part negative (to show people who think otherwise that they do not possess expert craft-knowledge of virtue) and two parts positive (to cure them of their hubris and to get them to care about wisdom, truth, and the best possible state of their psyche more than about money and honour).

In this section, we shall focus on third-stage elenctic examining. Our aim will be, by reflecting on its negative goal and on its antihubristic positive goal, to explain the existence and nature of Socrates' nonexpert ethical knowledge. In 3.4 and 3.10, we shall discuss the other positive goal of third-stage examining.

Socrates speaks in the *Apology* of examining people (21c3, 23b3–6, 28e4–6, 29e4–5, 38a4–5) and their lives (38a5–6; cf. 39c6–8) rather than of examining their beliefs about virtue. He makes it clear, nonetheless, that the examined life is precisely one in which elenctic discussion of virtue has a central place: "It is the greatest good for a human being to discuss virtue every day and the other things about which you hear me conversing and examining both myself and others, for the unexamined life is not worth living for a man" (38a2–6). Hence beliefs about the virtues, which have a profound effect on the lives of those who hold them, are the *primary* focus of an elenchus: "What I chiefly examine is the proposition [*logon*]. But the consequence may be that I the questioner and you the answerer may also be examined" (*Prt.* 333c7–9).

Only *sincere* beliefs have such profound effects, however; only their refutation counteracts hubris. Insincere beliefs have little effect on the lives of those who hold them and are abandoned without any humility-inspiring loss of self-esteem. It is easy to see, then, given the aim of third-stage examining, why Socrates often instructs his interlocutors to answer his questions only with their own sincerely held beliefs (*Cri.* 49c11–d2; *Grg.* 495a8–9, 500b5–c1; *Prt.* 331c4–d1; *R.* 350e5).[55]

---

55. See Vlastos (1983b, 27–38). Thrasymachus refuses to go along with this requirement: "What difference, he said, does it make to you whether I believe it or not? Isn't it my account that you are refuting?" (*R.* 349a9–10). The significance of this refusal for Plato's criticisms of Socratic ethical theory is discussed in Reeve (1988, 21–24).

Sincerity is one thing; dogmatism is another. And implicitly, at least, the difference between them is marked in the Socratic dialogues. Some interlocutors, like Polus in the *Gorgias*, exhibit dogmatic confidence in their ethical opinions. They are already hubristic and need to be cured through forceful refutation. Others, like Cleinias in the *Euthydemus* or Lysis and Menexenus in the *Lysis*, are sincere but modest and undogmatic. With them Socrates is gentler and more exploratory, aiming to counteract hubris by encouraging the intellectual openness and awareness of difficulties in received opinion which prevent its formation.

Let us imagine now that a candidate for an elenchus, C, produces a sincere belief P about a virtue. Provided Socrates believes that P is false, his initial goal is to refute P in a way that C will find compelling. Under what circumstances can Socrates honestly achieve his goal? There are essentially three. First, P might entail a contradiction just by itself. But that would be a very rare occurrence; most people do not have beliefs of this obviously self-contradictory sort. Second, C might accept a proposition Q which conflicts with P. That is more likely to happen but is still not all that common. Third, C might accept a set of propositions, Q and R (or Q, R, S, and so on), which entail not-P. This is much more likely to happen; people are often unaware of the concealed entailments of sets of propositions they accept.

Suppose that Socrates has found such a set of propositions and has demonstrated to C's satisfaction that they entail not-P. Must C accept that he was mistaken to believe P? No. For all that has been said so far, C might decide instead that he was wrong to accept Q or R (as Critias threatens at *Chrm.* 164c7–d3). To prevent this happening, Socrates must be sure that C's commitment to the set of propositions from which he derives not-P is greater than his commitment to P itself.

Given its goals and these few facts about logic and psychology, we would expect a standard third-stage elenchus to fit the following schematic description:

Under questioning, the candidate for the elenchus, C, produces a sincere belief P about a virtue.

Under questioning, C accepts Q and R.

Q and R entail not-P.

C's commitment to Q and R is sufficiently strong that, faced with the contradictory conclusion, he finds P to be problematic, not Q or R.

P is refuted.

An elenchus, then, is typically an argument directed against one of a person's sincere ethical beliefs, the premises of which are drawn from other propositions to which his commitment is greater: "the target is an opinion held by the respondent of the moment and the only worthwhile form of attack is through premises which have and keep his assent" (Burnyeat 1971, 214).

Day after day, Socrates must use an elenchus of this form to refute a wide variety of people he does not know. What would he need in the way of equipment to insure success? First, he would need as values for Q and R propositions which almost everyone would find it difficult to deny but which entail propositions which contradict likely values for P. Call the values for Q and R *acceptable propositions*.[56] Second, he would need *unacceptable propositions*. These are propositions which most people will reject because they contradict likely values for P but which are entailed by acceptable propositions. After nearly a lifetime of elenctic examination, then, Socrates should be in possession of both sorts of propositions. And, indeed, he is.

Socrates' favourite unacceptable proposition is this:

(A) It is better to suffer injustice than to do it.

He knows that most people will reject it on sight: "I know that only a few people believe this view or will believe it. And there is no common counsel between those who hold this view and those who do not, but of necessity they despise each other's views" (*Cri.* 49d2−5). But even though most people would reject (A), Socrates argues in the *Gorgias* that everyone implicitly believes it: "I think that I and you and other men believe that doing injustice is worse than suffering it" (474b2−5). Why does he think this? To find out we must look at the argument he uses to establish it.[57]

56. "The most conspicuous characteristic of Meno's answers is their conventionality and lack of originality" (Stokes 1986, 16). The same could be said for the views expressed by the majority of Socrates' interlocutors. When Thrasymachus rejects the acceptable proposition that justice is a virtue (*R.* 348b8−350c11), Socrates says (revealingly) that he cannot then refute him "by appeal to conventional principles [*kata ta nomizomena*]" (348e8−9).

57. Socrates' claim that everyone implicitly believes (A) and his later claim (479e8) that he has proved by elenctic argument that (A) is true are without exact parallel in the other Socratic dialogues. See Vlastos (1983c). But they are implicit in those dialogues. Socrates' frequent disclaimers of teaching are intelligible only if he presupposes that the conclusions of elenctic arguments are always implicitly believed by an interlocutor who accepts their premises (3.8). His injunction to

Polus claims that the contrary of (A) is true:

(1) Suffering injustice is worse [*kakion*] than doing it (474c5−6)

He also agrees, however, that

(2) Doing injustice is more shameful [*aischion*] than suffering it (474c7−8).

By presenting Polus with various cases or examples, Socrates then gets him to accept

(3) Something is fine [*kalon*] because it is pleasant or beneficial [*ōphelimon*] or both (474e5−475a1).

Since the shameful is the opposite of the fine, and the bad the opposite of the beneficial, Polus agrees that

(4) Something is shameful because it is painful or bad [*kakon*] or both (475a4−5).

On the basis of (3) and (4), he agrees that

(5) When one of two fine things is finer than the other, it is finer by being more pleasant or more beneficial or both, and when one of two shameful things is more shameful, it is more shameful by being either more painful or worse or both (475a5−b2).

On the basis of (2) and (5), he accepts

(6) Doing injustice is either more painful than suffering it or worse than suffering it (475b5−8).

But Polus also accepts

(7) Doing injustice is not more painful than suffering it (475b8−c3).

Hence he is forced to accept

the jury at *Ap.* 30c6−8, which we shall discuss below in 3.6, is intelligible only if he thinks that elenctic arguments can lead to knowledge. Given the form of such arguments, this is good evidence that he considers at least some of them to be proofs. It seems legitimate, therefore, to use these aspects of the *Gorgias* to illuminate elenctic argument generally. For further discussion of the *Gorgias* see Cooper (1982); Irwin (1986c). The argument with Polus which follows is discussed in Irwin (1979, 152−159); Vlastos (1967, 454−460).

(8) Doing injustice is worse than suffering it (475c7−9).

Socrates is now ready to justify his claim that everyone believes (A).

(9) Now didn't the mass of people [*tōn pollōn anthrōpōn*] and you yourself agree with us earlier that doing injustice is more shameful than suffering it? (475d1−3)

Socrates concludes that the mass of people believe (A).[58] He admits later, however, that repeated refutation may be necessary to convince them of this (513c7−d1).

Socrates' claim that most people believe his prize unacceptable proposition is based, then, on his belief that they would all accept (2)— together, no doubt, with the other propositions Polus accepts along the way. And, in fact, propositions like (2) and these others very frequently occur as premises in elenctic arguments.[59]

What epistemic status does Socrates attribute to these acceptable propositions? He does not tell us. But a plausible answer can be derived from what he does say. First, as (9) makes explicit, Socrates thinks that everyone really does accept or believe them. Second, he thinks that everyone will find them sufficiently compelling that they will continue to believe them even when they are shown to lead to something as antecedently unacceptable as (A)—otherwise he could not hold that even those people who deny (A) really believe it. Third, he thinks that (A) is true and that he has proved this: "In reality, then, agreement between you and me will finally reach the goal of truth" (*Grg.* 487e6−7); "And hasn't it been proved [*apodedeiktai*] that it [A] was said truly [*alēthē elegeto*]?" (479e8). Fourth, Socrates strongly implies that he *knows* (A): "I know well that [*eu oid' hoti*], if you agree with what my psyche believes, these very

---

58. What Socrates actually concludes is stronger. From (9) together with

(10) No one would choose the worse and more shameful over the less (475d4-e3)

he infers

(11) No one would choose injustice over suffering it (475e3-6).

But (10) and (11) presuppose that people believe (A).

59. Inferences from good or beneficial to fine are common (*Cri.* 48b8−9; *Prt.* 351b7−c3, 359e4−7). Virtues must be good (*agathon*), fine (*kalon*), and beneficial (*ōphelimon*) (*Chrm.* 159c1; *Euthd.* 278e5−282d3; *La.* 192c5−7; *Men.* 87e1−3; *Prt.* 349e3−5, 359e4−7). Virtues are, or are exactly analogous to, crafts (*Chrm.* 173a7−175a8; *Grg.* 460a5−461b2; *R.* 332d2−3). See Irwin (1977, 37−101).

beliefs are the true ones" (486e5−6). And in the *Apology* he represents a proposition with the same status as (A) as something known:

> (B) For know well [*eu gar iste*] that if you kill me, since I am the sort of man that I say I am, you will not harm me more than your-selves. (30c6−8)[60]

It seems reasonable to conclude that those acceptable propositions Socrates uses to establish unacceptable ones are, in his view at least, obvious truths. For unless they have this status, we cannot easily explain why they are generally believed, why they are found very compelling, and why as premises of proofs they can yield knowledge of the conclusions.[61]

It seems, then, that Socrates claims to know the conclusions of some of his arguments. But he is explicit that his knowledge of the conclusions is no more certain or secure than the arguments used to establish them:

> These things [(A)], having thus become evident [*houtō phanenta*] in the foregoing argument to be as I state them, have been clamped down and bound by arguments of iron and adamant which if you, or someone more energetic than yourself, is not able to undo, then it will not be possible for anyone to speak rightly unless he speaks as I do now. (*Grg.* 508e6−509a4; cf. 474a2−b2)

Polus has not been able to resist Socrates' argument, but another inter-locutor might succeed where he has failed and manage to undo the

---

60. Like (A), (B) is an unacceptable proposition. But, as we shall see in 3.6, it follows from acceptable propositions rather similar to those Socrates uses to support (A).

61. Gulley (1968, 43−44) argues that acceptable propositions must be self-evident. Kraut (1983, 65) argues that they "must be so eminently reasonable that they are *as yet* in no need of justification." Xenophon (*Mem.* IV.vi.15) claims that they must be "the most generally accepted opinions"—a view more recently defended in Polansky (1985, 247−253). Vlastos (1983b, 38−44) argues that a proposition is acceptable if it is sincerely held by the person being examined. Kraut, Xenophon, and Polansky are right to think that acceptable propositions must have a broad appeal. Vlastos is right that they must be sincerely believed. But it is not enough that they have these features; they must have them because they are obviously *true*. Truth and not just acceptability or reasonableness must enter the picture. To that extent Gulley is right. But he exceeds the evidence in suggesting that the truths in question must be self-evident.

"arguments of iron and adamant" which seem to establish (A). It would be hubris, therefore, to claim that (A) has been established with absolute certainty, once and for all, or to refuse to reexamine it or the premises on which it rests. In an elenchus, the interlocutor is under examination, but so is Socrates himself: "How could you think that I would refute you for any reason other than the one for which I would refute myself, fearing lest I might inadvertently think I know something when I don't know it?" (*Chrm.* 166c7−d2; cf. *Grg.* 506a3−5; *Hp. Ma.* 298b5−c2; *Prt.* 348c5−d3).

Moreover, Socrates couples his claim that he has proved that (A) is true and the strong implication that he knows that it is true with a version of his characteristic disclaimer of knowledge:

> But as for me, my position is always the same: I do not know how these things are [*tauta ouk oida hopōs echei*], but [I do know] this, that of all those I have encountered, as I have now, no one has been able to speak differently without coming off covered with ridicule. (509a4−7)

Socrates knows *that* (A) is true. But he does not know *how* it can be true, how it can be better to suffer injustice than to do it.[62]

Socrates claims not to know (A) with certainty, then, and not to be able to explain why it is true. Presumably, he would make parallel claims about (B). It follows that Socrates cannot have expert craft-knowledge of these propositions; craft-knowledge is certain and explanatory. Yet he implies that he knows (A) and claims that he knows (B). His knowledge of (A) and (B) must, therefore, be *nonexpert* knowledge. We must now try to determine what it is and whether it lacks all the features of expert craft-knowledge or only some of them.

Socrates does not know (A) and (B) with absolute certainty; he acknowledges the possibility that they might be overturned by arguments presented in the future. For the same reason, he does not have elenchus-proof knowledge of these propositions but only *elenchus-resistant* knowledge of them. Thus far they have proved irrefutable, but there is no guarantee that they will not be refuted in the future. Neither is Socrates'

---

62. In the *Republic*, Adeimantus says that he does not want a proof that justice is more choiceworthy for its own sake than injustice (367b2−3, 367e2−3). Like Glaucon, he already believes that (368a7−b3). What Glaucon and Adeimantus want is an *explanation* of how, in the face of Thrasymachus' arguments, justice can be more choiceworthy. Elenctic philosophizing alone cannot provide this sort of explanation. See Reeve (1988, 33−41).

knowledge luck-independent; bad luck may insure either that he does not notice the flaws in his own arguments or that he never meets someone who could in fact point them out to him. We are left with explanatoriness and teachability. Socrates claims explicitly, as we have just seen, that he does not know how (A) can be true: proofs are one thing; explanations are another. He also claims that elenctic examination is not teaching because it imparts no beliefs not already "in" the person being examined: (A) and (B) follow from propositions that the mass of people find acceptable and that are, in Socrates' view, (implicitly) believed by the mass of people. Thus nonexpert knowledge has none of the features definitive of expert craft-knowledge.

Turning back to human wisdom, we might characterize it more adequately as follows. Someone has human wisdom only if he recognizes that he has no explanatory, teachable, luck-independent, elenchus-proof, certain knowledge of virtue but that he does have some knowledge, of the sort (implicitly) possessed by all human beings, which, though elenchus-resistant, is nonexplanatory, unteachable, luck-dependent, and uncertain.

We have seen why, given the aims of third-stage examining, Socrates would need a supply of acceptable and unacceptable propositions. We have seen that he claims to know these. We have seen, too, that this claim does not compromise his characteristic disclaimer of expert craft-knowledge. These conclusions have not, certainly, been clamped down by arguments of iron and adamant. But perhaps enough has been said to show how the account of human wisdom developed in 1.6 might accommodate Socrates' initially perplexing claims to nonexpert ethical knowledge.

1.9 SOCRATES' DISCLAIMER OF KNOWLEDGE

Armed with these findings of 1.6−8, we are ready to discuss one of the central puzzles about Socrates, namely, the paradox of Socratic ignorance or the *disclaimer-of-knowledge paradox*. Socrates claims that he is wiser than others because he neither has knowledge of virtue nor thinks that he does. But he also frequently seems to claim or imply that he does have knowledge of virtue. These claims seem contradictory. Hence the paradox. The foregoing discussion suggests, however, that the contradiction is only apparent, that properly interpreted both claims are true. What Socrates is disclaiming is the craft-knowledge of virtue; what he is claiming is nonexpert knowledge. We must now test this potential resolution of the paradox against the text of the *Apology*.

The most significant of Socrates' disclaimers of knowledge (D*n*) are already familiar:

(D1) I know [*epaiō*] neither a lot nor a little [about oratory or natural science]. (19c2–5)

(D2) Certainly, I would pride and preen myself, if I knew [*ēpistamēn*] these things [the craft of teaching virtue]. But I do not know them [*all' ou gar epistamai*], men of Athens. (20c1–3; cf. 20d6–e3)

(D3) I know [*sunoida*] myself to be wise in neither a great nor a small way. (21b4–5)

(D4) They [the craftsmen] knew things that I did not know [*ouk ēpistamēn*]. (22d2–3)

To these we may add:

(D5) I have no adequate knowledge [*ouk eidōs hikanōs*] of things in Hades. (29b5)

(D6) I do not know [*ouk eidenai*] whether it [death] is a good thing or a bad thing. (37b6–7)

Clearly, then, Socrates makes other disclaimers of knowledge beyond the canonical one which registers his possession of human wisdom. Provided all of them are sincere, however, this need not trouble us.

But are all of them sincere? Most seem to be. (D1) is sincere, as we saw in 1.3. (D4), (D5), and (D6) are not controverted in the *Apology* or elsewhere. (D3) is sincere when it is uttered, otherwise it would hardly have led Socrates to examine the Delphic oracle's pronouncement at such length and personal cost. It is more circumscribed than it might seem, however, amounting, as we saw, to no more than a disclaimer of expert craft-knowledge of virtue. The ultimate sincerity of (D3) depends, then, as does that of (D2), on the question of whether or not Socrates ever manifests or implies that he possesses the craft-knowledge of virtue.

To settle that question we need a list of the things Socrates claims to know (K*n*):

(K1) I knew [*ēidē*] that I would find that they [the ordinary craftsmen] knew many fine things. (22d1–2)

(K2) And yet I know more or less [*oida schedon*] that I incur hatred by these very things. (24a6–7)

(K3) Know well [*eu iste*] that this [K2] is true. (28a6)

(K4) But to do what is wrong, such as to disobey one who is better than oneself, whether god or man, that I know [*oida*] to be bad and shameful. (29b6−7)

(K5) Know well [*eu iste*] that the god orders this. (30a5)

(K6) Know well [*eu gar iste*] that if you kill me, since I am the sort of man that I say I am, you will not harm me more than yourselves. (30c6−8)

(K7) Know well [*eu gar iste*], men of Athens, if I had tried long ago to be politically active, I would long ago have perished, and I would have benefited neither you nor myself. (31d6−e1)

(K8) If someone asserts that he ever learned anything from me or heard privately what everyone else did not, know well [*eu iste*] that he is not telling the truth. (33b6−8)

(K9) Or instead of this [death], am I to choose something that I know well [*eu oida*] to be bad and propose that? (37b5−c2)

(K10) I know well [*eu gar oid'*] that, wherever I go, the young will listen to me speaking just as here. (37d6−7)

(K11) It is certain [*dēlon*] that it is now better for me to be dead and to leave my troubles behind. (41d3−5)

A less cautious list might also include the following items, which, even though they are not explicitly of the form "I know or am certain that P," are surely knowledge claims nonetheless:

(K12) It looks as though in this [human wisdom] I really am wise [*tōi onti gar kinduneuō tautēn einai sophos*]. (20d8−9)

(K13) It was apparent [*ephanesan*] to me that the poets were also affected in the same way. (22c3−4)

(K14) I am convinced [*pepeismai*] that I am not voluntarily unjust to anybody. (37a5−6; cf. 37b3−4)

The length of the list should disturb anyone who thinks that Socrates claims to know only that he knows *nothing*.

Most of these examples are irrelevant, however, to the disclaimer-of-knowledge paradox. They are not craft-knowledge claims of any sort. But some—(K4), (K6), (K11), and (K14)—look more promising. As we shall see when we examine them in more detail in Chapter 3, however, these claims no more compromise Socrates' disclaimers than the other members of the list.[63] (K4) is an acceptable proposition; (K6) an unacceptable one which everyone—expert and nonexpert—nonetheless believes. (K11) is based on a divine revelation peculiar to Socrates, not on craft-knowledge.[64] (K14) is based on views about the effectiveness of the elenchus in combating blameworthy ignorance. Thus none of the knowledge claims Socrates makes in the *Apology* threatens the sincerity of any of his disclaimers or gives us any compelling reason to treat them as nonseriously or ironically tendered.[65]

Have we resolved the disclaimer-of-knowledge paradox, then, at least as far as the *Apology* is concerned? Not quite. A major problem remains to be negotiated. According to Socrates, someone who believes that he possesses craft-knowledge of virtue but who cannot defend his ethical views against elenctic scrutiny "does not . . . *possess* virtue, but only says that he does" (29e5–30a1). It follows that the craft-knowledge of virtue is necessary for virtue.

In addition to implying that the craft–knowledge of virtue is necessary for virtue, however, Socrates also says a number of things which seem to imply (I*n*) that he believed himself to be virtuous:

(I1) For know well that if you kill me, since I am the sort of man that I say I am, you will not harm me more than yourselves. For Meletus and Anytus would not harm me—would not even be able to—since I do not suppose it is lawful for a better man to be harmed by a worse [*ameinoni andri hupo cheironos blaptesthai*]. (30c6–d1)

63. Nonetheless, these texts do present difficulties for solutions to the disclaimer-of-knowledge paradox which suggest that Socrates claims only to have true belief about the virtues and ethical matters, not knowledge. This proposal is defended by Irwin (1977, 39–41, 61–63, 138–140); Santas (1979, 118–122, 311 n. 26); Woodruff (1982, 138–141). Vlastos (1985, 1–11) is convincingly critical.

64. (K11) threatens solutions to the disclaimer-of-knowledge paradox which argue that Socrates disclaims only certain or infallible knowledge. Vlastos (1985) owns the patents on this approach. He is followed by Teloh (1986, 1–23). Lesher (1987, 275–280) is critical.

65. Solutions to the disclaimer-of-knowledge paradox, therefore, which rely on irony are seriously problematic. See Gulley (1968, 69); Cornford (1939, 244–245); Teloh (1986, 30–32). It is important to note in this regard that Aristotle (*SE.* 183b6–8) takes Socrates' disclaimers of knowledge at face value: "Socrates asked questions but gave no answers himself; for he used to confess that he did not know [*ouk eidenai*]."

(I2) It does not seem fine [*kalon*] to me to do these things, being of the age I am and having the name that I have—for whether truly or falsely it is believed at any rate that Socrates in some way surpasses [*diapherein*] the majority of men. (34e3–35a1)

(I3) I thought that I was really too good [*tōi onti epieikesteron*] to survive if I went into these things. (36b9–c1)

(I4) What, then, am I worthy to suffer, being such a man? Something good [*agathon ti*], men of Athens, if you give what I deserve according to my true worth. (36d1–3; cf. *Grg.* 521b4–6)

(I5) For he [the Olympian victor] makes you seem to be happy [*poiei eudaimonas dokein einai*], while I make you be it [*egō de einai*]. (36d9–e1)

(I6) I am convinced [*pepeismai*] that I am not voluntarily unjust to anybody. (37a5–6)

(I7) Being convinced then [*pepeismenos dē*] that I do not do injustice to anyone . . . (37b2–4)

(I8) But you, too, members of the jury, should be of good hope towards death, and you should think this one thing to be true, that there is nothing bad for a good man, whether alive or dead, and his affairs are not neglected by the gods. (41c8–d2)

If these texts do indeed imply that Socrates believed he was virtuous, the disclaimer-of-knowledge paradox is regenerated. Socrates disclaims the craft-knowledge of virtue. He believes that possession of that knowledge is necessary for being virtuous. Yet he implicitly claims to be virtuous.

But do the texts carry this paradox-regenerating implication? As we shall see in 3.5 and 3.10, they do not. According to Socrates, most people falsely believe that they possess expert craft-knowledge of virtue. As a result, they not only lack virtue, they are guilty of hubris—of "the most blameworthy ignorance"—and of the vice to which it gives rise. But by regularly submitting themselves to elenctic examination (38a1–6), they could avoid blameworthy ignorance and its vicious consequences and become as good as it is possible for men to become in the absence, perhaps permanent, of the craft-knowledge of virtue (39d3–8). Because Socrates has spent each day for many years talking about virtue, "conversing and testing myself and others," he has been able to avoid all voluntary, because knowing, vice: (I6) "I am convinced that I am not voluntarily [*hekōn*] unjust to anybody." That, and not the possession of virtue, is the reason Socrates is happier and more virtuous (or more nearly virtuous) than Meletus and Anytus and most other people (*Phd.* 118a15−17).[66]

As far as the *Apology* goes, then, we do seem to have a promising resolution to the disclaimer of knowledge paradox. What Socrates disclaims is the craft-knowledge of virtue, and this he nowhere in the *Apology* either claims to possess or implies that he possesses.

We must now consider two problems for this solution which stem from other Platonic works often held to be continuous in doctrine and method with the *Apology*.

The first problem is this. In several places, Socrates defends the principle of "semantic monism" (Lesher 1987, 277−279):

> When we employ a term 'F' there is, in general, a single property F which 'F' designates, and which, when identified, can serve as a distinguishing feature of all the things designated by 'F' (*Euthphr.* 6e3−6; *Hp. Ma.* 287b4−289d5; *La.* 192a1−b8).

Presumably, he would apply this principle to 'knowledge'. But the solution we have been exploring to the disclaimer-of-knowledge paradox seems to involve a violation of it. When Socrates says "I know," he means that he has *ordinary* knowledge—justified, true belief, or whatever. But when he makes his canonical disclaimer of knowledge, he means that he has no *craft*-knowledge.

To see how our solution avoids this problem we need to reflect on the difference between *senses* of the word 'knowledge' and *kinds* of knowl-

---

66. Vlastos (1985, 6 n. 14) argues that in (I7) Socrates claims that "he is convinced that he does no wrong to anyone." And that he must, therefore, be "serenely confident" that he has achieved both virtue and, with it, happiness. But (I7) does not show this. In (I6) Socrates says, "I am convinced that I am not voluntarily [*hekōn*] unjust to anybody." And it is to this claim that he is referring back in (I7)—notice that he begins, "Being convinced then [*pepeismenos dē*] . . ." Hence what he is actually denying is only that he has *voluntarily* wronged anyone. And he can deny this simply on the grounds that he has not done wrong to anyone out of blameworthy ignorance. So (I7) does not imply that Socrates believed that he was virtuous. The same seems to me to be true of *Grg.* 522c8−d2, which Vlastos also cites in this regard. Socrates exhibits confidence about his postmortal fate because he "has never wronged man or god in word or deed." But such confidence is justified by a belief that he has avoided voluntary wrongdoing (*Grg.* 488a2−4); for Socrates is explicit that involuntary wrongdoing merits only instruction not punishment (*Ap.* 26a1−4).

edge. Ornithology and bacteriology are kinds of knowledge. But their existence does not entail that the word 'knowledge' has many senses (cf. *R.* 438c6−e8). Ornithology is justified, true belief (or whatever) about birds; bacteriology is justified true belief (or whatever) about bacteria. In the same way, craft-knowledge (*technē*) is justified, true belief (or whatever) about a craft. But, unlike birds and bacteria, crafts themselves have epistemic features. They are teachable, explanatory, luck-independent, elenchus-proof, and certain. Hence one cannot have justified true beliefs (or whatever) of the sort that make one a craftsman unless the justifications one has are teachable, explanatory, luck-independent, elenchus-proof, and certain. The reason craft-knowledge is not ordinary knowledge, then, is not that it involves a nonordinary sense of 'knowledge', but that it is knowledge—in the ordinary sense of the word—of something only experts know. Hence its existence in no way compromises the principle of semantic monism.

The second problem is more complex, and a fully adequate discussion would take us too far afield. Nonetheless, it is important to indicate, at least in a provisional way, how our solution to the disclaimer-of-knowledge paradox might accommodate it.

Socrates strongly suggests on a number of occasions that he cannot know whether a given virtue has a certain feature because he does not know *what* the virtue in question is (*Hp. Ma.* 286c8−d2, 304d5−e3; *La.* 190b7−c5; *Ly.* 212a4−7, 223b4−8; *Prt.* 361c2−6; *R.* 354c1−3). Then, in the *Meno*—which is not usually classified as a Socratic dialogue—we find the quite general claim that all knowledge is *what-presupposing*:

If I do not know what something is [*ti estin*], how can I know of what sort [*hopoion*] it is? (71b1−4)

What does this claim amount to? A natural thought is this. Socrates' elenctic questioning about a virtue is frequently designed to elicit knowledge of what it is (*ti esti*); hence, when he claims that knowledge is what-presupposing, he must mean that it presupposes knowledge of the kind of answer to the question about what it is that he himself is seeking in the case of virtue, namely, craft-knowledge of what it is.[67] But if this is the case, our solution to the disclaimer-of-knowledge paradox seems to be seriously threatened. For Socrates would be committed to holding that knowledge about how virtue is—which might well be taken to include the various kinds of knowledge that he exhibits in the *Apology*—

---

67. See Geach (1972, 34); Robinson (1953, 51−53). Irwin (1977, 294 n. 4); Kraut (1984, 274−279); Nehamas (1987, 277−293) are critical.

presupposes the very craft-knowledge of what it is that we are committed to holding he altogether disclaims. The question we must pursue, then, is whether the doctrine that knowledge is what-presupposing should be understood in this way.[68]

Immediately following the claim that knowledge is what-presupposing, Socrates gives this illustration of what he has in mind: "Or do you think that someone who does not know at all [*parapan*] who Meno is could know whether he is fine or wealthy or well-born, or the opposite of these?" (*Men.* 71a4–7; cf. *La.* 190a6–c3). But surely this cannot be an illustration of the principle that knowledge of how something is presupposes craft-knowledge of what it is. For Socrates can hardly be saying that, unless someone has craft-knowledge of who or what Meno is (whatever exactly that would be), he cannot know whether he is fine or wealthy or well-born. All he seems to be claiming, as his characterization of his example strongly suggests, is that if someone does not know "at all" who or what Meno is, he cannot say whether or not he has these qualities.[69] And this seems to be a perfectly reasonable view—an acceptable proposition. Imagine yourself being asked, "Is Meno wealthy?" when you have no idea who Meno is. The natural response is to say, "How can I know whether he's wealthy or not when I haven't the slightest idea who he is?"

<hr>

68. Not everyone believes, however, that this is the right question to pursue. "The early dialogues, taken as a group, do contain a contradiction, for the epistemic principle laid down in the *Meno* and followed by both the *Gorgias* and *Republic* I is violated in the *Apology*. But it is hardly surprising to discover that Plato's description of Socrates changes, as he begins to develop his own views" (Kraut 1984, 277). If Kraut is right, the principle that knowledge is what-presupposing is irrelevant to the disclaimer-of-knowledge paradox, and the discussion which follows in the text is unnecessary. But the matter is controversial. See Irwin (1986b, 407–410).

69. "If Meno does have an 'essence,' this is an intuitively obvious one: it is his provenance. And knowing this is indeed necessary in order to know (in any sense you like) whether nobility, wealth, and a distinguished birth, all of which are a function of his provenance and to that extent 'essential' to him, do or do not belong to him" (Nehamas 1987, 283–284). This ingenious proposal seems somewhat problematic, however; for it is not obvious that we do have to know Meno's provenance in order to know (or believe) that he is *wealthy*. If we have access to his bank balance (or the equivalent), that will usually be sufficient. Cf. Euripides (*El.* 367–390). Nehamas (1985, 5–6) adopts a view closer to the one defended in the text: "His [Socrates'] point is simple and intuitive: if he has *no* idea who Meno is, how can he answer any questions about him?"

Now, some kinds of knowledge of what a thing is are very easy to acquire. We all know that justice is justice, or that Meno is Meno. Some are more difficult to acquire. Only a few have craft-knowledge of what a shuttle or a flute is. Some are very difficult to acquire indeed. No human being, not even Socrates, seems to have craft-knowledge of what justice or any other virtue is. But it certainly does not follow that no one has any knowledge of the other, easier kinds. Indeed, as many have noticed, Socrates himself actually claims to have some of them: "To live well is the same as to live honourably and justly" (*Cri.* 48b4−10); "Wisdom is clearly virtue, either the whole of it or a part" (*Men.* 89a3). We shall examine these and related texts in 3.4.

Socrates' principle about what-presupposition seems to amount, then, only to the relatively uncontentious claim that all knowledge of whether a thing has a certain property presupposes *some* knowledge of what it is. And this principle would pose a problem for the solution we have proposed to the disclaimer-of-knowledge paradox only if Socrates had no knowledge whatsoever of what virtue is. Since he does have such knowledge, the problem seems to be averted.

One final difficulty deserves mention. At *Men.* 71b1−3, Socrates says: "I myself, Meno, am as poor as my fellow countrymen in this regard and confess to my shame that I have no knowledge of virtue at all [*ouk eidōs peri aretēs to parapan*]" (71b1−3). Taken in isolation, this text strongly suggests that Socrates is claiming to be totally ignorant about virtue, to know nothing at all about what it is or (consequently) about what it is like. But if we look at it in context, it seems much more likely that it is a disclaimer only of expert craft-knowledge of these things. Here is the preface Socrates makes to his disclaimer:

> In the past, Meno, the Thessalians had a great reputation among the Greeks for their wealth and their horsemanship. Now it seems they are philosophers as well. . . . The reason for this is Gorgias. He went to that polis and won the love of the leading Aleuadae because of his wisdom and also of the leading Thessalians. He accustomed you to give bold and magnificent [*aphobōs te kai megaloprepōs*] answers to any question you are asked, the sort that those who know [*tous eidotas*] are likely to give, just as he himself invites questions of any kind from any Greek who wishes to ask them and never fails to give an answer. But here in Athens, dear Meno, it is just the opposite. There is a dearth of wisdom, as though it had migrated from our part of the world to yours. If you ask any of us your question, he will laugh and say, You must think me fortunate indeed to know whether virtue can be taught or how it is acquired. The fact is that,

far from knowing whether or not it can be taught, I have no idea at all what virtue is [*pot' esti to parapan aretē tugchanō eidōs*]. (70a5–71a7).

Socrates is contrasting the wisdom of the Thessalians with that of the Athenians: the latter, unlike the former, cannot give the sort of "bold and magnificent" answers to questions about virtue that Gorgias and other experts are likely to give, the sort of answers for which he himself is unsuccessfully searching (71c3–4), the sort that earn one a reputation for real wisdom. Socrates then says that he himself is like his fellow Athenians in this respect (71b1–2). He does not have any of the kind of knowledge Gorgias claims—any expert knowledge—of what virtue is. He then appeals to the principle that knowledge is what-presupposing to derive the conclusion that he has "no knowledge of virtue at all" (71b3). On the reasonable assumption that *expert* knowledge of what something is like presupposes *expert* knowledge of what it is, while nonexpert knowledge of what it is like often presupposes no more than nonexpert knowledge of what it is, this conclusion should be understood as a disclaimer only of all expert knowledge of virtue. Like his fellow Athenians, Socrates has nonexpert humdrum knowledge of what virtue is and what it is like. He knows "plenty of things, at least plenty of small ones [*polla, smikra ge*]" (*Euthd.* 293b7–8).[70]

1.10 SOCRATES' ETHICAL RELIGION

The Delphic oracle commended elenctic examination; other dreams and oracles explicitly commanded it. Socrates repeatedly claims that Apollo has "ordered" him to philosophize and that to cease would be to "disobey" that order (23a5–c1, 28d6–29a1, 29b6–7, 30a5, 31a7–b1, 33c4–7, 37e5–38a6). It is tempting to conclude that his mission is based entirely in religion, that he carries it out simply and solely because Apollo has ordered him to do it. Some writers have succumbed to this temptation:

> The certainty of Socrates' assessment of the moral significance of his mission is logically independent of whatever beliefs he may have about the nature of virtue. . . . [H]is certainty about the moral im-

---

70. But we should not infer from this that Socrates has *complete* nonexpert knowledge of what virtue is like. In particular, he may not have nonexpert knowledge of whether or not virtue is teachable; for he may not have elenchus-resistant beliefs about its teachability. Cf. Kraut (1984, 288–304).

portance of his mission is derived from various forms of divination, and not from whatever conception of virtue he has developed and continues to test by means of the *elenchos*. (Brickhouse and Smith 1988, 107)

But others have argued that Socrates never does anything just because a god or an oracle has commanded or encouraged it:

There is, in my opinion, not a trace of voluntarism in Socrates' "obedience" to the god; on the contrary, he only does, as he always did, what he thinks is, on independent grounds, the best thing. (Nehamas 1987, 305–306)

We shall see, as we probe the nature of Socratic religion, that the truth lies between these views, although much closer to the second than the first.

The primary source of theology for the Greeks is the myths embodied in the writings of the poets. Homer and Hesiod, Herodotus tells us, "created for the Greeks a genealogy of the gods, gave the gods their epithets, distributed their honours and competences, and stamped them with their form" (2.53).[71] The primary source of knowledge about the gods for Socrates, as we see from the *Euthyphro*, is elenctic argument. This is a significant difference, certainly. But there are two important reasons not to overdraw it.

First, cliché notwithstanding, the writings of Homer, Hesiod, and the other poets never had the status of a Bible. They were not supported by a church and clergy, for example, and they did not have to be believed on pain of heterodoxy or excommunication—terms of doubtful application in Greek religion.[72] By the time of Socrates' trial, moreover, it is possible to speak of a "collapse of the authority of the poets and the myth administered by them" and of "the creation of a typical enlightened attitude of the average educated man towards religion" which represented the poet's myths, literally understood, as "untrue and impious" (Burkert 1985, 317–321). It is significant that "even such a zealot as Euthyphro expresses neither horror nor surprise" when Socrates refuses to believe the traditional stories about Zeus castrating his father (Taylor 1911, 16 n. 1).

Second, elenctic arguments rely on premises which must prove acceptable to the people Socrates examines. It is scarcely a surprise, therefore, that Socratic theology has at least one foot in Homer and Hesiod.

71. See Burkert (1985, 119–125).

72. See Burkert (1985, 8); Lloyd-Jones (1971, 134); Taylor (1911, 15–16).

Socrates never questions the existence of the gods, for example. Nor, more important for present purposes, does he question the traditional view that the gods are supremely wise and knowledgeable (Homer, *Od.* 4.379, 20.75−76; Hesiod, *Op.* 267; *Thg.* 886−900). In the *Hippias Major* (289b3−6), he endorses the claim of Heraclitus that "the wisest man is to the god as an ape is to a man." Part of the message he extracts from the Delphic oracle is that "it is really the god who is wise, and in this oracle he is saying that human wisdom is worth little or nothing" (23a5−7). But of course the conclusions Socrates reaches from acceptable premises are not themselves always equally acceptable. And this is as true in moral theology as it is in morals proper.

Piety, as traditionally conceived, is largely a matter of ritual, of knowing how to pray and offer sacrifice.[73] Euthyphro, who claims expertise in religious matters, finds an account of this sort congenial: "If a man knows [*epistētai*] how to say and do things acceptable to the gods in prayers and sacrifices, those things are pious." (*Euthphr.* 14b2−4). But Socrates rejects this answer:

> You could be much briefer than that, Euthyphro, if you wished, if you tell me the principal thing [*to kephalaion*] I asked for. But you aren't eager to teach me, that is certain; for just now, when you were on the point of doing so, you turned away; and if you had answered, I would have received adequate instruction about piety from you. (14b8−c3)

Now, the account of justice under examination at this point in the dialogue is that piety is "service to the gods [*hupēretikē theois*]" (13d7).[74] And the question from which Euthyphro turns aside is that of explaining what "the principal thing [*to kephalaion*] is" which the gods produce, using us as their servants (13d9−14a10). This is the thing which Socrates

---

73. See Dover (1974, 246−254); Mikalson (1983).

74. A number of commentators on this argument have suggested that "service to the gods" is, or is part of, the definition Socrates wants. See Brickhouse and Smith (1988, 91−96); McPherran (1985). But this cannot be right. First, it is inconsistent with Socrates' claim that it is "the principal thing" (14a1−2, 14b9)—the thing the gods produce using us as their servants—that holds the key to the definition he seeks. Second, it prevents us from taking literally his claim (14b8−9) that Euthyphro's account of piety could have been "much briefer"; for the account he gives at 14b1−7 does not contain the phrase *hupēretikē theois*. Finally, and perhaps most important of all, it is inconsistent with the view, which as we shall see Socrates expresses elsewhere, that piety, in common with the other virtues, is identical to knowledge.

claims would yield the account of piety he wants. But what is it? A few lines later, Socrates himself suggests the answer: "What the gods give us is certain; for there is nothing that is good which they do not give us" (14e11–a2). What the gods produce, using us as their servants, then, must be a good thing. As we shall see in 3.4, however, there is really only one good thing, namely, knowledge or wisdom. A servant who could produce knowledge could, therefore, produce all good things. But a servant who could do that would not just be pious; he would be completely virtuous:

> Therefore, do you think, my friend, there could be anything lacking in the virtue of someone who knew all good things and how they are and have been and will be produced and all about evil things likewise? Do you think that such a person would be lacking in justice or moderation or piety, when he alone, because of his knowledge of how to deal correctly with them, knows how to take proper precautions in his dealings with gods and men, both in regard to what is to be feared and what not, and in regard to getting good things?—I think, Socrates, that there is something in what you say.—But, then, what you describe [the knowledge of good and evil] will not be only a part of virtue, but the whole of virtue [*sumpasa aretē*]. (*La.* 199d4–e4; cf. *Grg.* 507a5–c7; *Prt.* 331a6–b8)

Piety is simply knowledge, then. And that is why Euthyphro's answer, though it is right in mentioning knowledge (14b3), could, by omitting the other things he mentions, have been much briefer.

These two doctrines, the traditional one about the superlative wisdom of the gods and the nontraditional one about the identity of virtue and wisdom, are at the basis of another Socratic departure from tradition. The gods are not only superlatively wise, they are *ipso facto* superlatively virtuous as well. That is why they are the source only of good things (*Euthphr.* 14e11–a2; cf. *R.* 335b2–e6, 379b1–c7). That is why they are in harmony with one another, loving and hating in unison (*Euthphr.* 7c10–9e3). That is why, presumably, Socrates is already confident, when he learns of the oracle to Chaerephon, that Apollo could not be lying (*Ap.* 21b6–7). To an unenlightened Athenian brought up on traditional stories about the disagreements between the gods and their casual and cruel treatment of mortals, this conclusion could only come as welcome, albeit perhaps rather shocking, news.[75] There are more shocks in store for him.

75. The general topic of the justice of the gods of tradition is, however, unsettled and controversy-ridden. See Adkins (1960); Dodds (1951); Griffin (1980, 179–204); Lloyd-Jones (1971).

The virtues are paradigmatically instantiated by the superlatively wise gods. But they are totally independent of the gods and of their approval or disapproval. Piety is loved by the gods because it is piety; it is not piety because it is loved by the gods (*Euthphr.* 10a1–11b5).[76] This may or may not be a "heterodox" view. Most people are unlikely to have very clear opinions about the metaphysics of morals. But it certainly conflicts with the suggestion in Homer that the ultimate ethical sanction on Zeus is the disapproval of the other gods (*Il.* 4.24–29, 16.439–443, 22.177–181). The virtues are not just independent of the gods, however; they are more important. For the demands of virtue are supreme and override *all* others, divine or human. The *only* thing a person should take into account is "whether his acts are just or unjust, the deeds of a good or a bad man" (*Ap.* 28b5–9; cf. 28d6–10; *Cri.* 48c6–d5).

The consequences of these elenchus-based conclusions for the authority of the gods are profound. Because we know that the gods are good and virtuous, we know that whatever they command must itself be good and virtuous. Because we know that the demands of virtue override all others, we know that we must obey those commands. But because virtue is independent of the approval or disapproval of the gods, the authority divine commands have over us derives entirely from the independent and overriding ethical authority of the virtues. The authority of the gods is therefore derivative. We should obey them because, on the basis of elenctic argument, we have discovered that we have an independent ethical reason to do so. The gods are better than we are, and "it is bad and shameful" to disobey someone better than ourselves (*Ap.* 29b6–7).

The general reason Socrates pays such heed to the Delphic oracle, therefore, the reason he is guided by the approval of elenctic examination he discovers in it, is not fundamentally a religious reason but an elenctically based ethical reason. That is why he can say with such confidence: "Not now for the first time, but always, I am the sort of man who is persuaded by nothing in me except the argument [*tōi logōi*] that when I reason [*logizomenōi*] seems to me to be the best" (*Cri.* 46b4–6).[77]

So far we have been discussing religious belief—dogma. But the most important aspect of Greek religion "was not dogma, but cultus, the practice of the proper rules of 'giving and receiving between God and

76. The argument has been widely discussed. See Cohen (1971); Geach (1972); Sharvy (1972).

77. My attention was drawn to this important passage by Vlastos, "The Paradox of Socratic Piety."

man' " (Taylor 1911, 16). When Plato comes to deal with this aspect of religion in the *Republic*, he recognizes that it is largely inaccessible to philosophical argument:

> What legislation, he [Adeimantus] asked, remains for us to discuss?—For us, none remains, I said. But for Apollo at Delphi, the most important, the finest, and the first remain.—What are these?—The founding of temples, sacrifices, and other types of service to gods, daimons, and heroes; and, again, funeral services, and the kinds of services which will insure the favour of those in that other place; for we do not know anything about these things ourselves, and, in establishing our polis, we won't, if we are wise, be persuaded by anyone except our ancestral interpreter. And the ancestral interpreter of these things to all men is the god who sits in the middle of the earth at its navel and delivers his interpretations. (427b1−c4)

A similar recognition is implicit in the thought and practice of Socrates. Ancestral and household gods, religious festivals and sacrifices, which were so prominent a part of Athenian life,[78] were a part of his life as well. In the *Euthydemus*, he says that he has "domestic and ancestral altars and shrines of the sort that other Athenians do," at which he worships "Apollo, Zeus, and Athena" (302c4−303a3; cf. *Ap.* 35d5−7). "All who happened to be near at the time," he proclaims in Xenophon, "have seen me—as Meletus himself could have done if he had so desired—sacrificing at the public festivals and on the public altars" (*Ap.* 11−12; cf. *Mem.* I.i.2). There is no suggestion in Plato or elsewhere, however, that Socrates thought that the elenchus should guide him in these matters. Nonetheless, this aspect of his religion, too, is transformed by the elenchus-based doctrines we have been exploring.

First, Socrates completely rejects the magical elements which almost invariably form part of ritual for the vast majority of worshippers.[79] The gods, being wise and virtuous, respond to our goodness (*Ap.* 41c8−d2; *Euthphr.* 15b1−2), to the justice and piety of our psyches, not to our gifts

---

78. See Burkert (1985, 216−275); Parke (1977).

79. This difference is emphasized by Vlastos, "The Paradox of Socratic Piety." In Murdoch (1986, 119)—a subtle dramatic exploration of Socratic religion— Socrates is made to say: "But of course, religion mustn't become magic. There's no secret knowledge, no complete explanation; we must be humble and simple and see what we know and respect what we don't know."

and sacrifices (*Alc. 2* 149e3–150b3). If it were otherwise, piety would be nothing but "a commercial craft" (*Euthphr.* 14e6–7), and the gods would be "like evil moneylenders" (*Alc. 2* 149e4–5). But, second, the gods *are* inevitably pleased by our virtue: the affairs of a good man "are not neglected by the gods" (*Ap.* 41c8–d2).[80] Traditional religion offered no such comfort. It is better that whole cities—even cities whose sacrifices have made them dear to Zeus—should fall than that gods should quarrel over the fate of mere mortals (Homer *Il.* 4.20–72). This has been aptly described as "a nightmare picture for men" (Griffin 1980, 196–197). In Socratic religion, it is an impossible picture.

The general authority of a divine command in Socratic religion is based, as we have seen, on the independent, elenchus-established authority of virtue. But is more required than that? Does Socrates also think that each particular command needs to be independently justified before being obeyed? Does he think, for example, that he is not obliged to obey the oracles and dreams which ordered him to undertake his mission simply because they are the commands of an ethically perfect god, unless he can establish on wholly independent grounds that it is the best thing for him to do? To answer this question it is useful to explore one of the strangest aspects of Socrates' religion, his *daimonion*.

Socrates first mentions his *daimonion* in the *Apology* when he is cross-examining Meletus. He argues that his *daimonion* is a daimonic activity the occurrence of which presupposes the existence of a substantive daimon who is the child of a god (26b2–28a1).[81] Later on, he says that this daimonic activity is vocal:

A divine and daimonic thing [*theion ti kai daimonion*] comes to me . . . This began in childhood—a certain voice comes [*phōnē tis*], and whenever it comes, it always turns me away from what I am about to do, but never urges me to go ahead. (31c8–d4; cf. *Thg.* 128d1–7)

80. Aeschines of Sphettus, one of Socrates' closest friends and himself the author of Socratic dialogues, credits Socrates with the doctrine that "the fine and good get a better deal from the gods because of their greater piety" (Dittmar 1912, Fr. 8, lns. 61–62).

81. Zeller (1885, 85–86) overlooks this passage: "By the *daimonion* in the sense of Socrates, no genius, no separate or distinct personality can be understood, but only vaguely some heavenly voice or divine revelation." Cf. Burkert (1985, 179–181); Guthrie (1971a, 82–85); Riddell (1877, 109–117).

Later still, he claims that the daimonic voice is "the sign of the god" [*to tou theou sēmeinon*] (40b1) and characterizes it as restraining him if he was "about to do something that was not right" (40a4−6). This strongly suggests—as does his acceptance as fact that it is the voice of a child of the gods—that the *daimonion* is subject to the same elenctically based ethical constraints as the gods themselves. Presumably, then, we can take Socrates' responses to daimonic prohibitions as evidence of his attitude to divine commands.

So how does Socrates respond to these prohibitions? Does he apply some independent rational test to determine whether they are really daimonic prohibitions and not some other, ethically unreliable ones? Does he always resort to critical reason in order to determine their meaning? Does he always try to justify them independently? All the evidence suggests that he does none of these things. He never mentions having to interpret the *daimonion*'s prohibitions, which seem always to have been entirely unequivocal and straightforward. He never submits them to any test either of authenticity or of truth. He simply acts on them without reflection. In the *Euthydemus*, for example, Socrates is about to leave the gymnasium "but as I was getting up there came the usual daimonic sign [*to eiōthos sēmeion to daimonion*]. So I sat down again" (272e1−273a1). Here nothing—no elenctic examination, no interpretation, no exercise of critical reason—intrudes between the sign and the action it enjoins. In *Alcibiades 1*, we learn that "a certain daimonic opposition [*ti daimonion enantiōma*]" prevented Socrates from abandoning Alcibiades (103a4−6). Nothing is said, however, about his having had trouble understanding what the *daimonion* was saying or wondering whether it was really his *daimonion* talking or testing its instructions to determine on independent grounds whether following them was really the best course of action (cf. *Thg.* 128d7−129e9).[82]

But perhaps the most dramatic example of Socrates' willingness to accept the prohibitions of his *daimonion* without independent justification—although not, in this case, without some small resort to interpretation—occurs in the *Apology* itself. Prior to being sentenced to

---

82. These facts about how Socrates responds to the *daimonion* make it difficult to accept the view developed by Vlastos, "The Paradox of Socratic Piety," that Socrates' exhibits his commitment to critical reason in always using it to determine the meaning of divine signs. Socrates does resort to the elenchus to determine the meaning of the Delphic oracle. But, then, it is a *riddle*. There is no reason to believe that the other dreams, oracles, and daimonic prohibitions Socrates received were equally in need of decoding.

drink the hemlock, Socrates makes three claims about death: "We have no adequate knowledge of things in Hades" (29b5); "No one knows whether death may not be the greatest of all goods for a man" (29a6−b1); "I do not know whether death is a good or a bad thing" (37b6−7). Prior to being sentenced, therefore, Socrates does not know whether it is better for him to be alive than dead. Perhaps what will happen to him in Hades will make any earthly life seem glorious by comparison. Having been sentenced, however, Socrates gets a new piece of evidence about death, namely, that his *daimonion* has not opposed the course of action which has led to the death sentence. On the basis of this new evidence and that of the previous behaviour of the *daimonion*, he concludes: "It is certain [*dēlon*] that it is now better for me to be dead and to leave my troubles behind. Because of this the sign did not hold me back" (41d3−6). If, as seems clear, Socrates could not achieve certainty on this head except from a divine source (who else could know about the postmortal fate of the psyche?), we may conclude not only that he obeys the prohibitions of the *daimonion* without independently justifying them, but that he uses the *daimonion* to establish truths which he could not establish in any other way.

Socrates is willing, then, to obey divine commands and prohibitions simply on the basis of the elenctically established goodness of the gods. He does not need to justify each particular command and prohibition independently of the fact that he believes it to have a divine source. Thus the dreams and oracles which he believed to contain a divine command to examine his fellows would have constituted a sufficient reason for him to undertake his mission. That reason is not, however, logically independent of—indeed, it crucially depends upon—his elenctically sustained beliefs about virtue and the gods. For the authority of divine commands stems from those beliefs.

Socrates does not need an independent reason, beyond that provided by his dreams and oracles, to undertake his elenctic mission to Athens. But does he nonetheless have such a reason? The following passage suggests that he does:

> Perhaps someone might say, "But, Socrates, if you go into exile, will you not be able to be silent and live quietly?" This is the most difficult thing of all to persuade some of you about. If I say that it is impossible for me to keep quiet because that means disobeying the god, you will not believe me, because you will think I am being ironical. On the other hand, if I say that it is the greatest good for a human being to discuss virtue every day and the other things about which you hear me conversing and examining both myself and

others, for the unexamined life is not worth living for a human being, you will believe me even less. (37e3−38a6)

On the one hand, Socrates has a religious reason to live the examined life: the god has ordered him to do it (29b6−7). On the other hand, he has a prudential reason to live the examined life: it is the best life for a human being, and a person must do what he thinks best, even at the risk of death (28d6−10). [83] *Prima facie*, then, religion gives Socrates one reason to live the examined life, and prudence gives him another, independent reason to do so. The question we must now pursue is whether these reasons are fully independent.

One basis for thinking they are not has do with certainty. As we shall see in 3.10, Socrates has an elenchus-based reason, which makes no reference to the gods, to believe that the examined life is best. Thus, in one quite straightforward sense, his religious reason and prudential reason are independent. But precisely because the latter is elenctically based, it cannot provide Socrates with certainty. The conclusions of elenctic arguments are always uncertain and corrigible, always open to revision. Yet it seems that Socrates' certainty about the value of the examined life and of his mission is absolute. He would die rather than abandon philosophy. It has been suggested, therefore, that his confidence in his mission must have another source and that this is provided by his religious reason and his belief in divination generally. [84] But this view of the matter is unconvincing.

First of all, there is no reason to believe that Socrates has the kind of certainty about his mission—absolute infallibility—that elenctic arguments cannot provide. He is quite explicit, for example, that his interpretation of the Delphic oracle is conjectural. He "supposed and assumed [*ōiēthēn te kai hupelabon*]" that Apollo had "ordered me to lead the philosophic life examining myself and others" (*Ap.* 28d10−29a1). He *supposed* and *assumed* this. But the next elenctic encounter may show his supposition to be mistaken. He would then be forced to admit that he was wrong about what Apollo was trying to tell him, just as he would have to abandon his views about justice if someone proved able to undo the arguments of iron and adamant which hold them fast. [85]

But, secondly, Socrates is also explicit that the *only* thing that would

---

83. McPherran (1986, 542) is mistaken, therefore, in claiming that the Delphic oracle, though it is not what initiated Socrates' philosophical career, is what "initiated his obligation to pursue it *even at the cost of his life.*"

84. See Brickhouse and Smith (1988, 100−108).

85. See Nehamas (1987, 306); Vlastos, "The Paradox of Socratic Piety."

convince him that he was wrong on any of these matters is an argument (*Cri*. 46b4−6; quoted above). Death threats, opinion polls, none of these carry any weight. His elenchus-based beliefs are not infallible. But in the absence of arguments he cannot answer, his confidence in them is always immense (see, for example, *Grg*. 508e6−509a4). We do not need to bring in religion, therefore, to explain Socrates' confidence about his mission or his willingness to face death rather than abandon it.

A second reason to doubt the total independence of Socrates' reasons for living the examined life concerns their scope. Socrates' religious reason is clearly intended to justify his *mission*, which involves elenctically examining pretty well everyone, "young and old, citizens and strangers" (30a2−4). But does Socrates' prudential reason have the very same scope? Is Socrates saying that the best human life must, like his, involve being a full-time elenctic missionary, or is he saying only that it must involve daily elenctic examination with others, on the order of the daily exercise our physicians recommend?

The goal of Socrates' mission is to persuade "young and old among you not to care primarily or passionately about your bodies and about wealth but about how your psyche can be the best possible" (30a7−b2). The goals of elenctic examination *per se* are to avoid the hubris of thinking he knows when he does not (*Chrm*. 166c7−d2) and "to get to the bottom of the problems that always puzzle me" and discover the truth (*Prt*. 348c5−7; cf. *Euthphr*. 14e9). If Socrates' religious and prudential reasons are completely independent, we ought to be able to explain how indiscriminate elenctic examination would enable Socrates to better avoid hubris and discover the truth.

A plausible explanation of this sort is not, however, easy to find. The reason that the desire to avoid hubris and discover the truth gives us to examine others, rather than engaging exclusively in autoexamination, is that another may see what we overlook. As Socrates puts it, we do everything better when we do it together with someone else (*Prt*. 348c5−d3). But this reason does not iterate. Two may be better than one. But it is not obvious that increasing the number of people one examines pays better dividends than repeatedly examining the same reasonably large and diverse group. The increase in dialectical skill developed through practice should more than compensate for novelty of perspective. It seems likely, therefore, that Socrates' reasons for living the examined life do indeed differ in scope and are not entirely independent. Both explain why Socrates leads the examined life. But only his religious reason explains why he is an Apollonian missionary.[86]

86. Cf. Brickhouse and Smith (1988, 105−107); McPherran (1986).

Socrates' mission, although not his practice of the elenchus, began with the Delphic oracle, then, and continues because of it. But *au fond* his reasons for obeying the oracle are elenchus-based ethical reasons. Socrates is a religious man. But he is not Kierkegaard's Abraham. He is a man of philosophy not of faith. A man who, as he says, "is persuaded by nothing in me except the argument that when I reason seems to me to be the best" (*Cri.* 46b4−6).

THE
DEFENSE
AGAINST
MELETUS

A man's character is his fate [*daimōn*].   —HERACLITUS

Nothing in the *Apology* has evoked more unanimous response than the section we are about to discuss—the cross-examination of Meletus. Almost everyone, even the most cautious, is convinced that it does not establish, is perhaps not even intended to establish, that Socrates is innocent. Socrates "entraps" Meletus into saying things he does not mean—the story goes—and then "refutes" him with arguments at once irrelevant to his charges and fallacious. Odd behaviour for the servant of Apollo, preaching concern for virtue. Odd enough, indeed, to cause skepticism. Is this really what Socrates does to Meletus and his charges? We shall have to see.

2.1 THE NEW CHARGES

The actual text of the *graphē asebeias* (2.3, 3.9) or writ of impiety, brought by Meletus against the historical Socrates is as follows:

> This indictment is entered on affidavit by Meletus son of Meletus of the deme Pitthus against Socrates son of Sophroniscus of Alopeke. Socrates does injustice by not believing in the gods in whom the polis believes [*hous men hē polis nomizei theous ou nomizōn*] and by introducing other *kaina daimonia*. He also does injustice by corrupting the youth. The penalty demanded is death. (Diogenes Laertius 2.40; Burnet 1924, 102)

It does not differ in any significant way from the summary Socrates produces in the *Apology*: "[Meletus' *graphē*] asserts that Socrates does injustice by corrupting the young, and by not believing [*ou nomizonta*] in the gods in whom the polis believes, but in other *daimonia kaina*" (24b8–c1). Meletus seems, then, to have brought as many as three separate charges:

(1) Corrupting the youth.

74

(2) Not believing in the gods in whom the polis believes.

(3) Believing in other *daimonia kaina*.

We must try to determine what they amount to.

In the course of his examination of Meletus, Socrates asks him to explain the content of (1):

> Nevertheless, tell us, Meletus, how do you say that I corrupt the youth? Or is it clear according to the charge you wrote [*kata tēn graphēn hēn egrapsō*] that it is by teaching them not to believe in the gods in whom the polis believes but in other *daimonia kaina*? Do you not say that it is by teaching this that I corrupt them? (26b2–6)

Meletus' answer is unequivocal: "I certainly do say that, most vehemently" (26b7). A closely similar view is expressed in the *Euthyphro*. Socrates is asked what Meletus thinks he does to corrupt the young. He replies:

> Strange things, to hear him tell it. He says that I am a maker of gods [*poiētēn einai theōn*], that I make new gods [*kainous theous*] and do not believe in the old ones, and that he has indicted me for the sake of these. (3b1–4)[1]

It seems certain, then, that (2) and (3) provide the basis for (1).

Nevertheless, some have seen an obstacle to this interpretation in the very form of Meletus' *graphē* itself:

> It is plain that the indictment would not have had its actual form, in which the charge of corruption is carefully put forward as a *separate* charge from that of irreligion, if, as Socrates suggests, the corruption consisted in his teaching irreligious doctrines alone. (Hackforth 1933, 105)

But this obstacle is illusory. It is one thing to be irreligious oneself; it is another thing to teach irreligion to others. Hence, even if corruption consisted only in religious perversion, (1), (2), and (3) would all still be

---

1. Josephus (*Ap.* 2.267) refers to an Athenian law which forbade the importation of "foreign gods." Burkert (1985, 317), apparently with this law in mind, claims that from "a legal point of view the introduction of new gods was the actionable fact" in Meletus' *graphē*. His implicit argument is that, since nothing in Meletus' *graphē* is an actionable fact except (3) interpreted as a charge of introducing new gods, (3) must be such a charge. In fact, as we shall see, there is compelling evidence that atheism was also an actionable fact and that (2) is a charge of atheism. Hence the meaning of (3) cannot be settled in this way.

separate charges. Moreover, there is no reason to take Meletus to be agreeing that corruption consists only in religious perversion. What he agrees to is that Socrates caused the corruption of the youth by teaching them irreligion. But no doubt he thought that the corruption Socrates caused involved all sorts of things beyond heterodox religious views: religion and morals usually go hand in hand. Again, (1), (2), and (3) are distinct.

(2) and (3) present difficulties of their own, however. At 31c8–d2, Socrates remarks that "a divine and daimonic thing [*theion ti kai daimonion*] comes to me, the very thing that Meletus wrote about in his *graphē* ridiculing it." So it is clear that he associates the *daimonia kaina* of (3) with his *daimonion*, his divine voice. Xenophon's Socrates also does this: "As for introducing *kaina daimonia*, how could I be guilty of that merely by asserting that a divine voice manifests itself to me, telling me what I must do?" (*Ap.* 12; cf. *Mem.* I.i.2). In the *Euthyphro*, too, this association is suggested. Socrates explains that Meletus has accused him of creating "new gods while not believing in old ones." Euthyphro responds: "This is because you say that the divine sign keeps coming to you" (3b5–6). Finally, the association is suggested by the actual text of the historical *graphē*: "It is hardly mere chance that the same word [namely, *daimonion*], unusual in this sense, and not the word 'gods', is also used in the official charge" (Ehrenberg 1973, 378). (3) must, then, refer in some way to Socrates' divine voice.

But if this is really so, why does (3) employ the plural form *daimonia* rather than the singular *daimonion*? One answer frequently suggested is this.[2] Part of the prejudicial caricature is that Socrates believed in the same sort of materialistic forces as the Ionian natural philosophers—Air, Clouds, Chaos, and so on—in place of the conventional gods. By using the plural rather than the singular, the prosecution wanted to exploit that belief to support, not just (2), but also (3). Now, there may be some truth in this suggestion—later in the *Apology* Meletus actually attributes some of Anaxagoras' heterodox religious views to Socrates (26d4–5). But it is not the whole story, or even the most important part of it. The real reason the plural is used is given in the *Apology* itself: *daimonia kaina* refers to *kaina daimonia pragmata* (27c1). (3) charges Socrates not with believing in strange divinities, but with believing in strange daimonic *doings*. The reference is not to a daimonic thing—that would require the singular adjective *daimonion* or the singular noun *daimōn*—but to the doings of a daimon, to its utterances, visitations, and pronouncements.

2. See Brickhouse and Smith (1988, 35–36); Burnet (1924, 14–15, 105); Hackforth (1933, 70).

This is established beyond reasonable doubt by the lengthy argument 27b3–d2, whose conclusion runs as follows:

> Is there anyone who believes that there are daimonic doings who does not believe in daimonic beings [*esth' hostis daimonia men nomizei pragmat' einai, daimonas de ou nomizei*]?—There is not.— Thank you for answering, if reluctantly, when the jury made you. Now you say that I believe in daimonic doings [*daimonia*] and teach about them . . . and you swore to this in your indictment. But if I believe in daimonic doings [*daimonia*], then surely there is also a great necessity that I believe in daimonic beings [*daimonas*]. (27b9–c9)

If (3) actually charged Socrates with belief in daimonic beings, this entire argument would be otiose.

It is sometimes argued against this proposal that it makes (3) into something that could not be an indictable offense at all, because belief in portents, signs, and familiar spirits was too much a commonplace in Athens to be the basis of an indictment of any sort.[3] This is true, as Xenophon has Socrates himself point out:

> As for introducing *kaina daimonia*, how could I be guilty of that merely by asserting that a divine voice manifests itself to me, telling me what I must do? Surely those who take their omens from the cries of birds and the utterances of men base their judgement on voices. Will anyone dispute either that thunder has its voice or that it is an omen of the greatest moment? Does not the very priestess who sits on the tripod at Delphi divulge the god's will through a voice? But more than that, in regard to the god's foreknowledge of the future and his forewarnings about it, I assert that this is how everyone speaks and what everyone believes. The only difference between them and me is that, whereas they call the sources of their warnings birds, utterances, coincidences, oracles, I call mine a daimonic thing [*daimonion*]. (*Ap.* 12–13)

But this fact has no decisive bearing on the interpretation of (3); for Meletus does not rest his indictment on (3) alone, but on (1) and (2) as well. The fact that (3) was almost certainly not an indictable offense, however, does make it reasonable to suppose that it is intended to be taken together with (2): What makes belief in strange daimonic doings criminal is that Socrates believes in them *instead* of the gods of the polis; part of what makes it credible that he does not believe in those gods is

---

3. See Burnet (1914, 184); Taylor (1933, 107–108).

that he believes in the daimonic doings. Again, this view receives some support from the *Euthyphro*, where it is suggested that Meletus has referred to the well-known fact of Socrates' *daimonion* in order to lend credence to the charge of "making innovations in the things that concern the gods . . . knowing that such things are easily misrepresented to the many" (3b6—9).

Taken together, then, (2) and (3) amount to this: Socrates does not believe in the gods in whom the polis believes, but instead in those other strange daimonic doings he is always talking about.

This brings us to (2). It has been suggested that this charge, which we have represented as being concerned with failure to believe, is really a charge about failure to worship: "*ou nomizonta*, 'not acknowledging' by giving them the worship prescribed by nomos . . . The charge is one of nonconformity in religious practice, not of unorthodoxy in religious belief" (Burnet 1924, 104). But this suggestion is untenable. Throughout the *Apology* (26b8—d5, 29a1—4, 35d2—5), *nomizein theous* (believing in gods) is used in the sense *nomizein theous einai* (believing gods to be or to exist). Since the latter phrase cannot mean to worship the gods, neither can the former.[4]

(2) is, then, a charge about failure to believe. The real problem is to determine what it accuses Socrates of failing to believe in. At 26c7, in response to a carefully formulated question from Socrates (26b8—c6), Meletus unequivocally asserts that (2) charges Socrates with not believing in any gods at all: "That is what I say, that you do not believe in gods at all [*Tauta legō, hōs to parapan ou nomizeis theous*]." The trouble is that this is not what (2) seems to say. Taken at face value, (2) charges Socrates not with out-and-out atheism but with "heterodoxy," with not believing in the gods in whom the Athenian polis believes.

One way that has been suggested to reconcile Meletus' written indictment with his oral interpretation of it is this.[5] Meletus believes that only the gods recognized by the Athenian polis are genuine gods and that anyone who rejects them is *ipso facto* an atheist, even if he acknowledges the existence of other things he falsely believes to be gods. Hence Meletus does not distinguish between heterodoxy and atheism, and neither does (2). Anyone who rejects the only genuine gods, the gods of the Athenian polis, is an atheist, no matter what else he believes.

This proposal has charm. But on balance the text tells firmly against it. Here is the question Socrates puts to Meletus:

4. See Tate (1936, 1937).

5. See Brickhouse and Smith (1988, 34—35). Cf. Hackforth (1933, 106—107).

Then by those very gods about whom we are talking, Meletus, make this clearer to me and to the jury; for I am not yet able to learn whether you are saying that I teach that there are some gods— and I myself, then, believe that there are gods and am not completely an atheist and am not unjust in this way—although I do not believe in the gods in whom the polis believes, but in others, and that this is what you charge me with, that I believe in others, or do you assert that I myself do not believe in gods at all and that I teach this to others? (26b8−c6)

The question offers Meletus a clear choice between theistic heterodoxy and atheism. And it is signal that Meletus does not respond by denying that these are genuine alternatives or by asserting that there are no real gods beyond those recognized by the polis, as we would expect if the line of thought under discussion were his own. Instead, he plumps unequivocally for atheism. Consequently, there seems to be little room for fancy footwork. Meletus claims that (2) charges Socrates with out-and-out atheism. And that—for a reason we shall explore in 2.2—means that, despite the seeming incongruity between the written charge and its oral interpretation, the real charge, the charge that Socrates must answer, is a charge of atheism. It is significant that both Xenophon (*Mem.* I.i.5) and Aristotle (*Rh.* 1419a8−11) accept this without demurral.

Since Socrates claimed that the ancient caricature of him as a generic intellectual is prejudicial to his defense against Meletus' charges, because it is widely believed that such people are atheists (18c1−3), this conclusion about the identity of Meletus' charges is precisely the one we have been led to expect.

The question we must now investigate is whether atheism was an indictable offense under Athenian law.

Plutarch tells us that a *psephism* or decree introduced by Diopeithes sometime in the 430s provided for the impeachment of "those who do not believe in what has to do with the gods or teach theories about what is up in the sky" (*Per.* 32.2). Many scholars believe that this decree was the legal basis of Socrates' indictment and that of a good many other intellectuals as well:

About 432 B.C., or a year or two later, disbelief in the supernatural and the teachings of astronomy were made indictable offenses. The next thirty-odd years witnessed a series of heresy trials which is unique in Athenian history. The victims included most of the leaders of progressive thought in Athens—Anaxagoras, Diagoras, Socrates, almost certainly Protagoras also, and possibly Euripides.

In all these cases save the last the prosecution was successful: Anaxagoras may have been fined and banished; Diagoras escaped by flight; so, probably, did Protagoras; Socrates who could have done the same, or could have asked for a sentence of banishment, chose to stay and drink the hemlock. (Dodds 1951, 189)[6]

Others are skeptical about whether all these trials ever took place, about whether there ever was an anti-intellectual witch-hunt in Athens. And there are, indeed, ample grounds for skepticism.[7] But skepticism on this larger issue should not be carried over to the narrower issue of the supposed legal basis for Socrates' trial.

The case for skepticism on this smaller head is threefold. (1) Our only authority for the existence of Diopeithes' psephism is Plutarch, who wrote almost five centuries after the death of Socrates. (2) Plutarch describes the psephism as providing for the legal action of *eisaggelia*,[8] whereas Socrates was prosecuted by *graphē*, a different legal action altogether. (3) The Amnesty of 403, which followed on the end of the Peloponnesian War, involved a complete revision and codification of the laws not completed until 401/400, the major provisions of which were as follows:

> No law passed before 403/2 was valid henceforth unless it was included in the new inscriptions made in the years from 410 to 403; no uninscribed law was to be enforced; no decree could override a law; and no prosecution could be brought henceforth for offenses committed before 403/2. (MacDowell 1978, 47)

Now (1) is not by itself compelling. Plutarch provides considerable detail about Diopeithes' psephism, down to its exact provisions, and the precise nature of the legal action it prescribed. This gives it—as opposed to some of the other things Plutarch tells us in this regard—a ring of historical authenticity which it would be overly skeptical to dismiss.

6. Cf. Momigliano (1973b, 565−566). The evidence relating to the trials is surveyed by Derenne (1930). Kerferd (1981, 21−22) points out that Aristotle, *Rh.* 1397b24 (quoted in 3.1) should be added to that evidence. On the trial of Anaxagoras in particular, see Mansfeld (1980).

7. The case is forcefully made in Dover (1976, 40−41). Stone (1988, 230−247) raises many interesting issues in an engaging way. It is important to keep a sense of perspective, however. Even half a dozen or so trials over thirty years hardly amounts to a witch-hunt.

8. See Harrison (1968, 2: 50−59, 74−82); below.

It seems reasonable to believe, consequently, that atheism and other forms of religious skepticism were once against the law in Athens. But it is unlikely that a society which outlawed atheism would reform its laws so as to forbid heterodoxy but not atheism. The fact, therefore, that Socrates was charged with not believing in the gods in whom the polis believed—whether construed as a charge of atheism or of heterodoxy— makes it probable that there was a law against atheism in force when he was charged. Could this law have been Diopeithes' original psephism? (3) establishes that it could not. But (2) gives us some reason to believe that it resulted from the latter by reform.

One major effect of the reforms of 403 was that action by *graphē* replaced action by *eisaggelia* except in the case of treason.[9] The explanation for this is straightforward. An *eisaggelia* had to be brought before the Assembly (*ekklēsia*) of all male citizens or before its steering committee, the *boulē* or Council of Five Hundred,[10] either of which could elect to hear the case or refer it to the dikastery for jury trial. A *graphē*, by contrast, was brought before the appropriate archon—the *archon basileus* or King Archon[11] in the case of a *graphē asebeias*—who referred the matter for jury trial if he determined that the prosecution had a case worth hearing (2.3). The initiator of a *graphē*, unlike the initiator of an *eisaggelia*, was subject to a fine of a thousand drachmai if he failed to secure one fifth of the jury votes or if he dropped his suit. The substitution of *graphē* for *eisaggelia* replaced a cumbersome and time-consuming procedure with a much more efficient one, then, and also deterred frivolous suits. Consequently, the fact that the law under which Socrates was prosecuted provided for action by *graphē*, while the original psephism provided for action by *eisaggelia*, actually increases the probability that the former resulted from the latter by reform, rather than being cut from whole cloth.

There is some reason to believe, then, that in 399 there was a law against atheism (and perhaps other kinds of impiety as well), which was the reformed offspring of Diopeithes' psephism, and that it was the legal

9. See MacDowell (1978, 184–186).

10. The Council is discussed in Aristotle, *Ath.* 43.2–44.3. The most authoritative modern treatment is Rhodes (1972).

11. The King Archon "introduced cases connected with religion (impiety, disputes about the duty to perform a sacrifice or the right to claim a priesthood) and also cases of homicide and deliberate wounding" (MacDowell 1978, 25). Cf. Aristotle, *Ath.* 57.1–4.

basis for Meletus' indictment of Socrates. Those who have portrayed Socrates as one of Diopeithes' victims may not, therefore, have been completely wide of the mark.

Vastly more secure than this speculative argument, however, is another which is firmly grounded in the *Apology*. Socrates describes those who have given currency to the caricature of him as a scientist and orator as his "dangerous accusers" on the grounds that "their hearers believe that investigators of these things do not believe in gods [*oude theous nomizein*]" (18c1–3). But why is it dangerous to be thought an atheist? The only reasonable answer is that the danger is a legal one, that atheism was an indictable offense. There must, therefore, have been a law under which atheists could be charged. For after the reforms of 403, as we saw, defendants had to be charged under a specific inscribed or written law.

These facts about the legal situation underwrite the conclusion we reached earlier, then, about the identity of the charges Socrates faces: Socrates is an atheist who believes in strange daimonic doings. He corrupts the youth by teaching these beliefs to them.

2.2 The Examination of Meletus

Armed as we are with very un-Athenian presuppositions about the law, Socrates' formal response to the charges we identified in 2.1 is a strange one—and it has certainly provoked strange interpretative responses.[12]

Many writers implicitly or explicitly accept some version of the following argument: (1) Socrates "entraps" Meletus into substituting a charge of atheism, which he then addresses, for the written charge of heterodoxy, which he ignores. (2) Socrates is legally obliged to answer the written charges, not their spoken replacements. (3) Therefore, his arguments are irrelevant to the legal task he faces. (4) In any case, the arguments are so bad that they cannot be taken seriously. (5) It follows that Socrates never denies the actual charges against him.[13]

Now if we suppose that Socrates does entrap Meletus into substituting an ersatz charge of atheism for the real charge of not believing in the

12. Perhaps the strangest is the suggestion by West (1979, 135) that the examination of Meletus is really a comic competition between Socrates and Aristophanes. His defense of this view presupposes—among many other contentious things—that Socrates' arguments are ridiculous. And that, as we shall see, is simply not the case.

13. See Allen (1980, 6–7); Burnet (1914, 181–185); Grote (1888, 7: 152–163); Hackforth (1933, 104).

gods in whom the polis believes, we must also suppose that he had a compelling reason for doing so. But what could this reason have been?

One suggestion is this. Socrates could defend himself against the charge of atheism because, as he demonstrates (26b2–28a1), it contradicts the charge of believing in daimonic doings. But because of his self-proclaimed ignorance he could not consistently answer the written charges, which involve no contradiction:

> To deny such charges on the basis of knowledge . . . one must first understand what they mean; that understanding requires inquiry into precisely the things of which Socrates knew himself to be ignorant—for example the real nature of virtue, the real nature of piety. . . . Whatever else we may think of Meletus and Anytus and Lycon . . . they had seen deeply enough into the character of the man they pursued to draw up an indictment distinguished by its lawyerly cunning, an indictment Socrates could no more have answered than a child. . . . This then is the second level of irony in the *Apology*. (Allen 1980, 7, 14)

Now, it is true that Socrates does not possess expert craft-knowledge of virtue. But it does not follow that he does not know enough about it to know that he is innocent of Meletus' charges. At 37a5–6 he says: "I am convinced that I am not voluntarily unjust to anybody." And at 28a2–4 he claims that his arguments are sufficient to show that he is "not unjust after the fashion of Meletus' *graphē*." On Socrates' own view of the matter, then, he has answered *the written charges*, not evaded them for lack of knowledge.

A second suggestion along these lines is that Socrates could not answer the written charges in good faith because of his skepticism about the traditional myths about the gods:

> He [Socrates] later denies atheism in stated terms (35d); but he does not deny, presumably for the reason given in the *Euthyphro* (6a–b; cf. 5a–b), namely, that he finds it difficult to accept the traditional stories of the gods' hatred and enmity towards each other, the charge of not acknowledging the gods the City acknowledges. (Allen 1980, 7)

This suggestion has some merit. Socrates himself speculates that his skepticism about the traditional theological myths might be the basis of Meletus' charges: "Could this be the reason, Euthyphro, that I face this *graphē*, that I shrink from accepting things like that being said about the gods [namely, that Zeus bound and castrated his father]?" (*Euthphr.*

6a6–9;[14] cf. *Phdr.* 229b1–230a7). But in the end it is unconvincing; for we know that Socrates did not consider such limited skepticism an obstacle to his belief in the gods of the polis. If he had, he would not have worshipped them at their public and domestic altars or participated in the great festivals in their honour (Plato, *Euthd.* 302c4–303a3; Xenophon, *Ap.* 11; 1.10). He would not, for that matter, have spent his life in service to one of them.

All this may well be true. There may be no evidence that Socrates had a motive not to confront the "real" charges and to get Meletus to substitute other charges which he could answer. But, whatever his motive, if he "entraps" Meletus, if he actually gets him by illegitimate dialectical tricks to say something other than he means, it will be cold comfort. So does Socrates' entrap Meletus? It seems clear that he does not. At the places at which Socrates gets Meletus to explain what his written charges mean, all he does is ask clearly formulated questions (26b2–7, 26c1–6); he does not argue or use the elenchus or bamboozle at all. If this is entrapment, everyone who has ever been cross-examined on a witness stand has been entrapped.[15]

We turn now to the question of where Socrates' legal responsibilities lie. In our legal system, criminal charges have a different legal status from evidence. A criminal charge has a precise identity determined by the written law—whether breaking and entering, or grand larceny, or second-degree manslaughter, or what have you. It is brought by the district attorney, who introduces witnesses and evidence, not to identify the charge, but to establish it. It is this legally defined charge that the defendant must answer. With evidence, on the other hand, things are reversed. Here the witness, and not the law, has final authority. His

14. Beckman (1979, 41) comments: "This . . . remarkable passage . . . tells us in no uncertain terms that Socrates belongs to the tradition of rational criticism of the gods of popular religion and that it is this habitual agnosticism which is at the root of the charges brought against him." But surely the passage tells us no such thing. The *Euthyphro* presents Socrates as being on his way to the *anakrisis* or preliminary hearing (2.3) at which he will hear the case against him for the first time (2a1–b11). Consequently, he does not yet know for sure what precisely Meletus is charging him with. That is why he says that his skepticism about some of the traditional myths about the gods "is likely [*eoike*] the reason he [Meletus] will say [*phesei*] that I do wrong." But what he actually discovers is that his *daimonion*, and not his skepticism about the myths, led to the charges.

15. Phillipson (1928, 306–311) is a generally sensible discussion.

testimony means what he says it means. Given this legal model, it becomes natural to assume that Meletus' written charges had the legal status we assign to criminal charges, that their identity was determined by the law, not by Meletus, and that Socrates' primary obligation was to answer them.

The question is whether this model fits the legal system of classical Athens. And in fact, as we shall see, the fit is less than perfect in two crucially relevant respects. First, the "charges" embodied in a *graphē* did not have to have any precise legal definition. A person could be the victim of (say) a *graphē asebeias* for teaching astronomy or introducing strange daimonic doings even if the laws concerning impiety did not specifically outlaw such activities by name: "To be the victim of a *graphē* at Athens it was not necessary to have committed an act which was forbidden by the law in so many words" (Dover 1976, 41). It was up to the jurors to determine whether such unmentioned activities nonetheless constituted a breach of the relevant laws. The oath of office taken by fourth-century jurors at the beginning of each year refers specifically to this discretionary power: "I will judge according to the laws and decrees of Athens, and matters about which there are no laws I will decide by the most just opinion."[16] We cannot conclude, therefore, from the fact that the formula "Socrates does injustice by not believing in the gods in whom the polis believes [*adikei Sōkratēs hous men hē polis nomizei theous ou nomizōn*]" appears in Meletus' written *graphē*, that this form of words had any specific legal significance or that it referred to a charge identified in those terms by Athenian law.[17]

16. See MacDowell (1978, 43–46, 60). Allen (1980, 22–32) concludes a spirited attack on this aspect of Athenian law as follows: "A procedure requiring laymen to find not only fact but law is incompatible with the technical precision required by legality." Meletus' charges, however, are much more specific than Allen makes them out to be. For example, Meletus does not make the vague charge that Socrates corrupts the youth, but the much more precise charge that he corrupts them *in a specific way*. See 2.1 and below.

17. "Athens had no legal equivalent of our public prosecutor, who is duly authorized by the state to prosecute charges in the state's name. Hence, the prosecutor's interpretation of the charges is *the only* interpretation that is legally at issue before the court" (Brickhouse and Smith 1988, 119). This conclusion is correct. But it does not follow from the fact that Athens had no public prosecutor. If Meletus' charges had independent legal meaning, he would not be free to interpret them as he wished, any more than the district attorney is free to interpret a charge of manslaughter as he wishes.

Second, under Athenian law, any citizen could bring a *graphē* against another whom he believed to be guilty of wrongdoing. And, indeed, most *graphai* were brought by private citizens and not by magistrates or state officials. As a result, a citizen who brought such an action typically played two roles which in our system of criminal law are kept separate, that of prosecutor, on the one hand, and that of chief witness for the ·prosecution, on the other:

> The role played by evidence in an Athenian court is quite different from its role in modern practice. . . . In Athens the diecasts looked to the speaker for the law and the facts and to the witnesses for corroboration; with us the jury looks to the witnesses for the facts and to the judge and counsel for the law and an integration of the results of examination and cross-examination of the witnesses. The litigants appear only as witnesses. (Bonner and Smith 1938, 2: 123)

Meletus is no exception. He is both charging Socrates with impiety and attesting (together with Anytus and Lycon) that Socrates did specific things that constituted impiety. This is made clear by the fact that he called no other witnesses beyond his fellow accusers to support his case (34a2–6, 36a7–b2). Consequently, Meletus' *graphē* is both a charge and a sworn affidavit supporting the charge. But if this is the case and if, as we have seen, there is no reason to believe that the charges he put in his written *graphē* had precise identities determined by law, we must conclude that Meletus is the final authority on what those charges amount to, just as a witness is the final authority on what his testimony means.

Consequently, it is clear that Socrates' primary responsibility must be to answer the charges as they are interpreted by Meletus and not, as would be the case in our legal system, the written charges as explicitly identified by the law. Far from Socrates' arguments being irrelevant to Meletus' written charges, then, they are exactly relevant to them.

Moreover, because Meletus is as much a prosecution witness as a prosecutor, because his *graphē* is both affidavit and charge, Athenian law allows Socrates to cross-examine him and obliges Meletus to answer his questions (27b3–c7). Consequently, Socrates can attack Meletus' *graphē* by discrediting him as a witness, by showing that he does not know enough about the things in his *graphē* for his testimony to carry any weight (think of how witnesses are discredited in our own legal system). This explains—what would otherwise be a complete mystery—why the professed aim of Socrates' examination of Meletus is to show that the latter is guilty "of dealing frivolously with serious matters, of irresponsibly bringing people into court, and of professing to be seriously concerned with things about none of which he has ever cared" (24c4−9). This is not an evasion, precisely because if Socrates can show these things, he will have seriously undermined not just Meletus, but his testimony and charges too.

Socrates does not entrap Meletus into saying what he does not mean, then, and does not argue against the wrong charges. His arguments are relevant to the charges, and his strategy of undermining Meletus' credibility is a reasonable and intelligible one. The question remaining is whether the arguments he employs to achieve these relevant purposes are worthwhile. For if they are as bad as many commentators claim, Socrates' defense will again be compromised.

The professed aim of Socrates' examination of Meletus is to show three things: (a) that Meletus has dealt frivolously with serious matters; (b) that he has irresponsibly brought Socrates into court; and (c) that he has professed to be seriously concerned with things about none of which he has ever cared (24c4−9). Consequently, the examination itself has three phases: the first (24c9−25c4) pertains to (c), the second (25c5−26b2) to (b), and the third (26b2−28a1) to (a).

The first phase begins as follows:

> Come here, Meletus, tell me: do you not consider it a matter of the greatest importance how the youth will be the best possible?— I do.—Then, come now, and tell these men, who makes them better? *Dēlon gar hoti oistha, melon ge soi*; for having discovered that I am the one who corrupts them, as you say, you bring me before these judges to accuse me. Come, inform the jury and tell them who it is that makes them better.—Do you see, Meletus, that you are silent and have nothing to say? Does this not seem shameful to you and a sufficient sign of what I say, that you have never cared? But tell me, my good man, who makes the youth better? (24d3−10)

Most translators and commentators give the impression that in the sentence left in Greek Socrates is presupposing that if Meletus cares about the youth, he must know who improves them.[18] Others argue that he is presupposing "that the one who knows who corrupts the youth also knows who makes them better" (West, 1979, 137). On either interpretation, Socrates' argument is certainly a bad one. It is not obvious that one cannot care sincerely about the youth without knowing who improves them. Nor is it obvious that one must know who improves them, if one

18. See Allen (1980, 44); Grube (1975, 28); Tredennick (1979, 54).

knows who corrupts them. In fact, however, Socrates is presupposing neither of these things. For the sentence in question, *Dēlon gar hoti oistha, melon ge soi,* does not carry the problematic implication that caring entails knowing. Instead it means this: "For it is clear that you know, or that you at least [*ge*] care."[19]

Socrates' argument, then, is actually this:

(1) Meletus considers it a matter of the greatest importance how the youth will be the best possible.

(2) It is clear, then, that he knows or that he at least cares who makes them better.

(3) For, having discovered, as he says, that Socrates corrupts them, Meletus has brought him to trial.

(4) Meletus is silent and has nothing to say about who makes the youth better.

(5) This is a "sufficient sign" that he has never cared about how the youth will be the best possible.

All Socrates presupposes, therefore, is that, if Meletus has absolutely nothing to say on the subject of who improves the youth, he cannot care about them as much as he claims and as his behaviour suggests. And this is surely reasonable. If Meletus is sufficiently concerned about the improvement of the youth to bring legal charges against their supposed corrupters and to claim that the question of how they are to be improved is most important, he ought to have given some thought to the question of who improves them and have something reasonable to say on the topic, even if it is only to point out that the topic is a complex one. The fact that he is at a complete loss for words, then, does cast doubt on the seriousness of his concern.

Meletus is not at a loss for long, however. When Socrates repeats the question of who improves the youth, he is ready with a whole battery of answers:

(6) The laws, the members of the jury, the members of the audience, the members of the Council of Five Hundred, the members of the Assembly of citizens, indeed all the Athenians, with the single exception of Socrates who corrupts them, educate the youth and make them better (24d11–25a11).

19. See Denniston (1987, s.v. *ge*).

But these answers do little to increase his credibility.[20] Meletus is not giving the answer—which it is alleged "every Athenian democrat would naturally give" (Burnet 1924, 107)—that young people learn their values from their society and their elders. He is claiming that every Athenian citizen makes the youth fine and good, with the single exception of Socrates, who corrupts them. As Socrates remarks, it would be a very happy state of affairs for the youth, if this claim were true. For it would be unlikely that one person could succeed in corrupting the youth if indeed everyone else was improving them (25b7—c1). But clearly the claim is absurd.[21]

To point up its absurdity, Socrates argues that the opposite is true:

Now answer me. Do you think that the same is true of horses? Do all men make them better, while one in particular corrupts them? Or is it wholly the opposite of this, that one in particular is able to make them better—or the very few who are horse-trainers—while the many, if indeed they *sunōsi kai chrōntai* horses, corrupt them? Isn't this so, Meletus; both with regard to horses and all other animals? Of course it is, whether you and Anytus agree or not. (25a12—c7; cf. *Cri.* 47a2—48a10)

Is Socrates saying outright that the many corrupt the youth? No. The clause "if indeed they *sunōsi kai chrōntai*" is restrictive. But what does it mean? The verbs *suneimi* (*sunōsi*) and *chraomai* (*chrōntai*) can mean something quite general, for example, 'to associate with' and 'to use', and most translations settle for that sort of rendering of them.[22] But this gives the clause doubtful application to the case in point. For though the many use horses, it is not clear what it would mean to say that they use the youth. *Suneimi* can also mean, however, 'to associate with in the manner of teacher and student'—Socrates uses it in this sense at 19e6 and 20a1.[23] And this is the clue to what he has in mind. The issue is precisely

20. Kraut (1984, 219) points out that Socrates makes no objection to Meletus' claim that the laws improve the youth. He sets that aside as irrelevant. His question is about which *human beings* improve the youth. Socrates believes that the laws of Athens, specifically the laws bearing on education, do contribute substantially to the improvement of the youth. See 2.3 and below.

21. Cf. Kraut (1984, 219); Phillipson (1928, 326).

22. See Allen (1980, 45); Grube (1975, 28); Tredennick (1979, 55); West (1979, 30).

23. See Liddell and Scott (1966, s.v. *suneimi*, II.2, 3). The verb is also used to refer to the homosexual relationship between an older male (*erastēs*) and a youth

one of who is able "to educate [*paideuein*] the youth" (24e4−5). And what Socrates is saying is this. Most people corrupt the youth rather than improving them, *if indeed* they associate with and use them, in the way that horse-trainers associate with and use horses, namely, for the purposes of giving them a complete education in virtue or excellence.

So did most Athenians associate with and use the youth in this way? Again, the answer is that they did not. A "complete education in virtue" consisted of instruction in "grammar, music, and gymnastics" (*Cleit.* 407b8−c3). The law required parents to have their children educated in these subjects to the extent that their means permitted,[24] and, as in our own culture, such education was largely in the hands of experts. A young boy had a *paidagōgos* who was responsible for his early "moral education." When he reached age seven (or so), the *paidagōgos* took him to school and stayed with him throughout the day. At school, he was under the instruction of a *grammatistēs*, who taught him reading, writing, and some mathematics, a *kitharistēs*, who taught him "music," and a *paidotribēs*, who taught him "gymnastics."[25] Socrates is not implying, then, any more than he is stating outright, that most people corrupt the young.

Neither is he making the arrogant claim, attributed to him by many writers, that he alone improves the youth.[26] The *Apology* suggests that his attitude to Athenian education was largely favourable. The few educational experts improve the youth, just as the few horse-trainers improve horses. And this suggestion is strongly underwritten by other early dialogues. In the *Laches*, Nicias remarks that Socrates advised him to hire Damon as a music teacher (*mousikēs*) for his son (180c9−d3; cf. *Ly.* 204a6−7). And in the *Crito* Socrates is presented as believing that

(*erōmenos*), through which the latter was supposed to learn virtue. See Dover (1978, 202); Henderson (1975, 159). *Chraomai* can also mean 'to use for sexual purposes'. See Liddell and Scott (1966, s.v. *chraomai*, IV.2).

24. The *Crito* (50d9−e1) refers to a law which required Socrates' father (who was a stonecarver, not an aristocrat) to educate him in music and gymnastics. Harrison (1968, 1: 78−79 n. 3) argues that the law in question may have been the Solonic law which required fathers to do no more than teach their sons a craft. But, as Kraut (1984, 91 n. 1) points out, there is no good reason not to take the *Crito* at face value.

25. See Beck (1964, 72−141).

26. See Guardini (1962, 39); Teloh (1986, 112); West (1979, 138, 150). Kraut (1984, 196, 220 n. 59) agrees that Socrates is claiming that the many corrupt the youth.

the laws of Athens, including those which provided for his own education and upbringing (*Cri.* 50d1−51c3), are very satisfactory, superior, indeed, to those of any other state, Greek or barbarian.[27]

The fact that the jury, which is so often agitated by his claims, is quiet here, offers some support for these rather low-key conclusions. For it is hard to imagine that they would sit idly by while a defendant on trial for corrupting the youth claimed that of all the Athenians—including themselves—he alone was innocent of that crime.

On the strength of this analogy between horse-trainers and educators, Socrates concludes again that Meletus is not concerned with the youth at all and has given no thought to the matters in his *graphē* (25c1−4); for if the analogy is sound, it is just silly to say that everyone improves the youth except Socrates alone.

Socrates' second argument is intended to show that Meletus has irresponsibly brought him into court. I have changed the order in which it is presented to make its inferential structure a little clearer. Despite its length when spelled out, it is a relatively straightforward argument.

(1) If Socrates corrupts the youths who associate with him, he must either do it voluntarily [*hekonta*] or involuntarily [*akonta*] (25d5−6).

(2) Everyone would rather be benefited than harmed by his associates (25d1−4).

(3) Wicked people harm their associates, whereas good people benefit them (25c7−10).

(4) Therefore, anyone who corrupts his associates or makes them wicked runs the risk of being harmed by them (25e2−3).

(5) Socrates knows that (4) is true (25d8−e3).

(6) Therefore, if Socrates corrupts his young associates, he does so involuntarily (25e5−26a1).

(7) Therefore, Meletus' claim (25d7) that Socrates corrupts the youth voluntarily is false (25e5−26a1).

(8) The law does not require that those guilty of involuntary wrongdoings be brought to court, only that they be instructed privately about the nature of their error (26a1−4).

27. See Kraut (1984, 48, 91−92, 177−180, 219−220); 2.3.

(9) Meletus has not instructed Socrates but instead has brought him to court (26a5–7).

(10) Therefore, Meletus has irresponsibly brought Socrates to court (implicit; cf. 24c6).

The first point to make about this argument is that, strictly speaking, (6) does not follow from the preceding premises. This is so for two reasons. First, even if no one voluntarily risks being harmed without cause, people do voluntarily risk harm if they think that they stand to gain enough by doing so. And nothing in the argument excludes the possibility that Socrates is such a person, that he voluntarily corrupts the youth, and voluntarily incurs the risk of being harmed, in order to get some other substantial benefit. Second, people often voluntarily do what they know or believe will harm them, out of *akrasia* or weakness of the will. Again nothing in the argument excludes the possibility that Socrates is weak-willed and that he has voluntarily corrupted the youth as a result.

Both these objections, however, presuppose that Socrates had a strong motive to corrupt the youth. And no such motive has emerged. Indeed, by far the most likely motive—namely, the desire for money—has been ruled out. For Socrates' poverty has already been mentioned (23b9–c1), will be mentioned again before his defense is over (31a2–c3), and was, in any case, sufficiently well known in Athens to be parodied in *Clouds*. Hence, in the context in which the argument is produced and in which the absence of motive can be fairly safely presupposed, it is, like its predecessor, a reasonable one.[28]

Nonetheless, many commentators have detected in the argument "the paradoxical notion of the involuntariness of crime" and perhaps for this reason have dismissed it as "sophistry" or as "ironically fallacious."[29]

28. "Do we suppose that Aristophanes saw any difference between the fees which Kallias paid to Protagoras and the friendship, patronage, and hospitality which Alkibiades made available to Socrates?" (Dover 1971, 73–74). If the jury, too, saw no difference between fees and gifts in kind, they may have sensed a lacuna in this Socratic argument. Still, Socrates' well-known poverty and frugality remain a powerful counterweight (31b5–c3) to such suspicion. Diogenes Laertius (2.74) reports Aristippus as responding as follows to the accusation that, although he was a student of Socrates, he took fees: "Most certainly I do, for Socrates, too, when certain people sent him corn and wine, *used to take a little and return all the rest.* His stewards were the foremost men in Athens. I've only got my slave Eutychides."

29. The first two quotations are from O'Brien (1967, 84–85), the third is from Shorey (1933, 81). Cf. Friedländer (1964, 2: 163–164); West (1979, 139–140).

But in fact this paradox is nowhere to be found in the argument. All that the argument really presupposes is the much less contentious view that people do not voluntarily run the risk of being harmed without having a strong motive.[30]

I turn now to Socrates' final argument against Meletus. Its aim is to show that Meletus has dealt frivolously with serious matters. But there is little doubt that it also mounts a powerful attack on his charges.

(1) Socrates corrupts the youth by teaching them not to believe that there are any gods at all (26b2−c7).

(2) Socrates corrupts the youth by teaching them to believe in strange daimonic doings (26b8−c7).

(3) Anyone who believes in the doings of horses, or flutes, or Xs of any sort must believe that there are horses, or flutes, or Xs (27b3−c2).

(4) Therefore, anyone who believes in daimonic doings must believe in daimons (27c1−2).

(5) Socrates believes in daimonic doings, indeed, Meletus actually accuses him of believing in them (27c4−8).

(6) Therefore, Socrates must believe that there are daimons (27c8−10).

(7) Daimons are either gods or the children of gods (27c10−d3).

(8) Anyone who believes that there are children of horses, or asses, or Xs must believe that there are horses, or asses, or Xs (27d10−e3).

(9) Therefore, anyone who believes that there are children of gods must believe that there are gods (27d9−e3).

(10) Therefore, Socrates believes that there are gods (27e5−28a1).

Brickhouse and Smith (1988, 118) agree that Socrates is relying on his doctrine of the involuntariness of wrongdoing. See 3.1, 3.4−6.

30. The parallels between the *Apology* and Gorgias, *Pal.*, discussed in 1.1, provide some indirect support for these interpretations. For, as Coulter (1964, 300−301 n. 6) points out, all that Gorgias has Palamedes say at the relevant point in the latter (*Pal.* 13) is that "no one incurs all sorts of dangers and risks the possibility of ignominy without the prospect of some considerable advantage." Coulter himself believes, however, that Socrates is relying on the doctrine that no one errs voluntarily.

(11) Therefore, (1) and (2) contradict one another.

(12) Therefore, Meletus' *graphē* is a self-contradictory riddle, and Meletus is guilty of dealing frivolously with serious matters (27a1−7).[31]

Dissatisfaction with this transparently valid argument rests largely on the perception of it as irrelevant, as being aimed at a charge that does not actually appear in Meletus' *graphē*. But this perception, as we saw above, is unjustified. Meletus' charges have the status of evidence; they mean what he says they mean. Hence Socrates' arguments are correctly targeted. It follows that Socrates really has shown that the charge of atheism is false; for Meletus actually accuses him of believing in daimonic doings, and he certainly does believe in them (31c8−d4). He also believes that daimons are children of gods (27c10−d2).[32] Since he is aware that the aforementioned beliefs entail that there are gods, he must believe that there are gods. Later, indeed, he makes this explicit: "I do believe in them [gods], men of Athens, as none of my accusers do" (35d6−7). And if he believes that there are gods, he cannot be an atheist.

It will not do to reject this argument on the grounds that it is hard to believe that Meletus would actually bring inconsistent charges against Socrates; for the charges of atheism and believing in strange daimonic doings are not *formally* inconsistent. They only become inconsistent when combined with the proposition that daimons are the children of gods (or stand in some other relation to them which insures that gods exist if daimons do). And we can easily imagine that this sort of inconsistency was overlooked by Meletus, Anytus, and Lycon; especially if it is true that, having little in the way of direct evidence to offer (33c8−34b5), they wanted to lend credibility to their *graphē* by referring in it to Socrates' well known belief in daimonic doings.

31. Notice that Socrates already knows at 24c5−6 (indeed at 18c1−3) that Meletus' *graphē* is self-contradictory (27e3−5). He must already know, therefore, that Meletus is charging him with out-and-out atheism. How did he know this? There are two possibilities. Either Meletus revealed it at the *anakrisis*, or preliminary hearing, or intimated as much in his speech of prosecution.

32. This is denied by Guardini (1962, 43) and West (1979, 146−147). But there is no support for their views. It is not true, for example, as West maintains, that Socrates' acceptance of the relationship between daimons and gods is only hypothetical. It is hypothetically stated at 27d8−10, but not at 27c10−d1. Nor is it to the point to refer to the fact that Socrates says later that he has "no adequate knowledge of things in Hades" (29b5−6), for even if that denial covered gods and daimons, it is belief that is at issue here, not knowledge.

Another fact, which is not part of Socrates' formal argument, but which emerges in the course of it, has bearing on the atheism charge. After Meletus has explained that his charge is indeed one of atheism, Socrates asks him the following question: "Why do you say this? Do I not believe, as other men do, that the sun and the moon are gods?" (26d1−3). Meletus replies, "No, by Zeus, for he says that the sun is stone, and the moon earth" (26d4−5). This is a damaging reply, because these are doctrines that everyone associates with Anaxagoras of Clazomenae.[33] Hence the fact that Meletus attributes them to Socrates helps substantiate the claim that he has no very clear idea at all of just what Socrates does teach and that he has charged him with teaching atheism simply because it is one of "those accusations that are available against all philosophers" (23d2−7). Again this undermines Meletus' credibility as a witness.

Finally, we must not forget in considering the atheism charge that Apollo was one of the gods of the Athenian polis and that Socrates spends much of his defense building a very strong case that he believes himself to be serving Apollo in elenctically examining his fellows. Few, indeed, could offer such compelling proof of their faith as a life of poverty and public service of the sort that he has to show (31b1−c3).

Now, it does not follow from the fact that Socrates is not an atheist that he cannot have taught atheism to his young associates—teaching does not have to be sincere. But, again, in the context in which the argument is produced, this fact has very little real weight. After all, Meletus cannot be charging Socrates with being an insincere teacher of atheism, for he is also accusing him of being an atheist. More important, Meletus does not simply charge Socrates with teaching atheism. He charges him with teaching atheism by teaching belief in *daimonia* (26b8−c7).[34] And that charge cannot be true; for teaching belief in *daimonia* is teaching belief in doings which entail the existence of gods. And this cannot, in any obvious way, amount to teaching atheism. Indeed—although this is a marginally more controversial conclusion—it cannot even amount to teaching heterodoxy; for Socrates' daimon is not

33. Anaxagoras' doctrines are discussed in Kirk, Raven, and Schofield (1983, 352−384) and Reeve (1981).

34. Teloh (1986, 112−113) overlooks this fact: "Socrates does not deny directly the charge of corruption. The charge is vague, and there is no point to deny a charge whose tentacles spread out to all facets of one's life." Meletus is precise about the way in which Socrates corrupted the youth. Hence, by denying that he can have corrupted the youth *in that way*, Socrates is explicitly denying the corruption charge.

the offspring of some strange god, but "the sign of the god," Apollo (40b1).

Finally, Socrates also argues against the corruption charge later in the *Apology*, pointing out that Meletus has not introduced any direct evidence bearing on it and that what direct evidence there is would actually tell against it:

> Now, if I corrupt some of the youth and have already corrupted others, then surely some of them, who have grown older and who realize that I gave them bad advice when they were young, should now come forward themselves to accuse me and get their revenge. Or, if they were unwilling to do so themselves, then some of their families, their fathers or brothers or other relations, should have remembered and taken their revenge, if their family had been harmed by me. I see many of them present here. . . . And I could mention many others, some of whom Meletus should surely have called as witness in his own speech. If he forgot to do so, then—I yield time to him—let him do it now. You will find, gentlemen, that it is wholly the opposite, that everyone is ready to come to my aid, the corrupter, the man who has harmed their families, as Meletus and Anytus claim. Now, those who were corrupted might well have reason to help, but the uncorrupted ones, their relatives, who are older men, what reason to help me could they have other than the right and just one, that they know Meletus is speaking falsely and that I am telling the truth? (33c8–34b5)

This, besides being an important argument in itself, reinforces Socrates' earlier defense. For it makes it likely that Meletus has rested his corruption charge directly on the atheism charge, arguing or presupposing or giving it to be understood, in effect, that because Socrates is an atheist he must contaminate or pollute his followers with his own atheistic beliefs.[35]

At the end of his cross-examination of Meletus, Socrates explicitly claims to have proved that he is not guilty of his charges: "But, in fact, men of Athens, that I am not unjust after the fashion of Meletus' *graphē*

---

35. That Meletus and the others did think in this way is further evidenced by the fact that they characterized Socrates as a "most polluted fellow [*miarōtatos*]" (23d1). For the adjective *miaros*, of which *miarōtatos* is the superlative, refers to "a condition that has some, and usually all, of the following characteristics: it makes the person affected ritually impure and thus unfit to enter a temple: it is contagious: it is dangerous, and this danger is not of familiar secular origin"

does not seem to me to need much defense; these things are sufficient [*alla hikana kai tauta*]" (28a2–4; cf. 36a6–b2). And his arguments amply support his claim. He has seriously undermined Meletus' credibility and with it the credibility of his charges. Moreover, he has shown, in part on the basis of Meletus' actual charges themselves, that he is not an atheist and that he cannot have corrupted the youth in the way that Meletus has alleged, namely, by making them atheists through teaching them about his *daimonion*. Far from its being the case, then, that Socrates does not deny the formal charges brought against him or that the arguments he offers against Meletus are all ironically fallacious, he both explicitly claims that he is innocent of the charges and justifies his claim with reasonable and pertinent arguments. He is innocent of the specific legal charges brought against him, and he demonstrates his innocence.

2.3 MOTIVES

Even if the specters of irony and fallacy have now been laid to rest, even if we are persuaded that Socrates does prove that he is innocent of Meletus' charges, there are other reasons why this part of his defense can continue to seem somehow problematic. In this section, we shall consider the most compelling of these reasons, specifically those stemming from the motives, or supposed motives, of the various parties to the trial.

The first of these reasons is based on a widely credited account of what led Meletus to bring a *graphē asebeias* against Socrates. It will be useful to set it out in a schematic form, so that its various components can be more easily distinguished.

(1) Charged with the grave impiety of having profaned the Elusinian Mysteries and suspect in connection with the mutilation of the Herms, Alcibiades, the most brilliant of the Athenian generals, defected to Sparta, where he greatly contributed to the subsequent defeat of democratic Athens at Sparta's hands. Critias, archenemy of the democracy, implicated in the mutilation of the Herms, and possibly the author of the atheistical play *Sisyphus*, was one of the bloodiest of the notorious Thirty Tyrants, the oligarchy installed in Athens in 404 by the victorious Spartans. In the eight months of their reign, the Thirty executed some fifteen hundred and banished some five thousand of their countrymen.

(Parker 1983, 3–4). Cf. Liddell and Scott (1966, s.v. *miaros*). Bonner and Smith (1938, 2: 192–231); Burkert (1985, 75–84); and Parker (1983) discuss the important role pollution played in the moral, religious, and legal life of the Greeks.

Socrates was the companion and supposed teacher of these "monsters of impiety."[36]

(2) Anytus was a democratic leader who helped restore democracy to Athens in 403 after the overthrow of the Thirty, under whom he had lost most of his wealth. As general, he was accused over the loss of Pylos in 409 but "bribed the court and was acquitted" (Aristotle, *Ath.* 27.5). He may also have been involved in some further political corruption in 413/412 (Aristophanes, *Thesm.* 809). There is evidence that he was the lover (*erastēs*) of Alcibiades (Plutarch, *Alc.* 4.4−6), that he believed that Socrates was responsible for the ruin of his son (Xenophon, *Ap.* 29−31), and that he was passionately opposed to the sophists (Plato, *Men.* 89e6−92c5).[37] Meletus, who brought the *graphē* against Socrates, is usually represented as little more than a cat's-paw of Anytus. But if, as others argue, he is the same Meletus who brought a charge of impiety against Andocides in 399, then he was not only one of the people who participated in the arrest of Leon of Salamis under the Thirty (something Socrates refused to do), he was also a religious fanatic and may well have been the chief instigator of the charges.[38]

(3) It was the distrust aroused by Socrates' connection with Alcibiades and Critias—traitors as suspect on religious as on political grounds—that provoked Meletus and Anytus to bring him to trial: "You [Athe-

36. This characterization is from the appeal of Cleocritus, the herald of the communicants in the Elusinian Mysteries, to the adherents of the tyranny at the battle of Munychia (403). On Alcibiades, see Davies (1971, 9−22); Thucydides (6.15, 27−29, 60−61, 89, 93, 7.27); Plutarch, *Alc.* On Critias, see Davies (1971, 322−335). The Thirty are discussed in Grote (1888, 6: 431−499), Krentz (1982), and, more briefly, in Hammond (1959, 442−449). Socrates' relations with Alcibiades and Critias are discussed in Xenophon, *Mem.* I.ii.12−16, 24−25, 31, 39, 40−46.

37. See Davies (1971, 40−42).

38. At *Ap.* 18b3, Socrates refers to his accusers as "Anytus, and those with him [*tous amphi Anuton*]"; in the *Seventh Letter*, Plato (?) says that "some of those in charge [*dunasteuontes tines*]" brought the *graphē* against Socrates (325b1−c5). Both texts suggest that Anytus was the principal agent. Cf. Diogenes Laertius (2.38); Burnet (1924, 101). Hackforth (1933, 78) points out, however, that the sentiments attributed to Anytus at *Ap.* 29b9−c5 make him sound like a follower rather than a leader. The strongest cases for the identity of the two Meletoi have been mounted by Dover (1968, 78−80) and Blumenthal (1973). The strongest opposing case is MacDowell (1962, 208−210). The fact that "the name [Meletus] is irritatingly common in the late fifth century in Athens" (Davies 1971, 382) helps keep the waters somewhat muddy.

nians] put Socrates to death, because he was shown to have educated Critias" (Aischines, *In Tim.* 173); "And when your purpose was to accuse Socrates, as if you wished to praise him, you gave him Alcibiades as a pupil" (Isocrates, *Bus.* 5). However, the Amnesty of 403, which outlawed prosecution for offenses committed before that date, made it impossible for Meletus and Anytus to reveal the real nature and basis of their charges. Hence, they focused on the charge of impiety and mentioned no names in connection with the charge of corrupting the youth.[39]

If we accept (3) as the verdict of history, or at least of historians, the most we can infer is that Socrates failed to confront the real, but legally impermissible, basis of the charges against him. But if we also accept that Socrates *knew* that his association with Critias and Alcibiades lay behind the charges, we must ask why, knowing the real basis, he failed to confront it.[40] Such failure would not directly impugn his legal defense; his legal obligation is to answer the charges and the evidence presented to support them, not to confront evidence which the law itself excludes as impermissible. It would, however, raise questions about his honesty and integrity. Socrates has said that he will tell "the whole truth" (17b8). But it seems that only someone with something to hide would fail to confront what he knows to be the real basis of capital charges, especially if he could point to its illegality. For the Amnesty, which forbade his prosecutors from using his association with Alcibiades and Critias against him, did not impose any correlative restrictions on him. The crucial question is, then, whether we should accept that Socrates did, indeed, possess the knowledge at issue.

Socrates claims, as we saw in 1.2, that it was the anger and humiliation caused by the imitative elenctic activities of his young followers, and not his association with Alcibiades and Critias in particular, that led Meletus, Anytus, and Lycon to charge him with atheism and corrupting

---

39. See Ehrenberg (1973, 79); Grote (1888, 7: 144−146); Guthrie (1971a, 61−64); Vlastos (1983a, 495−497). Proponents of the argument have had difficulty in explaining why Meletus and Anytus waited from 403 until 399 to bring Socrates to trial. See Taylor (1933, 103) and Stone (1988, 133−139) for rather different suggestions. Many writers emphasize political motives over religious ones. But this is not warranted by the evidence—especially if Meletus was the chief prosecutor. Given (1), (2), and Socrates' own account of the motives of his prosecutors (23c2−d9), the case for a mixture of religious, political, and even personal motivation is much stronger. See Irwin (1989).

40. Burnet (1924, 106−107) implies that Socrates did believe this.

the youth. Implicitly, then, he is claiming not to believe that his association with them was the real basis of the charges. To reject these claims (explicit and implicit) as either rationalization or evasion would clearly be a very drastic step. Do we have a sufficiently compelling reason to take it? This involves two other questions corresponding to the two "sins" of Alcibiades and Critias—impiety and antidemocracy.

First, then, the question about impiety. Do we have any reason to think that Socrates could not have honestly and directly confronted the issue of his connection with Alcibiades and Critias and its bearing on the charges of atheism and religious or ethical corruption, if he had believed it to be germane? Surely, we do not: Socrates' response to the corruption charge (33c8–34b5), his refusal to obey the unjust orders of the Thirty (32c4–d8), and his public orthopraxy (1.10) provide a more than adequate basis for such a confrontation.

Turning now to the second question, we must try to determine whether there is any compelling reason to believe that Socrates could not have honestly and directly confronted the charge that he shared in the antidemocracy of his supposed pupils and associates.

Socrates is clear that the center of his life, his elenctic mission, does not discriminate on the basis of class, age, or nationality (23b4–6).[41] Though especially directed to his fellow citizens (30a4), his mission is to everyone in Athens, not just to the rich or the intellectually well endowed. The elenctically examined life is for all men, the many as well as the few (38a2–6):

> Why rank that method [the elenchus] among the great achievements of humanity? Because it makes moral inquiry a common human enterprise, open to every man. Its practice calls for no adherence to a philosophical system, or mastery of a specialized technique, or acquisition of a technical vocabulary. It calls for common sense and common speech. And that is as it should be, for how man should live is every man's business. (Vlastos 1971, 20)

In one very important sense, then, Socrates' mission is profoundly democratic, and he could and does defend it as such.

Socrates' mission was, moreover, specifically to Athens. And Athens was the most democratic society in existence. Yet Socrates is not de-

---

41. Socrates does not mention women. Their seclusion presumably prevented him from interviewing them. See Gould (1980). At 41b7–c4, however, Socrates mentions that he would question women in the afterlife, if he had the chance.

terred by this from thinking highly of his polis. Far from it. In the *Apology*, he characterizes her as "the greatest polis, with the greatest reputation for wisdom and strength" (29d7−8). In the *Crito*, he says that he prefers Athens and her laws to "any other polis, Greek or barbarian," including those of Sparta, Crete, Thebes, and Megera, which he admits are "well-governed" (51c4−53c8).

Socrates does not tell us, however, just what his preference for Athens is based on. But surely it must be some feature that distinguished her from the other poleis he mentions. This feature may have been Athens' democratic constitution:

> The salient difference—the one that would leap to the eye of any Greek juxtaposing Athens against that quartet of cities—would be in the area of constitutional law. In the Athenian constitution democracy reached its apogee in fifth-century Greece, while each of these four constitutions stood as clearly for oligarchy—extreme in the case of the Spartan and Cretan constitutions, moderate in the case of the Theban and Megarian. So while no mention is made of either democracy or oligarchy anywhere in the passage [*Cri.* 51c4−53c8], there can be no doubt that Socrates' preference for Athenian law is *a preference for Athens' democratic constitution.* (Vlastos 1983a, 499)

But equally well the distinguishing feature may have been intellectual freedom or freedom of speech:

> Athenian law permitted philosophical activity and moral criticism to a degree unparalleled by any other Greek city, and it surely was this "negative" feature of the legal system that made Socrates one of the great admirers of his native city. (Kraut 1984, 228)

We do not need to choose between these two contenders, however, for freedom of speech (*isēgoria, parrēsia*) was itself widely recognized as both central to and distinctive of Athenian democracy.[42] In his *Defense of Socrates*, written in the fourth century A.D., Libanius has Socrates himself draw attention to this fact and make it relevant to his trial:

> It is for this reason that Athens is a fair and delightful sight, and men come here from all quarters by land and sea. . . . It is because

42. See Griffith (1966); Momigliano (1973a); Woodhead (1967). Relevant ancient texts include Democritus, B226; Demosthenes, 20.106; Euripides, *Hipp.* 421−423, *Ion* 670−672, *Phoen.* 385−442; Herodotus, 5.78; Plato, *Grg.* 461e2, *R.* 557a2−b6; Ps-Xenophon, *Ath.* 1.12.

our polis is a factory of words. One man asks questions, another answers. One is content to learn, another teaches. . . . All this is worthy of the goddess on the Acropolis, and of those educated by the gods, and of Theseus, and of our democratic constitution. This makes the city more pleasant than Sparta. . . . This is what makes the difference between us and non-Greek peoples. And they [Meletus and Anytus] who are now taking away our freedom of speech [by indicting me for what I say] are destroying the customs of democracy. (74–76)

Absent a better explanation of Socrates' preference for Athens, then, and it is difficult to think of another nearly so compelling, we must conclude that, far from being antidemocratic, Socrates preferred a strongly democratic polis and the intellectual freedom and freedom of speech distinctive of it to any of the less democratic poleis, Greek or barbarian, with which he was acquainted.

We have uncovered strong evidence, then, that Socrates was not antidemocratic. We must now consider the evidence on the other side. The prime exhibit is Socrates' claim that *if* someone has the expert craft-knowledge of virtue, he alone should rule and be obeyed:[43]

Especially concerning the just and unjust, fine and shameful, good and bad, about which we are now deliberating—should we follow the opinion of the many and fear that, or should we go by the opinion of the one, *if* there is one who knows these things [*ei tis estin epaiōn*], and before whom we feel fear and shame more than before all others? If we do not follow his instructions, we shall corrupt and mutilate that part of us which is improved by just actions and harmed by unjust ones. Or is there nothing in this? (*Cri.* 47c8–d5; cf. *La.* 184e8–9)

But surely this is not in any politically interesting sense an antidemocratic view. A democrat might well admit that, *if* someone genuinely possessed the craft-knowledge of virtue and really knew how to arrange happy and thriving lives for all of us, then it would be madness to refuse to allow him to rule. The view becomes interestingly antidemocratic only when coupled with the claim that someone or some group, other than the citizen body as a whole, does or could possess the knowledge in question. But Socrates strenuously denies this. He does not have the craft-knowledge of virtue himself and has never met anyone who does. Indeed, he considered it impossible (or as near impossible as makes little

43. See Taylor (1933, 149–150); Stone (1988, 39–129).

difference) for human beings to acquire such "more than human wisdom."[44]

The second piece of evidence that Socrates was antidemocratic is the corpus of apparently harsh things he has to say—some of them in the *Apology* itself—about the many. In his cross-examination of Meletus, for example, he says that "the many, if indeed they associate with and use horses, corrupt them. Isn't this so, Meletus, both with regard to horses and *all other animals*?" (25b3–6). Later, in explaining why he has brought his elenchus-backed message of concern for virtue only to individuals, not to the polis as a whole, he seems to condemn both the many and the kind of political participation which is vital to the success of a democracy:

> No one will preserve his life if he genuinely opposes you or any other multitude and prevents the occurrence in the polis of many unjust and illegal things; for it is necessary for a man who really fights for justice and who is going to preserve his life even for a short time to lead a private but not a public life [*idiōteuein alla mē dēmosieuein*]. (31e2–32a3)

But are these passages really evidence of antidemocracy? When we examine them closely, we see that they are nothing of the kind. In the first passage, Socrates is claiming only that the many, if indeed they try to do what the *grammatistēs*, *kitharistēs*, and *paidotribēs* are trained to do, botch the job. But this is not antidemocratic, any more than it would be prodemocratic to argue that children should be educated by those with no special training. The second passage, as we shall see in 3.7, is not a damnation of democratic politics or a justification of being apolitical, but a comment on the limited powers of an elenchus, which, being essentially a one-on-one affair, must always be conducted *idiōteuein alla mē dēmosieuein*—with individuals (or in private) not with the demos.

The final piece of evidence of Socrates' antidemocracy we shall consider is his supposed opposition to the practice, central to Athenian democracy although not to democracy *per se*, of electing public officials

---

44. This marks an important difference between Socrates' attitude to democracy and Plato's. It may be fair to say that neither was a "practical opponent" of Athenian democracy. But Plato is a "theoretical opponent" of it because—unlike Socrates—he believes that rule by philosopher-kings is a real possibility, that human beings could acquire (the equivalent of) the craft-knowledge of virtue (*R.* 375e6–7, 456b12–c2, 472d9–473b2, 499c2–5). Cf. Irwin (1986b, 410–414); Kraut (1984, 218–228).

by lot. This is attested to by Aristotle (*Rh.* 1393b5−9) and by the accuser (possibly Polycrates) cited in the following passage of Xenophon:

> But, his accuser said, he [Socrates] taught his companions to despise the established laws by insisting on the folly of appointing public officials by lot, when no one would choose a pilot or a builder or a flautist by lot, nor any other craftsman for work in which mistakes are far less dangerous than mistakes in the craft concerned with the polis. Such sayings, he argued, led the young to despise the established constitution and made them violent. (*Mem.* I.ii.9−10)

The nature of Socrates' opposition to election by lot evidenced by these sources, however, is as follows: *if* someone possesses "the craft concerned with the polis," he should occupy public office, not someone elected by lot. But opposition of this sort is entirely hypothetical unless Socrates believed that someone actually possessed the craft of politics. And, as we shall see in 3.4, he did not believe this. Indeed, he believed that the craft of politics, being identical to the craft-knowledge of virtue, was likely to remain the exclusive prerogative of the gods forever. This no doubt explains why he himself accepted appointment to public office by lot. He served as a member of the Council in 406 (*Ap.* 32a9−c3) and was chairman of its standing committee on what seems to have been a second occasion (*Grg.* 473e6−474e1).[45] And all three—Council, standing committee, and chairman—were chosen by lot (Aristotle, *Ath.* 43.2−44.3).[46]

Any fully confident claim about Socrates' attitude to democracy would have to be based on a wider and more detailed survey of the evidence than has been attempted here. But enough of the chief witnesses cited in this regard have been reviewed to make it reasonable to

---

45. See Dodds (1959, 247−248).

46. Rhodes (1972, 2) points out that those citizens "who stayed in Athens in 411 to perform military service under the Four Hundred were debarred" from serving as members of the Council. The fact, therefore, that Socrates served as a member in 406 is compelling evidence that he was not a supporter of that oligarchic faction or seen as such. This is scarcely what we would expect if indeed he "shared with his conservative friends at least one overriding interest: the replacement of the . . . democracy by the rule of an aristocratic-oligarchic elite" (Wood and Wood 1978, 97). Kraut (1984, 177−180, 218−228) is a clearheaded discussion of Socrates' often misrepresented admiration for the oligarchic Spartans, against whom he fought on three occasions (*Ap.* 28e2−3).

believe that, had he thought it crucial, Socrates could have defended himself directly against a charge of having corrupted Alcibiades and Critias in the political sense of having poisoned them with his own antidemocratic views, just as he could have defended himself against a charge of having corrupted them in the religio-ethical sense. We have no sufficiently compelling reason to believe, therefore, that Socrates is engaging in rationalization or evasion or doing anything other than stating his honest opinion, when he traces the charges against him, not to his association with Alcibiades and Critias, but to the anger and hurt pride caused by the activities of his young followers.

The second source of suspicion of the defense against Meletus' *graphē* focuses on Socrates' own motives. It is best expressed as a series of questions. Why does Socrates set out primarily to discredit Meletus rather than to demonstrate his own innocence directly? Why does he not say in so many words that he believes in the gods in whom the polis believes? Why does he never say outright that he has not corrupted the youth?

Socrates does not believe that Meletus' *graphē* is his major problem. At the beginning of his defense he says that he fears his old accusers, who represent him as a generic intellectual, "much more" than "Anytus, and those with him" (18b1–c2). At the end of his examination of Meletus he returns to this theme:

> But, in fact, men of Athens, that I am not unjust after the fashion of Meletus' *graphē* does not seem to me to need much defense; these things are sufficient. On the other hand, what I said earlier, that I am much hated by many, know well that this is true. This is what will convict me, if I am convicted—not Meletus and Anytus, but the prejudice and envy of the many. This has convicted many others, good men, too. There is no danger that it will stop with me. (28a2–b2)

The *graphē*, just by itself, is frivolous (24c5–6) and unsupported by direct evidence (33c8–34b5). The prejudice caused by his long-standing reputation as an intellectual is serious and gives the *graphē* an appearance of weight. It is these beliefs, surely, that explain why Socrates devotes so little time to Meletus (four pages out of eighteen) and why he focuses on discrediting him and his charges rather than on directly proving his own innocence. Socrates does prove his innocence, as we have seen. But he does so indirectly in the course of showing that Meletus' charges are in fact inconsistent. This may not have been a wise stratagem. But we can explain it in an entirely nonsinister and unproblematic way. For to deny charges that one believes one can show to be frivolous and to spend one's defense attempting to demonstrate directly that one is innocent of them, when one believes that the real threat lies elsewhere, would be to accord the charges the very seriousness one believes them to lack and to adopt a strategy irrationally at odds with one's beliefs about the facts of the case.

Two final reasons for uneasiness with Socrates' defense draw upon the supposed motives of two other important parties to his trial, namely, the King Archon and the jurors.

An action by *graphē asebeias* of the sort brought by Meletus required an *anakrisis* or preliminary hearing before the King Archon. We do not know very much about what the *anakrisis* involved, because it took place before the speeches, which provide the bulk of the available evidence about Athenian court procedure, took place. But it certainly involved questions put to the litigants by the Archon and by each other, and "there may have been adjournments of the procedure to enable one or other litigant to furnish correct answers to these questions" (Harrison 1968, 2: 95). The principal aims of the *anakrisis* were to determine whether there was an issue to be put before a jury and, if there was, to define it "juristically in such a way that a straight condemnation or acquittal of the defendant could be pronounced" (Harrison 1968, 2: 95).

We may assume, then, that the King Archon determined that Socrates had a case to answer. This makes it difficult to believe that Meletus' charges were as frivolous or as easy to refute as Socrates makes them out to be. And this, in turn, provides a foothold for uneasiness about the defense he gives. Was Socrates unaware of what the Archon saw in the case? Was he unable to convince him that the charges were frivolous? Or, having seen what the Archon saw, did he, for some—possibly unsavory—reason, decide not to confront it openly?

Turning, now, to the jury, we find a similar problem. If Meletus' charges are as frivolous as Socrates believed and if he actually demonstrated that he was innocent of them, why did 280 of his peers find him guilty?[47]

We shall never know the answers to all these questions. We shall never know why the King Archon acted as he did or why those jury members voted as they did. But it is at least as likely that they were influenced by

47. A tied jury vote secured acquittal. At 36a5–6 Socrates says that if 30 more people had found him not guilty, he would have been acquitted. Assuming a normal jury of 500, this entails that the vote was 280 to 220. See Burnet (1924, 150–151).

the prejudicial caricature that Socrates feared so much or that they were motivated by the same concerns that history has attributed to Meletus and Anytus, as that they saw something in the charges or in the defense against them that we ourselves have been unable to see. We must not forget either the 220 jurors who proved as blind as ourselves in this regard and found Socrates innocent.

It is impossible to discuss all the reasons that Socrates' defense against Meletus' charges has been found strange and disturbing. But a sensibly charitable reader of the *Apology* should not be swayed by those considered here. We may believe that Socrates was wrong about the motives of Meletus and Anytus. We may believe that he would have done better to take the formal charges more seriously and to have rebutted them directly. We may be right. Who can say? But it does not follow that Socrates' defense is dishonest, or evasive, or the outcome of unsavory motives. All that follows—and this only if we are right—is that it is not forensically the best defense he could have given.

THREE

THE
TRUE
SOCRATES

> We achieve, if we do achieve, in little sedimentary stitches as though we were
> making lace.   —YEATS

Having exposed the falsehood and explained the genesis of the ancient
caricature, having refuted Meletus' formal charges, Socrates turns to a
broader characterization and defense of the philosophic life he has led.
Previously, he has been attacking the false Socrates of rumour and writ.
Now he turns to a positive account of what he is, to the true Socrates.

3.1 THE SOLDIER OF APOLLO

Socrates begins this positive phase of his justificatory self-portrait with a
hypothetical question:

> Are you not ashamed, Socrates, to have followed the kind of oc-
> cupation *ex hou kindouneueis nuni apothanein*? (28b3—5)

He is often taken to be asking whether he is not ashamed of an occupation *from which he is at risk of being put to death*.[1] And this makes his
question at least somewhat intelligible: judicial execution, even for
someone who believes himself innocent, is a shameful death. But it
cannot be what Socrates means; for he argues that anyone who asks the
question he has in mind is committed to holding that "all the heroes
who died at Troy are despicable [*phauloi*], especially the son of Thetis
who was so contemptuous of danger compared with disgrace" (28b9-
c4). But Achilles and the other heroes of Troy were not judicially executed. They died glorious and honourable deaths, not shameful ones.
What Socrates' imaginary interlocutor is really asking is, "Are you not
ashamed, Socrates, to have followed the kind of occupation *from which
you are now at risk of dying*?" And this is not a readily intelligible question
at all. Why should anyone think that it is shameful to have an occupation
that puts his life at risk?

---

1. See Allen (1980, 49); Brickhouse and Smith (1988, 128—129); Tredennick
(1979, 59).

The answer is that no one is thinking such a thing. What is finally being presupposed is not that it is shameful to risk death, only that it is shameful to risk death *in some ways*. We can see this from a chance remark of Aristotle's—although the fact that Socrates goes on to argue that he has nothing to be ashamed of, even if he does risk death, because he is relevantly like a soldier under orders, suggests the same view. In the course of arguing that the rejection of a more probable statement can be used to show that a less probable one should also be rejected, Aristotle gives the following as an illustration: "If generals are not despicable [*phauloi*] because they risk death [*thanatountai*], neither are sophists" (*Rh.* 1397b24).[2] Generals run a greater risk of death than sophists but are not despised, so that sophists who are in fact despised because they risk death (presumably in impiety trials) should not be despised either. The clear implication is, first of all, that sophists or philosophers—the two were not popularly distinguished (20a2−5, 23d4−7)—were indeed despised in Athens because their profession put their lives at risk and, second, that not all practitioners of risky professions were despised. It was something about sophistry, then, that made it shameful to risk death by doing it, not something about risking death in general.

This does not tell us, of course, just what it was about sophistry or philosophy that made it shameful in this way, but it does suggest an intelligible answer, namely, that it was thought shameful to risk "the greatest of evils" (29a6-b1) through practicing an unsavoury profession (cf. *Prt.* 312a3−6). Hence—and this is another piece of evidence that might be cited in favour of the present interpretation—we can see that it is a particularly good question with which to begin a defense of the philosophic life.

Socrates' response to this question hinges crucially on the fact that he has been ordered to lead the philosophic life—to elenctically examine his fellows—by Apollo and on a principle, itself based on three other principles and a factual claim. Once the reasoning behind this crucial principle is understood, the remainder of the argument falls readily into place.

The principle in question is this:

(1) Wherever a man posts himself, thinking it is the best place for him to be, or wherever he is posted by a commander, there he must, as it seems to me, stay and face the risks, and not take into account death or anything else before what is shameful. (28d6−10)

2. I owe notice of this text to Kerferd (1981, 21−22).

(1) cannot mean that someone must always do whatever his commander orders. For Socrates concedes that the Thirty were in command (*archē*; 32d4, 32d8) when they ordered him to arrest Leon of Salamis (32c4–e1), yet he disobeyed them.[3] Some have argued, therefore, that (1) should be understood as

(1a) Someone must always do what he believes to be best and obey his commander, provided that what the latter orders him to do is what he himself independently believes to be best.[4]

But while (1a) clearly avoids the problematic implication that someone must always obey a commander, it cannot be what Socrates intends. For his strategy, as we are about to see, is to use the fact that he has been ordered to live the philosophical life by his commander Apollo to prove that it would be wrong of him not to live it (28d6–29a1). And to that strategy (1a) is simply irrelevant.

Finally, (1) is silent on the question of what one is to do if obedience itself involves doing something wrong and shameful, as would have been true in the case of obeying the Thirty's unjust command (32d2–3). All (1) tells us is that a person must do what he thinks best or what a commander has told him, rather than giving more weight to death or to anything else than to avoiding what is shameful.[5]

The first of the principles Socrates uses to justify (1) is

(2) But to do what is wrong, such as [*kai*][6] to disobey one who is better than oneself [*tōi beltioni*], whether god or man, that I know [*oida*] to be bad and shameful. (29b6–7)

What does (2) mean? "Everything depends," it has been correctly noted, "on how we take *beltion* ('superior')."

---

3. It may be significant, however, that Socrates characterizes his military commanders at Potidea, Amphipolis, and Delium, to whom, in the first instance, (1) applies, as "the commanders you [the Athenian democracy] had chosen to command me [*hous humeis heilesthe archein mou*]" (28e1–2); for this suggests that (1) may be restricted to *legitimate* rulers. Socrates may not have believed that the Thirty fell into this class.

4. See Woozley (1979, 48–49); Nehamas (1987, 304–307).

5. Cf. Kraut (1984, 23 n. 38).

6. *Kai* is epexegetic. If it functioned as an ordinary conjunction, the argument would be missing the vital connective tissue which enables Socrates to explain why it would be wrong to disobey the god. Cf. Kraut (1984, 234–235 n. 74).

> If someone is superior merely by being in a position of political power or authority, then Socrates is committing himself to an extremely conservative political doctrine—and he is also contradicting the position he took when he disobeyed the Thirty. . . . But a "superior" can mean someone who is more virtuous (*Protag.* 320b3, cf. *ameinon* at *Ap.* 30d1), and surely that is what Socrates means here. He will always obey someone who is at a higher moral stage than the one he has reached, for he assumes that such a person will never give orders that are contrary to justice. (Kraut 1984, 23 n. 38)

This is an attractive proposal. But it overlooks one crucial piece of evidence. Socrates clearly includes his military commanders at Potidea, Amphipolis, and Delium among those who are his superiors in the requisite sense. Otherwise (2) would fail to be relevant to him both as philosopher-soldier of Apollo and as Athenian soldier (28d6−29b7). He can hardly be supposing, however, that these commanders had all reached a "higher moral stage" than himself.[7] So it is back to the drawing board.

Beltion is the comparative of the adjective *agathon* ('good'), and one's better is therefore someone who is, literally speaking, "more good" than one is. Part of what (2) says in effect, then, is that it is a bad thing to disobey someone who is "more good" than oneself. Since 'bad' is the contrary of 'good', this is surely an *acceptable proposition*. In addition, (2) says that it is wrong to do what is bad or shameful. And this is also an acceptable proposition. Thus (2) as a whole is precisely the sort of proposition we would expect to find as a premise in a Socratic argument.[8]

---

7. This problem also plagues the account of (2) proposed by Nehamas (1987, 306−307): "The central idea is that at 29b6−7 Socrates is saying that it would be bad and shameful to fail to be convinced or persuaded by either a human or by a divine moral expert. The question of submission, I think, is not raised." But neither were Socrates' commanders at Potideia, Amphipolis, and Delium moral experts, nor did they try to persuade him to stay at his post. They simply gave him orders. The question of submission is not only raised, then, it is answered. The commands of our betters must be obeyed, if our only reason to disobey is fear of death or "anything else whatever" (29a1).

8. Brickhouse and Smith (1988, 128−137) argue that in (2) Socrates is "only professing confidence in what, as the result of numerous elenctic tests, he has found to be justified." But their argument is implausible; for Socrates clearly expects the jury to follow his reasoning and to be convinced by it. If he did not think that (2) would be found to be justified on first hearing, we would expect him to explain and justify it. Since he does neither, it seems more reasonable to believe that he took (2) to be acceptable as it stands.

Imagine, now, that X believes (2) and that he also believes, as Socrates does, that he is like a soldier who has been assigned to his post by a commander. In this situation, it is reasonable for X to believe that his commander is in the relevant sense his better. For unless there is strong evidence to the contrary, X's commander must be presumed to be in a better position to know what it is best for him to do on the battlefield or its analogue, the Athenian polis, than X is himself. But, in the context envisaged in (2), the only contrary evidence X has is that staying at his post puts him at risk of dying. And that, as the remainder of the argument will show, has insufficient weight to justify disobedience. Thus (2) explains why disobeying a commander is bad, wrong, and shameful.

If this reconstruction is on the right lines, (1) follows from acceptable propositions which anyone would find it difficult to deny. And because (1) has this status, because, like (2), it clearly does not constitute expert craft-knowledge of virtue, it in no way compromises Socrates' disclaimer of such knowledge.

The remaining two principles Socrates uses to support (1) are as follows:

(3) I shall always fear and avoid the things I know are bad rather than the things which, for all I know, may be good. (29b8–10)

and

(4) How is this not just that most blameworthy ignorance of thinking that one knows when one does not know? (29b1–2)

(4) partly explains why (3) is true: to choose what one knows to be bad over what may, for all one knows, be good, is to act as if one actually knows that the latter is worse than the former. And this, Socrates claims, is blameworthy.

Why? Why is acting as if one knows what one does not know blameworthy? The answer seems to lie in the fact that, through self-examination or examination at the hands of others, someone can come to recognize his ignorance or, failing that, render himself nonculpable through an honest and protracted attempt to discover the truth. Socrates sometimes seems to suggest that daily elenctic examination is required to achieve either of these results (38a1–6). And this might be thought to be a totally impractical suggestion which would put the examined life outside the realm of the possible for the vast majority who must work to earn their bread.[9] But this is not the case. Virtue is the most important

9. Mrs Poyser puts a similar objection to Dinah Morris (*Adam Bede*, Ch. VI): "But for the matter o' that, if everybody was to do like you [be a Methodist

thing; without it nothing else is unequivocally good (30b3−4). It cannot be practical, therefore, to make anything besides trying to be as virtuous as possible the center of one's life. This does not mean, however, that one must starve in the process. Earning a living, too, must find a place in most people's examined lives. But its place is at the periphery, not at the center. We must care more for virtue and our psyche than for making money (30a8-b4). This is a revolutionary proposal, no doubt, but not— given its presuppositions—a silly one (1.10, 3.5, 3.10).

This brings us to the factual claim:

(5) [We] have no adequate knowledge of things in Hades. (29b5)

Socrates concludes from it that

(6) No one knows whether death may not be the greatest of all goods for a man. (29a6-b1)

If we do not know what happens in Hades, we do not know whether death is a good or a bad thing.

(2) has placed disobeying a commander in the class of things we know to be bad. (6) puts death in the class of things which may, for all we know, be good. To disobey a commander out of fear of death is thus doubly bad. On the one hand, it involves disobeying a better, which is a bad thing. On the other, it involves acting as if we know what we do not in fact know, namely, that death is "the greatest of evils" (29b1). And this is also blameworthy and bad.

It follows that, if the only reason to disobey a commander is that obedience puts us at risk of death, we must obey him. As Socrates puts it in his opening formulation:

> It is not a fine thing to say, sir, if you think that a man who is the least bit of good should take into account the risk of living or dying rather than considering this alone when he acts: whether his actions are just or unjust, the deeds of a good or of a bad man. (28b5−9)

This is so, we can now see, not because the demands of justice are categorical imperatives, which must be obeyed whatever the con-

preacher], the world must come to a standstill; for if everybody tried to do without house and home, and with poor eating and drinking, and was allays talking as we must despise the things o' the world, as you say, I should like to know where the pick o' the stock, and the corn, and the best new-milk cheeses 'ud have to go. Everybody 'ud be wanting bread made o' tail ends, and everybody 'ud be running after everybody else to preach to 'em, instead 'o bringing up their families, and laying by against a bad harvest. It stands to sense as that can't be the right religion."

sequences, but because to choose what one knows to be bad, over what may, for all one knows, be good is to act out of blameworthy ignorance.

Armed with (1), Socrates is ready to explain why he must continue to lead the philosophic life, even if it puts him at risk of death:

> So I would have done something terrible, men of Athens, if, when the commanders you had chosen to command me stationed me in Potideia, Amphipolis, and Delium, I remained where they stationed me and ran the risk of dying, but when the god stationed me, as I supposed and assumed, and ordered me to live the philosophic life, examining myself and others, I had, out of fear of death or of anything else whatever, abandoned my post. (28d10−29a1)

Socrates has been ordered to philosophize by Apollo, who is, in the relevant sense, his better. To disobey that order out of fear of death would be terrible, for it would be to act hubristically—to suppose he knows when he does not know.

Notice, however, that Socrates actually claims a more general result. He says that he would have done a terrible thing if he had abandoned philosophy not just out of the fear of death but out of the fear of "*anything else whatever [all' hotioun pragma]*" (29a1). Is this, too, supposed to be justified by appeal to (4)? Yes. For acceptable propositions entail that only vice is bad (3.4). And this makes it likely that Socrates thinks that to believe bad anything other than vice is to be guilty of blameworthy ignorance.

Now it might reasonably be thought a weakness in Socrates' argument that it assumes that, if we cannot know our postmortal fate, if we have "no adequate knowledge of things in Hades" (29b5), we cannot know that death is a bad thing; for, after all, we do know that death deprives us of many things we value, that it causes suffering to those we love. And that alone is sufficient to make it bad (*Cri.* 44b5−8).[10] This weakness must be admitted. But it is surely remediable. Even if death is, for these reasons, a bad thing, it would still be irrational to abandon out of fear of death the very thing that made life good and worthwhile. And philosophy has that status for Socrates: elenctically discussing virtue every day, examining himself and others, is "the greatest good for a man" (38a1−6), something that makes him "the best possible" (39d8). We shall see why in 3.10.

10. See Nagel (1979, 1−10).

3.2. Obedience to the Law

With the foregoing argument to hand, Socrates draws a further conclusion:

> Therefore [hōste] if you let me go now and disobey Anytus—who said that either I should not have been brought here in the first place or, since I have been, that it isn't possible not to condemn me to death, for he said that if I am acquitted, your sons, following what Socrates teaches, will soon be completely corrupted—if you said to me with regard to this, "Socrates, for the present we will disobey Anytus; we will release you; but on the condition that you no longer philosophize, nor spend time on this investigating; and that if you are caught still doing this, you will die." If, as I say, you were to acquit me on those terms, I would say to you, men of Athens, I salute you and I am your friend, but I will obey the god rather than you, and as long as I breath and am able I will not stop philosophizing. (29b9-d5)

This further conclusion stirs up a nest of questions. Is Socrates saying that, if the court ordered him to stop philosophizing, he would disobey? If so, is he saying that he would disobey something he believes to have the status of a valid law? If he is, how exactly is this supposed to be mandated or justified by his previous argument? And, however it is justified, is it not inconsistent with what he says in the *Crito* about obeying the law?

Socrates supposes that the court releases him, specifies a condition under which he stays free—no philosophizing—and tells him what will happen if he fails to meet that condition—they will have him put to death.[11] So what the court is being supposed to say is: "We unconditionally release you, and you will stay free on the condition that you do not philosophize, but if you are caught philosophizing, you die." Now, this statement is not an explicit imperative or order such as "Thou shalt not philosophize." But it cannot reasonably be doubted that it is an order nonetheless, that it has the force of a command. For conditionals with threatening consequents are standardly used to order or command someone not to make the antecedent true. When I say, "If you touch my books, I will kill you," I am not giving you permission to touch my books provided you pay a certain price. I am positively ordering you not to touch them and giving you an incentive to obey by telling you what will happen if you do not. There is good reason to believe, consequently,

11. Cf. Woozley (1979, 44).

that Socrates is supposing the jury to have ordered him not to philosophize, and that is why he says, "I will obey [*peisomai*] the god rather than you" (29d3−4).[12]

Socrates is supposing, then, that the jury orders him to stop philosophizing, threatening death for noncompliance, and he is stating unequivocally that he would disobey that order. Does this mean that he is saying he would disobey something that he believes to have the status of a law?

Some have argued that it does not, on the grounds that such a court order would have no binding force in Athenian law and would, in fact, itself have been illegal.[13] But this—even if true—is largely irrelevant to the point at issue. It is what Socrates is *supposing* that is crucial to the question of whether he is showing willingness to act illegally, not the actual legal situation, his beliefs about it, or his own views about legal validity. And what he is supposing is surely this: if the jury were—even *per impossibile*—to enact a legally valid prohibition on elenctic examination, he would disobey it. That is why he does not say that he would disobey the court because the order he is supposing it to make would be legally invalid. His purpose in bringing up the hypothetical court order is not to exploit the fact that counterlegals with false antecedents are true, but to make it clear to the jury that absolutely *nothing*—not even death many times over (30c1)—would get him to abandon philosophy.

There seems to be nothing for it, then, but to take Socrates to be committing himself to break a law (or law-equivalent) forbidding him to philosophize on pain of death.

The situation, therefore, appears to be this. Socrates has been ordered to philosophize by Apollo. He cannot disobey simply out of fear of death. He knows that would be wrong. That is the first conclusion he

---

12. Woozley (1979, 45−46) argues that because *peithesthai* "can mean anything that corresponds in the passive to the active 'persuade'," Socrates could be saying not that he would disobey a court order, but simply that he would not be persuaded by the jury to abandon philosophy. Socrates does not just use *peithesthai* to describe what he will not do in regard to the jury, however; he uses it to describe what he will do in regard to Apollo. And he surely is not saying simply that he will be persuaded by the latter to continue to philosophize. Apollo has not tried to persuade him to philosophize; he has ordered him to do it. That, indeed, is the whole thrust of Socrates' argument here. See Kraut (1981, 658−659).

13. See Brickhouse and Smith (1988, 139−149). Cf. Kraut (1981, 657−658).

reaches. But now he says that it follows from this same argument—note again the strong sign of consequence (*hōste*) with which he begins (29b9)—that if the court ordered him to abandon philosophy on pain of death, he would disobey. The question is, why does he think this further conclusion follows? After all, if the court ordered him to abandon philosophy, surely he would be in the situation of having received conflicting commands from two different superiors, one from Apollo and one from the court.[14] And what his initial argument seems to say about that situation—insofar as it speaks to it at all—is that it would be wrong to disobey either command, that, so to speak, Socrates is damned if he philosophizes and damned if he does not.

Though this problem looks pressing, we should not concede anything to it. Socrates has argued that one must obey one's superior, someone who is relevantly wiser than oneself—the god in ethical matters, one's commanding officer on the battlefield—in any situation in which one's only reason not to obey is that obedience puts one at risk of death. He has *not* said at all that one must obey anyone in authority, no matter what they command. Socrates has been ordered to philosophize by Apollo, his superior in ethical matters. He knows himself that doing philosophy every day is the greatest good. Hence he knows—and on more than one ground—that not to philosophize would be wrong. Then the court orders him to abandon philosophy on pain of death. But the court is not his superior in ethical matters or in wisdom. Indeed, it is his inferior, as his many elenctic examinations of the jurors or their peers have shown. Moreover, he knows that what the court has ordered him to do is wrong. Even though he has received conflicting orders, then, the principles defended in his argument require him to obey only the god's command. They positively forbid him to obey the court.

The final question we must consider is whether this view about the obligation to obey a valid court order having the status of law—the Apology doctrine, as we may call it—is consistent with the famous Persuade or Obey doctrine, which plays such a prominent role in the *Crito* (51b3−4, 51b9-c1, 51e4−52a3).

Socrates has been sentenced to death and is in prison awaiting execution. He is explaining, in the person of the Laws of Athens, why it

14. Santas (1979, 38−40) takes 29b6−7 to mean that one should obey someone who is better than oneself and "better than any other orderer." But there is nothing in the text to suggest that 29b6−9 is intended to handle conflicting orders in this way. Socrates himself does not refer to the conflict between the court and the god at all. See Kraut (1981, 654−655).

would be unjust for him to accept Crito's advice to escape. Persuade or Obey is introduced as a crucial part of that explanation:

> We say that the one who disobeys us acts unjustly . . . because he agreed to obey us but neither obeys nor persuades us if we are doing something wrong. We do not harshly order [Socrates] to do what we command but allow either of two [alternatives]—either to persuade us or to do [*hē peithein hēmas hē poiein*], but he does neither of these. (51e4–52a3)

The Laws say only that *they* are to be persuaded. And this is an obvious metaphor, a trope made possible by their personification. But they say absolutely nothing about how that metaphor is to be cashed, about which of their representative bodies in Athens—the one that makes the laws (the Assembly) or the one that implements them (the courts)—is the appropriate one to hear persuasion. They do not say when persuasion is to occur, whether after a law is alleged to have been broken or before. Nor do they explain the kind of alleged injustice or wrong that it is appropriate to persuade them about. Is it unjust laws, unjust verdicts, or unjust sentences? Given these unclarities, it is hardly surprising that there is considerable dispute about just what Persuade or Obey means.

The Laws say that if Socrates escapes execution, he does not comply with Persuade or Obey, because he neither persuades nor obeys. What is it that he fails to obey? Some or other of the relevant Athenian laws, presumably. But which laws exactly? Only three have any bearing on his situation:

> The *law against impiety*—perhaps the descendent of Diopeithes' psephism; that is the law under which Socrates was indicted.

> The *counterpenalty law* which required the defendant against a *graphē asebeias* to propose a counterpenalty to the one demanded by the prosecution, requiring the jury to choose between them (3.9); that is the law which led to Socrates' death sentence.

> The *law on verdicts*, possibly more implied than expressed, which required the defendant to abide by the verdict of the court and not to try to prevent its sentence from being carried out (*Cri.* 50a8-b5).

But of these laws, the only one that Socrates would break or fail to obey if he escaped is the law on verdicts. So, whatever Persuade or Obey means, it must explain why Socrates is obliged to obey that law.

With that in mind, let us turn to the interpretations of Persuade or Obey which have been proposed.

(A) Either a citizen must persuade the Assembly to repeal or modify any law he thinks to be unjust or he must obey that law.[15]

(B) A citizen who disobeys his city "must, when summoned, persuade a jury that he was right to disobey. But if he was right, yet fails in his efforts to show this to the jury, he has done no wrong." (Kraut 1984, 69)[16]

(A) is a doctrine about our obligation to obey laws or to persuade the legislature to reform them. (B) is a doctrine about our obligation to persuade a jury that our law-violating actions were just.

(A) is inconsistent with the Apology doctrine. It requires Socrates to obey the court order forbidding philosophizing. That is a strike against it. But there is another. (A) says that Socrates must either reform the law on verdicts or obey it. The problem is that this law, being central to the very idea of the rule of law itself, is not the kind of law that Socrates— who is clearly in favour of that idea—could possibly want to reform. Indeed, it is because the law on verdicts has this special status that the Laws can say: "With this attempted act [escape], are you thinking of anything else than destroying us, the Laws, and the entire polis, for your part?" (*Cri.* 50a8-b5).[17] Consequently, in the pertinent circumstances, with the law on verdicts as its focus, (A) has no more explanatory force than a doctrine of simple obedience. For to be told in regard to such a law that one must either get it reformed or obey it amounts to being told simply to obey it.

(B) is consistent with the Apology doctrine. That is a significant point in its favour. But, like (A), (B) cannot explain why Socrates must obey the law on verdicts. (B) says that if Socrates disobeys the law on verdicts, he must, if summoned, persuade a jury that he was right to do so. It seems, however, that because of the special nature of the law on verdicts (and of the counterpenalty law, for that matter) such persuasion would have to focus on the law against impiety. Socrates would have to argue, in effect, that he was right to disobey the law on verdicts because the court was wrong to find him guilty of disobeying the law against impiety. But if that is what Persuade or Obey is saying, it cannot explain why Socrates must not escape. For Socrates thinks—and the Laws

15. See Allen (1980, 104); Grote (1865, 1: 300); Guthrie (1971a, 92−93); Woozley (1979, 71). Irwin (1986b, 400−404) accepts a version of (A). Kraut (1984, 54−60) is critical.

16. Cf. Irwin (1986b, 400−404); Vlastos (1984b, 931−932).

17. See Kraut (1984, 115−148).

agree—that the court was wrong to find him guilty of impiety (50c1−6). (B) would thus permit him to escape, although it would oblige him, if summoned, to return to Athens for what would in essence be a retrial on the charge of impiety. But Socrates believes that Persuade or Obey obliges him to obey the law on verdicts and not escape.

These arguments against (A) and (B) give us an incentive to look for an alternative interpretation of Persuade or Obey with more obvious explanatory bearing on Socrates' actual situation in the *Crito*. And in fact there is one which is as consistent with the actual text of Persuade or Obey as either (A) or (B), namely,

> (C) A citizen of Athens who has broken or been accused of break-
> ing one of its laws must, if summoned, either persuade a court
> that he has done nothing unjust or abide by the court's verdict
> and obey the law requiring him to submit to the sentence passed
> on him.

The Laws do not "harshly order" someone to obey. They give him the option of defending himself before a jury. But if he does not succeed in persuading the jury that he is innocent of wrongdoing, he must obey, not the law he has already broken (that would make little sense), but the law about accepting his punishment. If Socrates had been given no such option, he might with justice have tried to escape. But because he has had the chance to persuade the court of his innocence and has failed to do so, (C) requires him to obey the law on verdicts and accept his punishment. For if, having failed to persuade the court, he disobeys that law and escapes, then he "neither persuades nor obeys [*toutōn oudetera poiei*]" (52a3).

But suppose that the sentence chosen by the jury required Socrates to do something unjust. Suppose, for example, the sentence imposed was to cease philosophizing. What then? Socrates is absolutely explicit, as we have seen, that one must never, not even to save one's life, do anything unjust. So he would not do what such a sentence required of him. Would he thereby violate Persuade or Obey? No. He would violate Persuade or Obey only if, having been called before a court to account for his disobedience and having failed to persuade it that his disobedience was just, he tried to escape the sentence it imposed. Persuade or Obey continues to come into play in this manner as long as the court continues to impose sentences which require a defendant do something he believes to be unjust.[18]

18. The actual sentence chosen by the jury requires Socrates to kill himself by drinking hemlock: he is to be his own executioner, not just a passive victim. See

What Persuade or Obey requires of Socrates in the *Crito*, then, is that he not escape. He has tried to persuade the court that he is innocent, and having been found guilty, he has then tried to persuade it that he should be fined, not executed. He has failed. What Persuade or Obey requires of him in the *Apology* is not that he obey the court order, no matter what, but that he defend himself against a charge that he has disobeyed it and that, if he fails, he abide by the verdict and sentence of the court—provided it does not require him to do anything unjust—and not try to escape his punishment. And nothing in the *Apology* suggests that Socrates plans not to meet that requirement.

In both the *Apology* and the *Crito*, Socrates strongly advocates the view that an individual's most fundamental obligation is to avoid doing what he knows to be wrong (*Ap.* 28b5–9, 28d6–10; *Cri.* 48c6-d5). But in both works, implicitly in the former, explicitly in the latter, he manifests an equally fundamental respect for laws which do not "harshly order," which give an accused the chance to defend himself in court. No one must ever do what he knows to be wrong, even at the price of his life. But if he lives under laws of the sort in question and if he breaks or is accused of having broken one of them, justice requires him to answer the charges. He must try to persuade a court that what he did was right. If he fails, justice requires that he accept the sentence of the court (provided that it does not require him to do injustice). He is not the slave even of laws like these. But he is not above them either. His actions done, not he but the laws, or their representatives, have the final say about what is to happen to him as a result.

3.3 SOCRATES' MISSION

The account of his elenctic philosophizing that Socrates gave earlier in the *Apology* dealt primarily with what we called its *second stage*, the goal of which was to decode the oracle. But second-stage elenctic examining is not what he tells the court he would continue even if they outlawed it: it was not conducted in obedience to divine command, had no ethically

---

Frey (1978); Lesser (1980). Socrates believes he is innocent of the crime for which hemlock is the punishment. Does not the actual sentence, then, require Socrates to do something unjust? No. Socrates would be doing something unjust in (legally) killing himself if he knew that death was a bad thing (cf. 37b2–5). But he does not know this (37b6–7). By the end of the trial, indeed, he has become certain that it is better for him than the available alternatives (41d4–5; 3.11). He does not believe, therefore, that drinking the hemlock is doing something unjust. If he did, we can be sure he would refuse to do it.

reformative purpose, was carried out exclusively among those with a reputation for wisdom, and had long ago reached an uncontroverted conclusion. What Socrates would not abandon at any cost is *third-stage* examining—the stage in which, confident now of the command Apollo had sent him through Delphi, he took up his "service to the god" (23c1) and extended his elenctic examination to "anyone, citizen or stranger" (23b5−6; 30a2−4, 30a8), with the aim of getting them to care for virtue more than for anything else and releasing them from the hubris of the "most blameworthy ignorance." That is why, as he now characterizes it to the jury, the elenchus has the strong religio-ethical flavour and reformative purpose that in his earlier account it lacked.

Failure to notice this difference, clearly indicated in the text, between the various stages in Socrates' examinings has led some writers seriously astray:

> In the *Apology* Socrates is made to provide too many inadequate reasons for inflicting his elenctic interviews upon his reluctant victims. At one moment he cross-questions a public man in order, not very piously, to satisfy himself but not his victim that the Delphic oracle was wrong. At the next, he does so in order, not very piously, to satisfy himself, but not his victim, that after all the Delphic oracle was right. . . . Just in four or five sentences or phrases Socrates avers that his task is that of exhorting Athens to virtue, but he does not explain the connexion between this edifying task and the practice of puncturing the conceit of artisans, poets and others by pavement-questionings upon their specialities. . . .
> The factitiousness of these discordant reasons for Socrates forcing his pavement interviews upon resentful interlocutors has a simple explanation. Such interviews did not occur. They are Platonic inventions. (Ryle 1966, 177−178)[19]

But, as we now see, the conceit-puncturing negative examining belonged to Socrates' entirely pious search for the meaning of the oracle. His positive mission of exhorting Athens to virtue, on the other hand, followed upon his interpretation of the oracle as a divine command to disabuse his fellows of their hubris. The two stages are related, not by identity of purpose, but by the fact that the second resulted in the understanding of the oracle as mandating the third and giving it its new religio-ethical goal.

This third stage of elenctic philosophizing is a two-part affair. The first part consists of a reproach:

19. Cf. Hackforth (1933, 112).

Best of men, you are an Athenian, from the greatest polis, with the greatest reputation for wisdom and strength; are you not ashamed that you care about having as much money as possible, and reputation and honour, but that about wisdom and truth and how your psyche will be the best possible you neither care nor give thought? (29d7-e3)

The second part comes into play only if the reproach is resisted as unmerited. It consists of an elenctic examination on the topic of virtue:

And if one of you disputes this and says he does care, I will not immediately let him go, nor will I go away myself, but I will speak with him, examine him, and use the elenchus on him, and if he does not seem to me to possess virtue, but only says that he does, I will reproach him, saying that he attaches least importance to the most important things and treats the less important things as more important. I will do this to anyone I happen to meet, young and old, citizens and strangers, but especially to the citizens, since you are closer in kin to me. Know well that the god orders this. And I think that no greater good has come to be in the polis than my service to the god. I go around doing nothing but attempting to persuade young and old among you not to care primarily or passionately about your bodies and about wealth but about how your psyche can be the best possible. I say that wealth does not bring about virtue, but it is virtue that makes wealth and everything else, both public and private, good for a man. (29e3−30b4)

This, then, is what Socrates does. This, not arcane science, forensic oratory, or expert craft-knowledge of virtue, is what the jury should have in mind when they try to decide whether or not he is guilty of Meletus' charges:

If, then, by saying these things, I corrupt the youth, they must be harmful. But if someone asserts that I say something other than this, he is talking nonsense. In regard to these things, I would say to you, "Men of Athens, whether you believe Anytus or not, whether you let me go or not, I would not do other than this, not even if I were going to die many times." (30b5−c1)

A number of writers, noticing the conditional form of these remarks about corruption—"if, then, by saying these things . . ."—have argued that Socrates is not actually denying that he corrupts the youth, that he is expressing uncertainty about whether telling people to care for their psyches more than money is harmful: "He does not assert that his speeches do not corrupt. He admits that there is room for doubt" (West 1979, 172).[20] But there is little basis in the text for this view. For the natural way to take a conditional whose consequent its utterer clearly believes to be false or silly is as a strong denial of the antecedent. And Socrates shows absolutely no doubt about the falsity of the consequent of his conditional: elenctically discussing virtue every day is "the greatest good for a man" (38a1−6); "no greater good has come to be in the polis" (30a5−7) than his elenctic mission; he makes the Athenians, not just seem to be happy, but actually "be it" (36d9−e1). Therefore, he cannot have any doubt either about the falsity of its antecedent. He is denying, and denying in no uncertain terms, that his activities corrupt, because he is asserting in no uncertain terms that they are beneficial, not harmful.

Socrates does not believe, then, that third-stage elenctic examining corrupts. But his brief characterization of it is nonetheless problematic. Indeed, as we shall see, it draws upon two of the most perplexing Socratic doctrines.

3.4 KNOWLEDGE, VIRTUE, AND HAPPINESS

The primary target of the elenchus is a sincere belief about a virtue, very often a belief about what it is. And unless that belief is elenchus-proof it does not constitute expert craft-knowledge. Failure to withstand an elenchus, therefore, clearly condemns an interlocutor to nonpossession of craft-knowledge. That much is intelligible and reasonable. But, in characterizing his mission, Socrates draws an additional conclusion. He says that those whose beliefs about the virtues fail to withstand an elenchus do not "possess virtue [kektēsthai aretēn]" (29e5−30a1). We may infer that he thinks that craft-knowledge of virtue is necessary for virtue. But why does he think this?

In addition to claiming that elenchus-proof beliefs about virtue are necessary for virtue, Socrates also claims that "it is virtue that makes wealth and everything else [hapanta], both public and private, good for a man" (30b2−4).[21] This is surely an unacceptable proposition if ever there

20. Cf. Allen (1980, 7).

21. This passage is usually translated to say that virtue makes its possessor wealthy. See Grube (1975, 33); Tredennick (1979, 62); West (1979, 36). Burnyeat (1971, 210) argues that this is a mistake: "No doubt some listeners, like some modern translators, would understand Socrates to be making the implausible claim that virtue pays in a straightforward sense, although to confine the thrice-repeated 'valuables' (chrēmata) to money is to miss the Socratic challenge to

was one: money, pleasure, and health seem to be good things to have whether one is virtuous or not, and "age, ache, penury, and imprisonment" seem to be bad things even for the virtuous.[22] Yet Socrates claims that by elenctically examining people he is "attempting to persuade" them to share his views about virtue (30a7−8). It must be true, therefore, that he believes that this unacceptable proposition about virtue is—like the doctrine that it is better to suffer injustice than to do it—firmly based in acceptable propositions. These two problems, the one about virtue and craft-knowledge, the other about virtue and happiness, are best approached together.

One of Socrates' deepest commitments, his "supreme principle of practical choice," has been aptly dubbed the principle of the "Sovereignty of Virtue" (Vlastos 1984a, 186−189):

> It is not a fine thing to say, sir, if you think that a man who is the least bit of good should take into account the risk of living or dying rather than considering this alone when he acts, whether his acts are just or unjust, the deeds of a good or a bad man. (*Ap.* 28b5−9; cf. 28d6−10)

> But for us, since the argument thus compels us, the only thing we should consider is . . . whether we would be acting justly . . . or, in truth, unjustly . . . And if it should become evident that this action is unjust, then the fact that by staying here I would die or suffer anything else whatever should not be taken into account when the alternative is to act unjustly. (*Cri.* 48c6−d5)

Faced with a choice between acting unjustly and anything else whatever, we must always choose the latter. In 3.1, we traced Sovereignty of

common notions of what is a valuable possession." While he is surely right about this, it is not the whole story. If money and the like can be included among Socratic *chrēmata* (and surely they can be: at 36d1−37a1 Socrates says that free meals in the prytaneum would be a good thing), the false implication that money comes from virtue remains. For this reason, the account of the matter given by Burnet (1924, 124) is preferable: "The subject is *chrēmata kai ta alla hapanta* and *agatha tois anthrōpois* is predicate. We must certainly not render 'from virtue comes money'! This is a case where interlaced order may seriously mislead." Money does not come from virtue. But virtue makes money and other things good. This is a persistent Socratic doctrine, as we are about to see.

22. The list is Claudio's (*Measure for Measure*, III.1). But he draws the unSocratic conclusion that even a life filled with the evils which the items on it bring "is a paradise/ To what we fear of death."

Virtue—itself an unacceptable proposition—to part of its ground in acceptable propositions.

In addition to holding Sovereignty of Virtue, Socrates also holds the following doctrine about thought and action:

> The good is the end of all our actions; everything must be done for its sake [*heneka*]. (*Grg.* 499e7−8; cf. 468b1−4; *Def.* 413a3)

He holds, too, that the good and happiness are intimately related. And though the precise nature of their relationship is a matter for investigation, it seems certain, nonetheless, that Socrates embraces *eudaimonism*, that he holds that we all aim at the good because (in some way or other) it guarantees us eudaimonia or happiness (*Euthd.* 282a1−4; cf. *Smp.* 204e5−7).[23]

These doctrines naturally lead us to expect that virtue and happiness are intimately related. And, on this score, the Socratic dialogues do not disappoint:

> The more moderate you are, the happier you are. (*Chrm.* 176a4−5)

> I [Socrates] don't know how he is off for education and justice.— What's that? Is the whole of happiness in that?—Yes, so I say, Polus, for I say that the fine and good man or woman is happy, and the unjust and base is wretched. (*Grg.* 470e6−11; cf. 507c3−5, 507d6−e1)

> The just psyche and the just man, then, will live well [*eu biōsetai*], the unjust badly. . . . But the one who lives well [*eu zēn*] is blessed and happy [*eudaimōn*], and the one who doesn't is the opposite. . . . So the just man is happy and the unjust one is wretched. (*R.* 353e10−354a4; cf. *Alc. 1* 134d1−e2, 135b3−5; *Prt.* 313a6−9)

At least one text suggests, indeed, that living well or happily and living virtuously are so closely connected as to be one and the same thing:

> To live well is the same as to live finely and justly [*To de eu kai kalōs kai dikaiōs hoti tauton estin*]? (*Cri.* 48b8; cf. *Euthd.* 279d6−7)

23. *Eudaimonia* and *eu prattein* (doing well) are coextensive (*Alc. 1* 116b2−9, 134d1−e2; *Chrm.* 171e7−172a3; *Def.* 412d10−e1; *Euthd.* 278e3−279a2, 279a2, 280b6, 280b7). *Eu zēn* (living well) and *eudaimonia* are coextensive (*R.* 353e10−354a4). Wisdom (virtue) guarantees *eupraxia* (acting well), *eutuchia* (good luck) (*Euthd.* 281b2−4), and *eudaimonia* (*Euthd.* 292e4−5). Socrates' eudaimonism is provocatively discussed in Irwin (1977, 82−101). The issue of whether or not *eudaimonia* is best understood as happiness is discussed in Kraut (1979) and Vlastos (1984a).

We shall shortly have to reconsider whether or not this text really identi-fies virtue and happiness.

To live well is to live finely and justly, then. But what is it to live finely and justly? What is the fine? What is the just? Socrates' answer, frequently reiterated and clearly an unacceptable proposition, is that the conventionally distinguished virtues are identical to knowledge or wisdom. Here is the argument he uses to establish this in the *Meno*.[24] Each step is recognizably an acceptable proposition of the canonical sort discussed in 1.8; each is agreed to without hesitation by Meno:

> Do we say that virtue is something good [*agathon*], and will this hypothesis stand firm for us, that it is something good?—Of course.—If there is something good, but other than and different from knowledge, virtue might well not be a kind of knowledge. But if there is nothing good that knowledge does not encompass, we would be right to suspect that it is a kind of knowledge.-- That's so.—And it is by virtue that we are good?—Yes.—And if we are good, then we are beneficial; for all good things are beneficial, are they not?—Yes.—Therefore, virtue is beneficial.—Necessarily, given what we have agreed.—Then let us examine what kinds of things benefit us, taking each in turn. Health, we say, and strength, beauty and no doubt wealth too—we say that these things, and others of the same kind, benefit us, do we not?—Yes.—Yet we also say that these same things sometimes do harm. Do you agree or not?—But of course.—Then let us consider what guides these things when they benefit us, and what guides them when they harm us. Don't they benefit us when they are rightly used, and harm us when they are not?—Clearly.—Next, consider things hav-ing to do with the psyche. Is there something you call moderation, and justice and courage, and intelligence, and memory, and noble character, and all other such things?—Yes.—Now consider which-ever of these you believe not to be knowledge but other than knowledge, do they not sometimes benefit us and sometimes harm us? Take courage, for example. If courage is not knowledge but a kind of boldness, then if a man is bold without wisdom, he is harmed, but with wisdom, he is benefited. Isn't that so?—Yes.— And similarly with moderation and quick wits. Things learned or

24. The *Meno* is not usually included among the Socratic dialogues, although Allen (1984, 1: 6–16) places it after the *Prt.* and before the *Grg.* But the argument we are about to consider parallels arguments in dialogues, such as the *Alc. 1*, *Chrm.*, and *Euthd.*, which are thought to be Socratic.

acquired through training are beneficial when guided by wisdom, but harmful without wisdom?—Very much so.—In a word, then, everything the psyche either undertakes or undergoes, when guided by knowledge ends in happiness, and when guided by ignorance in the opposite?—Likely so.—Therefore, if virtue is among the things in the psyche which must itself be beneficial, it must be knowledge, since everything which has to do with the psyche is by itself [*kath' hauta*][25] neither beneficial nor harmful, but becomes one or the other by the addition of knowledge or ignorance. According to this argument, then, virtue, being beneficial, must be a kind of knowledge.—I agree.—Furthermore, the other things we were just discussing, wealth and the rest, are sometimes good, sometimes harmful. And just as knowledge, guiding the rest of the psyche, makes things having to do with the psyche beneficial, while ignorance makes them harmful, so, too, with these other things—the psyche, guiding and rightly using them, makes them beneficial, and wrongly using them makes them harmful.—Clearly.—But it is the wise psyche that guides rightly, and the ignorant psyche wrongly?—That is so.—Therefore one can say this about everything, in man all other things depend on the psyche, but things of the psyche depend on knowledge if they are to be good. According to this argument, knowledge would be the beneficial thing—and virtue we say is beneficial?—Clearly.—Therefore, wisdom is clearly virtue, either the whole of it or a part.—What you say, Socrates, seems rightly said to me. (87d2—89a5).

The precise interpretation of the conclusion of this argument and similar conclusions elsewhere (for example, *Prt.* 329b5—334c5, 349a6—361d6), which identify virtue and knowledge, is disputed. It seems likely,

25. It is common to translate *kath' hauto* as '*in* itself', and to infer that Socrates is here—and in *Euthd.* 281d2—e5—explicitly contrasting things desirable *for their own sake* (intrinsic goods) with things desirable for *the sake of something else* (extrinsic goods). See, for example, Kraut (1984, 211—212 n. 41). Vlastos (1987a, 187—196; 1984a, 210—211 n. 85) argues against this interpretation, claiming that *kath' hauto* means simply '*by* itself'. His view receives strong support from the Hippocratic treatises, where medical prescriptions often take some such form as "this may be taken (*auto*) *kath' hauto* or mixed with water." Here the problematic phrase clearly must mean 'by itself'. Gillespie (1912, 195—196) provides useful discussion and references. But if *kath' hauto* means no more than 'by itself', the contrast Socrates has in mind might be between goods which by themselves produce other intrinsic goods and (putative) goods which produce intrinsic goods only in collaboration with something else.

however, that Socrates does not mean simply that the names of the virtues or the predicates which denote them are coextensive, but that there is a single psychological state which makes men just, moderate, courageous, and so on, and that this state is a certain sort of knowledge or wisdom.[26] To live finely and justly, then, is to live virtuously, and to live virtuously is to live in accordance with knowledge or wisdom.

What sort of knowledge or wisdom? The *Charmides* suggests that moderation is the knowledge of good and evil (174b11−176a5). The *Laches* suggests that the knowledge of good and evil and how to produce them is courage and, indeed, the whole of virtue (197e10−199e12).[27] To live well or virtuously, on this showing, is to live in accordance with the knowledge of good and evil:

> It is not living according to knowledge that is doing well and makes us be happy [*to eu prattein te kai eudaimonein poioun*], not even if it is knowledge of all the other kinds of knowledge, but in accordance with one thing alone, the knowledge of good and evil. (*Chrm.* 174b11−c3)

But this is not Socrates' most informative word on this matter. For that we must turn to the *Euthydemus* (the relevant doctrine also appears in a more compressed form in *Alc. 1* 133b7−134a12).

As usual, Socrates argues in the *Euthydemus* from acceptable propositions to unacceptable ones, gaining the assent of his interlocutor, Cleinias, at each step. There is no one who does not want to do well and be happy (278e5−6). And what we need to do well is to have "plenty of good things" (279a1−4). What are these things? Here is what "everyone would tell us" (279a7): the good things are wealth, health, beauty, good birth, power, honour in one's own country, moderation, justice, courage, wisdom, and *eutuchia*, or good luck (279a7-c8). But it is not sufficient for happiness merely to possess these good things; we must also use them:

> And again, if a man were possessed of wealth and all the other goods we mentioned, but if he did not use them, would he be happy just because he possessed the good things?—Not at all.— Then it seems to be necessary, I said, that the one who is to be happy not only must get possession of such good things but also

26. See Burnyeat (1971, 225−232); Irwin (1977, 42−47, 86−90); Penner (1973, 39−41); Wakefield (1987).

27. See Irwin (1977, 88−89).

must use them, or else there is no benefit from having them. (280d1−7)

Indeed, we must not only possess them and use them, we must use them in the right way: "We all desire to be happy, and we have been shown to be happy by using things and using them rightly" (282a1−4; cf. *Men.* 78b3−79a1). It seems, therefore, that the text from the *Crito* (48b8) we encountered earlier must be understood to mean not that the state of being happy is identical to the state of being just, wise, or virtuous, but that the activity of living well or happily is identical to the activity of living justly, wisely, or virtuously (cf. Aristotle, *EN.* 1101a14−16).[28]

The *Euthydemus* (280d1−7) also seems to suggest, however, that virtuous activity needs things beyond virtue or wisdom itself—*externals*, as we shall call them. It seems to suggest that virtue is not sufficient for the virtuous activity which is happiness. But, as we are about to discover, this is a *suggestio falsi*.

Socrates frequently allows externals to be called good things (*Euthd.* 280d1−7; *Ly.* 218e3−219a4; *Men.* 78c5−d1). And in the *Gorgias* he lumps them together with wisdom and contrasts them with *intermediates*, things which are sometimes good and sometimes bad:

> Now is there anything in existence that isn't either good or bad or intermediate between the two: neither good nor bad? . . . And you [Polus] call [*legeis*] wisdom and health and wealth and other things of that sort good? . . . And you call [*legeis*] neither good nor bad things of this sort: which partake now of the one, now of the other, and at times of neither—for example, sitting and walking and running and sailing; and again stones and sticks and other things of that sort? . . . And when people do these intermediate actions, do they do them for the sake of [*heneka*] the good things, or the good things for the sake of the intermediates? . . . So it is in pursuit of the good that we walk when we walk, thinking this would be better, and, when, on the contrary, we stand, this too we do for the sake of the good? Or not? (467e1−468b4)

28. Vlastos (1984a, 189−196) seems to overlook this fact. He argues that if *Cri.* 48b8 is an identity statement, it must mean that "happiness *is* virtue—virtue is its sole component, the only thing that makes life good and satisfying." But if this text identifies activities, not states, we cannot infer from it alone, that being virtuous (or being in a virtuous state) is sufficient for being happy. Virtuous activity may require other things than merely being virtuous, just as the activity of playing the piano requires other things (such as a functioning piano) besides the ability to play it. And happiness or living well may require virtuous activity.

But this classification is conventional only. Polus, Cleinias, and Meno, like most people, call health, wealth, and the rest good things, things for the sake of which other intermediate things are wanted, things that are good to have by themselves. Socrates, though he is often willing to speak with the vulgar, is consistently critical of this view and consistently persuades his interlocutors to share his doubts. In the *Lysis*, he argues that if we value or love X for the sake of Y, there must be a *prōton philon*, or primary object of value or love that we value or love for its own sake and for whose sake we value or love everything else. It is only this thing, he argues, that we really value or love:

> In speaking of the things that are loved for the sake of some other loved thing [*heneka philou tinos heterou*], we are clearly speaking of them in terms appropriate to it; for it looks as though we really love only it, the thing in which all the so-called loves end. (*Ly.* 220a7−b3; cf. *Grg.* 467d6−e1; *La.* 185d5−7)[29]

In the *Meno* (87d2−89a5), as we saw, he argues that wisdom alone is good and beneficial. And, in the *Euthydemus*, he concludes the doublet of the *Meno* passage as follows:

> As regards all the things [*sumpanta*] we first called goods, it looks as though the argument isn't about how they are by themselves and by nature goods [*auta ge kath' hauta pephuken agatha*] but rather, I think, this: if they are led by ignorance, they are greater evils than their opposites, insofar as they are more able to serve an evil leader, but if understanding and wisdom lead them, they are greater goods, but by themselves [*auta de kath' hauta*] none of them is of any worth [*oudetera autōn oudenos axia einai*]. . . . Of all the other things, none is either good or bad [*tōn men allōn ouden on oute agathon oute kakon*], but of these two, wisdom is good and ignorance bad. (*Euthd.* 281d2-e5)

29. Vlastos (1984a, 212 n. 98) argues that this text advocates only the following more restricted doctrine: if we value X for the sake of Y, and X is either a nonmoral conventional good (such as health), or a conventional intermediate, then X is good only in a manner of speaking. Irwin (1977, 85) argues, correctly in my view, that the doctrine applies to any X we value for the sake of some Y that is "other [*heterou*]" than X. But this does not *by itself* entail, as Irwin claims, that no X of this sort is not also wanted for its own sake. It does not entail that all such Xs are "instrumental" goods only. For something can be wanted both for its own sake and for the sake of something else (*R.* 357c1−3). See Kraut (1984, 211−212 n. 41); Zeyl (1982).

Wealth, health, and the rest—unlike the conventional intermediates—seem to be good things.[30] Most people would choose to have them for their own sake. But acceptable propositions entail that they are not good things. They are good if led by wisdom, bad if led by ignorance. They are not desirable by themselves or for their own sake. In other words, they are really intermediates. The only thing on the conventional list of goods that is a genuine good is wisdom (cf. *Cri.* 44d6—8; Diogenes Laertius, 2.31).

But what is this wisdom? What is "the knowledge which will make us happy" (*Euthd.* 292e4—5)? Must someone get "all knowledge" in order "to be happy and a good man" or is there one knowledge that alone will make him good and happy (282e2—4; cf. *Chrm.* 174b11-c3)? Socrates' answer is that in order to make ourselves happy "we need such a knowledge as combines both how to produce something and how to use what it has produced" (289b4—6). For happiness, as we saw, involves not just the possession but also the use of good things. The argument now focuses on the question of what knowledge or craft combines production and use in the requisite way.

The crafts of harpmaking, flutemaking, or speechmaking are the first to be rejected. For in the case of each of them it is clear that "making is one craft and using is a separate one" (289d5—7). The next candidates are generalship and mathematical science, which are excluded by Cleinias on the grounds that generals cannot use what they have hunted and captured (290b8—9) but must hand it over to the politicians and that (smart) mathematical scientists—even though "they are not mere makers of diagrams but try to discover the beings [*ta onta aneuriskousin*]" (290c1—3)—hand over their discoveries to dialecticians to use (290c3—6).[31]

The final craft examined is the "craft of kingship" which is identified with the craft of politics: "For we believe the craft of politics and king-

---

30. Included in the list are the virtues, moderation, justice, and courage (*Euthd.* 279b4-c1). But these are not intermediates for Socrates, because they are identical to wisdom, which is a good by itself. Hence they are not other (*oudetera, allōn*) than wisdom. Cf. Penner (1973, 43).

31. Cleinias' comment causes consternation in Crito, who cannot believe him capable of such insight: "I think that if he said it, he did not need Euthydemus or any other man to educate him" (290e4—6). This response makes Socrates doubt his memory—could it have been Ctesippus who said it rather than Cleinias? (290e7—8). Finally, he speculates that it was a "higher power [*tōn kreittonōn*]" who spoke these words, and Crito agrees that it must have been (291a2—7). What is going on? The doctrine Cleinias introduces, that mathematical scientists

ship to be one and the same [*hē politikē kai hē basilikē technē hē autē einai*]" (291c4−5). This craft knows how to use the products of *all* the other crafts, "steering all and ruling all and making all useful" (291c7−d3). It follows that there cannot be a craft product—unless it is the product of politics itself—which the craft of politics does not know how to use. The problem is, then, to determine just what the craft of politics produces (292a4−5).

If the craft of politics is the one that would make us happy, "it must be beneficial . . . it must provide us with something good" (292a7−11). But the only good thing is "some kind of knowledge" (292b1−2). That was the outcome of the examination of conventional goods at 281d2−e5. What kind of knowledge? The very knowledge to which the craft of politics is itself identical: "It must not produce any of those products which are neither good nor bad; it must impart no knowledge but itself alone" (292d1−4). Initially perplexing, this outcome is in fact the only intelligible one. For we were led to the craft which used the products of all the other crafts by pursuing the identity of the craft that would make us happy. And the craft which used those products just turned out to be the craft of politics.[32] But if the craft of politics produces itself, it will clearly satisfy the requirement of combining knowledge of "how to produce something and how to use what it has produced" (289b4−6). For every craft knows how to use itself to produce its own products.

Of the conventional goods under consideration, then, only the craft of politics is a good thing, and it both produces itself and uses what it produces. Hence it must be the craft which makes us happy. For to be happy is just to get good things and use them rightly (280d1−7, 282a1−4).

What must the craft of politics be like to bring about this desirable result? There are two possibilities. First, the craft of politics could be an adaptive craft which enables us to be as happy as the circumstances with which luck presents us allow (we shall examine some texts which suggest this view below). In this case, the degree of happiness we achieve, which in some cases may be very small, depends on something over

try but fail to discover *ta onta*, is Plato's own (*R.* 525d5−526b3, 527a6-b6). See Burnyeat (1987); Reeve (1988, 71−79). The introduction of the doctrine here may, therefore, signal that Plato is filling out Socratic doctrine in a way he thinks necessary. It may also signal that the *Euthydemus* is a later dialogue than is usually thought. See Kahn (1981, 317−318); Vlastos (1988).

32. "When he [Socrates] inquired about whàt the virtue of a good ruler is, he stripped away everything but this: making his followers happy" (Xenophon, *Mem.* III.ii.4). Cf. Vlastos (1983a, 502−503).

which politics has no control. Second, politics could be a craft which masters luck. In this case, it controls circumstances to insure that our degree of happiness is the greatest it can be, absolutely speaking. Which of these possibilities does Socrates have in mind?

Individual texts in the *Euthydemus* suggest that politics masters luck:

Wisdom . . . just is good luck [*hē sophia dēpou . . . eutuchia estin*]; even a child would know that. (279d7—8)

For wisdom, I presume, could not make a mistake but must always do the right thing and achieve its end; for otherwise it would not be wisdom any longer. . . . When wisdom is possessed, the one who has it needs no good luck besides. (280a7—b3)

And the structure of the dialogue itself also suggests this. Cleinias says that politicians use the products of generalship, while dialecticians use those of the mathematical sciences (290b8—c6). We naturally expect, therefore, that the argument will proceed by trying to determine which of these two crafts—politics or dialectic—is the one that will make us happy. But this is not what happens. Instead dialectic seems to drop from sight, the claims of politics to be the craft in question are examined, and the argument ends in apparent aporia (291b1—292e5). However, the politics Socrates has in mind is certainly not what Pericles or Themistocles practiced or what we understand by politics. Politics as actually practiced—which the *Gorgias* identifies with sophistry (519c2—3; cf. *Plt.* 303b7—c5)—does not know how to use the products of all the other crafts. The craft Socrates has in mind seems rather to be the one practiced by the philosopher-kings in the *Republic*. And dialectic is a fundamental ingredient (*R.* 531c6—540c2; cf. *Cra.* 390b1—c12) of that craft. That is why dialectic only *seems* to disappear. That is why the closing moments of the *Euthydemus* are devoted to the relations between philosophy (dialectic) and politics (304c6—307c4). But if politics is indeed the craft practiced by the philosopher-kings, there is every reason to think that it masters luck as far as possible rather than simply adapting to it. For that craft enables the philosopher-kings to arrange for the production of a maximally stable, maximally self-sufficient polis whose members are as happy as possible throughout their lives.[33]

But to settle the issue in favour of mastery, without relying on such controversial evidence, we must turn to a neglected passage in *Alcibiades 1*:[34]

33. See Reeve (1988, 170—204).

34. In antiquity, there was no doubt that *Alc. 1* was a genuine Platonic work, even a paradigmatic one. See Diogenes Laertius 3.62; Friedländer (1964, 2: 231—243). Many modern scholars, however, have dismissed it as spurious. Clark

And if the psyche too, my dear Alcibiades, is to know itself, it must surely look at a psyche, and especially at that region of it in which the virtue of a psyche, wisdom, comes to be, and at any other which is like this?—I agree, Socrates.— And can we find anything in the psyche that we can call more divine than that with which we know and think?—We cannot.—Then this resembles god, and whoever looks at this and comes to know all that is divine [kai pan to theion gnous], both god and wisdom [theon te kai phronēsin], will thereby gain the best knowledge of himself.—Plainly.—And self-knowledge we admitted to be moderation?—Surely.—So if we have no knowledge of ourselves and no moderation, shall we be able to know our own belongings [cf. 131a2ff.], good or bad? . . . And anyone who is ignorant of his own belongings will also be ignorant, I suppose, of the belongings of others.—Quite.—And if ignorant of the things of others, he will be ignorant of the things of the polis?— Necessarily.—Then such a man can never be a politician.—No, indeed.—Nor a home-manager.—No, indeed.—Nor will he know what he is doing.—No.—And not knowing will he not make mistakes?—To be sure.—And when he makes mistakes, will he not do badly in private and in public?—How could he not?—And doing badly won't he be wretched?—Yes.—And what of those for whom he is acting?—They too [will be wretched].—Then it is not possible to be happy if one is not moderate and good. (133b7−134a14; cf. Chrm. 171e7−172a3; La. 199d4−e1)

This text states in no uncertain terms that the craft (see 133d12−e2) required for the successful practice of politics, which is identical to moderation and essential for happiness, cannot make mistakes and involves knowing "all that is divine, both god and wisdom."[35] Someone possessed of such a craft would, surely, no more have to adapt to luck,

(1955), one of the more recent treatments of this question, takes a middle road, arguing that "the first two-thirds of the dialogue are the work of a pupil or follower of Plato, while the last part is by Plato himself." Allen (1984, 1: 6−18) accepts Alc. 1 as genuine and dates it in the first eight of Plato's compositions, later than Ap., Cri., La., Ion, Hp. Ma., Hp. Mi., and Chrm., and earlier than Ly., Euthphr., Euthd., Prt., Men., and Grg. This dispute about authenticity is difficult to resolve. But most scholars would probably agree with Guthrie (1975, 169 n. 3) that "whether or not Alc. 1 is by Plato," it is "a reliable source for Socratic teaching."

35. Many other texts underwrite the attribution of these doctrines to Socrates. "And kingship [basilikē], tyranny, statesmanship, mastery, household management, justice, and moderation are one and the same craft" (Amat. 138c8−10; cf. Plt. 259c1−4). The same doctrine is suggested at Prt. 318e5−319a5,

rather than mastering it, than a god (cf. *Men.* 99e3—100b4; *R.* 497b7—c3).

We can now understand why Socrates thinks that possession of the political craft, the craft-knowledge to which virtue is identical, is both necessary and sufficient for happiness. As things stand, any ordinary craft can be crippled for want of externals, whether they are materials which it cannot make or chance catastrophes (bad luck) over which it has no control. If the papermaker has produced no paper, the writer cannot exercise his craft. If an unpredictable hurricane strikes, the ship's pilot may be helpless to get his ship to harbour.[36] The possession of ordinary crafts is not, in other words, sufficient for their successful use. But if we look at the superordinate craft of politics the *Euthydemus* posits and *Alcibiades 1* describes and if we imagine it guiding the totality of all the other crafts and using their products to promote happiness (cf. *Plt.* 305d1—4, 311b7—c6), we can see that for it there will be no paper shortages, no unpredictable or unavoidable catastrophes, that it will be, as we suggested in 1.7, *luck-independent*. Reverting to the language of externals, we might put the matter as follows. Ordinary crafts need externals for their exercise. Their possession is not sufficient for their use. But for the superordinate political craft, there are no externals. Its possession and use go hand in hand. That, in essence, is why it is a good "by itself" or without anything else. We all want to be happy. And all we need to satisfy that want is to possess virtue—the superordinate political craft.

If virtue is the superordinate craft of politics and is (at least) necessary and sufficient for happiness, is virtue something desirable for its own sake, is it intrinsically valuable, or is it valuable only as an extrinsic or

with 349e3—5. Cleitophon attributes to Socrates the doctrine that justice is the craft of politics and that we cannot live well without it: "Moreover, the conclusion of this argument of yours is a fine one, that it is better for every man who does not know how to use his psyche to have his psyche at rest and not to live than to live doing things by himself; but if it is necessary for him to live, it is better for him to spend his life as a slave rather than a free man, handing over the rudder of his reasoning, as of a ship, to another who has learned the craft of governing men, which is the name that you often give to politics [*politikēn*], Socrates, when you say that it is the same as judging and justice" (*Cleit.* 408a4—b5). Finally, Xenophon represents Aristippus as attributing the doctrine that the craft of kingship is happiness to Socrates: "But how about those who are trained in the craft of kingship [*basilikēn technēn*], which it seems to me you believe to be happiness [*nomizein eudaimonian einai*]?" (*Mem.* II.i.17; cf. III.ii.2—4).

36. See Irwin (1986a, 92—96).

instrumental means to something else?[37] This question has two components which must be carefully distinguished. First, is virtue wanted for its own sake? Second, what is the precise nature of the relationship between wanting something for its own sake and wanting it because it guarantees us happiness?

Everything we want, we want for the sake of the good (*Grg.* 499e7−8). Since the good is itself something we want to possess (cf. *Smp.* 206a6−13), it follows that we must want the good and only the good for its own sake. What is the good? The *Hippias Major* identifies it as that by which "all good things are good" (287c5−6). Other dialogues make the same claim for virtue: "Now we are good, and so is anything else which is good, when some virtue has come to be present?" (*Grg.* 506d2−4; cf. *Chrm.* 161a8−9; *Euthphr.* 6d9−e1; *Prt.* 332b4−6; *R.* 353d9−354a2). Since wisdom, or the craft of politics, is both the only virtue and the only good thing, we have double warrant for concluding that it is the good. If we are right, as seems likely, to discern a reference to Socrates in it, this conclusion is supported by the following passage from the *Republic*: "The many believe that pleasure is the good, while the more sophisticated believe that it is wisdom" (505b5−6).[38] But if wisdom, or the craft of politics, is the good, it must be wanted for its own sake. It follows that virtue is an intrinsic good, desirable for its own sake.

We want virtue for its own sake, then. But we also want virtue because (in some way or other) it guarantees us happiness. For virtue is the good, and according to eudaimonism we want the good because (in some way or other) it guarantees us happiness. The problem is to explain how both these things can be true.

One natural solution is to think that virtue and happiness must be identical; since then wanting virtue for its own sake and wanting it for the sake of happiness would amount to the same thing. There is no direct evidence, however, that Socrates believed that virtue and happiness are identical: no text explicitly states or straightforwardly entails this view.[39] Indeed, the formula Socrates most often uses to express the

37. Irwin (1977, 92−94) argues that virtue is an instrumental means to happiness. Vlastos (1978; 1984a, 207 n. 54) and Zeyl (1982) are critical. Irwin (1986a, 90, 105) defends the weaker claim that Socrates' doctrine that virtue is sufficient for happiness "is compatible with the purely instrumentalist conception of virtue."

38. Cf. *Cri.* 44d6−7; Xenophon, *Mem.* IV.v.6; Adam (1963, 2: 52).

39. Kraut (1984, 211−212 n. 41) argues that *Euthd.* 279c9-d7, 281b2−4, and 282c8−d1 together entail that "wisdom, virtue, good fortune, good action, and

relationship between virtue and happiness seems to entail that they cannot be identical. Virtue is something, he tells us, which *makes* us happy or *produces* happiness. This is the formula he repeatedly uses in the *Euthydemus* and throughout the earlier dialogues.[40] And we have it on the authority of the *Hippias Major* that producer and product cannot be identical (297a7−b1).

A second potential solution, which has found a number of supporters, is that virtue is identical to a part or constituent of happiness.[41] Controversy has focused, consequently, on whether as Socrates conceived of them, virtue and happiness are related as part to whole. In fact, however, controversy seems to have focused on a dubiously relevant issue. If someone wants a car and knows that an engine is a vital part of a car, he will, all things being equal, want a car engine. But if he wants the car for its own sake, it does not follow—simply from the fact that he knows an engine is a vital part of a car—that he wants the car engine for its own sake. Without the rest of a car around it, so to speak, a car engine may hold absolutely no charm for him whatsoever. Similarly, without happiness around it, virtue may not be desirable, even though it is a part of happiness. Thus even if virtue is a part of happiness, it is still difficult to understand how we can want it both for its own sake and for the sake of happiness.

The only remaining alternative is to treat the notion of wanting virtue for the sake of happiness as an explication or partial analysis of the

happiness are identical." But his argument is indecisive. First, though 279d7−8 does say that wisdom "just is" good luck, it also says that "even a child would know that." Together with the still prevalent tendency—manifested in such slogans as "Happiness is being a grandparent" and "Happiness is a warm blanket"—to identify happiness with what (purportedly) produces it, this significantly reduces its evidential value. Second, 281b2−4 and 282c8−d1, which employ the verbs *parechō* and *poieō* respectively, suggest that the relation between wisdom (virtue) and good luck expressed at 279d7−8 is the relation of production or making, not of identity. Finally, if Xenophon is to be believed, Socrates explicitly denied that good luck and good action are identical (*Mem.* III.ix.14). Other evidence that Socrates identifies virtue and happiness—including *Ap.* 30c5−d5 and 41c8−d2, which we shall examine in 3.6—is discussed and undermined in Vlastos (1984a, 192−196).

40. See *Alc. 1* 116b2−9; *Chrm.* 174a10−11, 174b11−c3; *Euthd.* 280a6, 280e4−6, 281b2−4, 282a1−6, 282c8−d1, 291b4−7, 292b7−c1, 292e4−5; *Grg.* 506c6−507e1, 508a8−b2; *Prt.* 313a6−9. Cf. *Smp.* 204e1−205a3.

41. See Irwin (1977, 82−94, 184); Vlastos (1984a). Cf. Reeve (1988, 28−33).

notion of wanting virtue for its own sake. The picture is, roughly speaking, this. Happiness is *the ideal object of desire*, something which renders desire superfluous, so to speak, by satisfying it once and for all. That is why it is pointless to ask why someone wants to be happy (*Euthd.* 278e3−6; *Smp.* 205a1−3): desire just is something that seeks satisfaction; happiness just is what satisfies desire. Virtue guarantees happiness. But it guarantees it in a unique way: it produces happiness *by itself* (*kath' hauto*), for the craft of politics to which virtue is identical produces happiness by itself. What this means is that we need nothing else besides virtue in order to be happy. Virtue is not a step on the way to happiness; it is the end of the journey. How are we to register this fact? If we characterize the lower steps on the ladder by saying that we want them for the sake of reaching the higher ones, it is natural to do so by saying that we want the highest step—virtue—for its own sake. Of course we also want virtue for the sake of the happiness which by itself it produces. But that does not mean that there is a further step beyond the top. Rather it is simply an explication of what it is to be the final step: the final step is the one that produces happiness, the one that once and for all satisfies desire.[42]

So far, then, we have seen strong reason to believe that Socrates holds that virtue just by itself produces happiness. The problem is that there are other texts which seem to be inconsistent with this view. We cannot take the view as established, therefore, until we have solved the problems these apparent inconsistencies create.

Some texts suggest that at least one external—namely, health—is positively necessary for happiness, that without it life is not worth living:

> Come now, if we ruin that which is improved by health and corrupted by disease by not following the opinions of those who know, is life worth living for us when that is ruined? And the thing in question is the body, is it not?—Yes.—And life is not worth living with a body that is corrupted and in bad condition?—In no way. (*Cri.* 47d7−48a4)

> For I suppose he [the ship's pilot] knows enough to reason that it is not clear which passengers he has benefited by not letting them drown and which ones he has harmed; he knows that he puts them ashore no better than they were when they boarded, either in body

42. See Engberg-Pedersen (1983, 3−36).

or in psyche. He reasons, then, that if someone suffering serious and incurable diseases in his body who has not expired is wretched because he has not died and has gained no benefit from him—if that is so, then, if someone has many incurable diseases in what is more honourable than his body, his psyche, it will not be worth living for him, and the pilot will not benefit him by saving him from the sea or the law court or anywhere else; the pilot knows that it is not better for the wretched man to live, for he is bound to live badly. (*Grg.* 511e6−512b2)

If, as these texts seem to say, the activity of living well is impossible without (some measure of) health, it seems to follow that virtue by itself cannot produce happiness.[43]

The second problem is this. If we accept that virtue by itself produces happiness, it seems that once we have settled the question of what virtue requires of us, we cannot have any eudaimonistic reason to prefer one state of affairs over another. According to eudaimonism, however, all our practical reasons are ultimately eudaimonistic. It follows that we can have no reason to prefer one state of affairs over another if both are equally compatible with virtue. Yet in the following text, for example, Socrates suggests that this is not the case:

Would you, then, wish to suffer injustice rather than do it? For myself, I would wish neither. But if I were forced to choose between suffering injustice and doing it, I would choose to suffer it. (*Grg.* 469b12−c2)

Both suffering injustice and neither doing nor suffering it are equally compatible with Socrates' virtue, yet he prefers the latter. This suggests that the doctrine that virtue by itself produces happiness is at odds with eudaimonism and that we cannot consistently attribute both of them to Socrates.[44]

Finally, there are texts which suggest that virtue produces happiness not because virtue or the superordinate craft of politics masters luck, but because it adapts well to the circumstances luck creates, squeezing out of them, so to speak, the maximum amount of happiness possible.[45]

If it [death] is complete lack of awareness, like a dreamless sleep, then death would be a marvelous gain; for I think that if someone

43. See Brickhouse and Smith (1987); Kraut (1984, 38−39 n. 21).

44. See Vlastos (1984a, 189−196).

45. See Irwin (1986a).

had to choose the night in which he slept so soundly that he did not even dream and had to put beside it all the other days and nights of his life and then decide how many of them had been better and more pleasant than that night, not only a private individual but the great king himself would find them easy to count compared with the other days and nights. If death is like this, I say it is a gain, for all time would then seem to be no more than a single night. (*Ap.* 40c9−e4)

[I want] to persuade you [Callicles], if I can, to change your mind and to choose to have, instead of the unsatisfied and uncontrolled life, the life that is ordered and always adequately supplied and satisfied with the things that are at hand on each occasion. But am I persuading you to change your mind at all and that orderly people are happier than uncontrolled ones? (*Grg.* 493c5−7)

For surely a true man should forget about how long he will live and should not love life, but should entrust these matters to the god and believe the women when they say that no man can escape destiny. (*Grg.* 512d8−e4)

The third of these texts suggests that the length of our lives is beyond our control and that we must accommodate ourselves to that fact. The second suggests that to be happy we must be able to so moderate our desires that we are satisfied by whatever is available. The first bears out this suggestion by claiming that a situation in which we have no awareness at all, whether of satisfaction or frustration, would be better and more pleasant than most of our days (cf. Xenophon *Mem.* I.vi.10).

So much for the problems. How are we to solve them?

The knowledge or wisdom to which virtue is identical is the superordinate craft-knowledge of politics. It follows that *the craft-knowledge of virtue must itself be the knowledge of politics*; for what it is knowledge of—virtue—is that very craft. Now, Socrates characterizes the craft-knowledge of virtue as "more than human" (*Ap.* 20e1), sincerely disclaims possession of it, never discovers anyone who does possess it, and finds in the Delphic oracle a strong suggestion that it may forever remain the prerogative of the gods (*Ap.* 23a5−7). Having seen what that craft-knowledge actually is, namely, the superordinate craft of politics, this is just what we would expect. Yet it holds the solution to the three problems we have identified.

The *Crito* and the *Gorgias* suggest that life is not worth living if our health is ruined. But this threatens the claim that virtue by itself produces happiness only on the supposition that we can both possess virtue and have ruined health. If virtue is the craft-knowledge of virtue, the superordinate craft of politics, there is no reason to grant this supposition. If we had virtue, we would be able either to insure our bodily health or—perhaps through the "knowledge of immortality" (*Euthd.* 289a7–b3)—arrange to live virtuously and happily without our bodies. But, of course, *we* do not possess the craft-knowledge of virtue, *we* are not virtuous. Our lives can be ruined by catastrophic illness.

Nonetheless, the *Crito* and *Gorgias* texts remain problematic because they seem to be inconsistent with Sovereignty of Virtue. By seeing how this inconsistency is to be resolved, we will be led to the solutions of the other problems under discussion.

If virtue brings *no* happiness unless it is accompanied by (some measure of) health, it seems that someone who "has many incurable diseases" can have no eudaimonistic reason to act virtuously or to avoid vicious action. If (some measure of) health is necessary for happiness, it seems that we can have no eudaimonistic reason to prefer a virtuous action which completely ruins our health to a vicious one which destroys our psyche. For, if bad health can indeed make life not worth living, either action will leave us utterly wretched or possessed of no happiness whatever. But Sovereignty of Virtue tells us that we must always do what we know or believe to be just and avoid what we know or believe to be unjust or vicious. How can Socrates' accept this doctrine, then, and also accept that health is necessary for happiness?[46]

We know or believe that without health bodily (or embodied) life is not worth living. But, ignorant of our postmortal fate, we cannot know whether or not *bodily* life is necessary for psychic life or life itself (cf. *Grg.* 492e8–493a5). Consequently, we cannot know whether or not health is necessary for living well or happily, only that it is necessary for living our embodied lives well or happily. Perhaps the end of our bodily life is just the beginning of an eternity of examining the great heroes of the past. If so, it would be a psychic life of "inconceivable happiness"

46. In the *Gorgias*, Socrates allows that it is possible for A to be more wretched than B without its being the case that B is happier than A (473d7–e1). This suggests an answer to our question. If A has a ruined psyche and B has ruined health, then, though neither is to any degree happy, A is more wretched than B. We should choose ruined health over vice, not to gain happiness, but to avoid wretchedness. Cf. Brickhouse and Smith (1987, 20 n. 28). If we accept this answer, however, we must modify Socrates' views on thought and action. The good is not the end of all our actions (*Grg.* 499e7–8). Happiness is not our only ultimate goal. We also act to avoid wretchedness. Rather than modifying such central Socratic doctrines, we should explore other options.

(*Ap.* 40b5−c7). Death may be the "greatest of all goods" (*Ap.* 29a6−8). But whatever happens to us when bodily life is over, it would still be "the most blameworthy ignorance" to choose vice even over catastrophic illness or death. That is why Socrates can consistently hold both Sovereignty of Virtue and the view that without health life—bodily life—is not worth living.

Not even so important an intermediate as health, then, is something we can know to be necessary for virtuous activity or for living well or happily. But neither can we be certain that bodily life is unnecessary for virtuous activity; for bodily life may, for all we know, be necessary for psychic life. Ignorance cuts both ways here. It is quite reasonable, therefore, to choose and (speaking with the vulgar) classify as goods intermediates which enable one to continue one's bodily life and to be actively as virtuous as it is possible for human beings to be and to avoid and (speaking with the vulgar) classify as bad things which would prevent one from doing these things. That is why (everything else being equal) we have a eudaimonistic reason to choose neither suffering injustice nor doing it over suffering it: suffering injustice will affect our capacity to be actively as virtuous as possible. That is why Socrates (speaking, in this case, *to* the vulgar) can say that he knows that imprisonment, for example, would be a bad thing, while free meals in the prytaneum would be a good one (*Ap.* 36d1−38a6). The former would prevent him from serving Apollo, which he knows to be just. The latter would enable him to serve Apollo better. It would never be reasonable, however, to choose an intermediate over virtue; for without virtue intermediates are not good things.

Because we do not possess and likely will never possess the craft-knowledge of virtue, we and the happiness of which we are capable are very often at the mercy of situations beyond our control. A virtuous person, possessed of that craft, could master them or arrange for them never to come about. But our best strategy is to adapt to them so far as we can without being voluntarily vicious, restricting our desires so that we can be satisfied even if we are very unlucky. There are limits to adaptivity, though. When, despite our best efforts or those of our physician, our health is irreparably ruined, life may not be worth living. Within those limits, however, if we cannot have mastery we must strain at least for adaptivity.

We can now see why Socrates believes that those who cannot defend their ethical views lack not only the craft-knowledge of virtue, but virtue itself, and why he believes that "it is virtue that makes wealth and everything else, both public and private, good for a man" (30b2−4).

Virtue just is the craft-knowledge of virtue, and the latter, being by itself productive of happiness, does indeed make everything genuinely good or beneficial for us. Moreover, we can understand why Socrates says that by examining people he is attempting to persuade them to share these views. For the arguments he uses to defend these views are intended to rely only on acceptable propositions, on obvious truths.

3.5 VOLUNTARY VICE AND INACCESSIBLE VIRTUE

Socrates' doctrine that virtue is identical to the craft-knowledge of virtue seems to entail both that voluntary (because knowing) vice is impossible and that virtue is inaccessible to human beings. And these entailments seem obviously paradoxical: it seems possible to be voluntarily vicious, and it also seems possible, albeit more difficult, to be virtuous. The question we face, therefore, is to determine whether the entailments hold, and if they do, whether or not they are in fact as paradoxical as they seem.

There are two obvious reasons why the doctrine that virtue is knowledge does not *entail* that voluntary vice is impossible. First, someone who knew that the action he contemplated was vicious and wanted not to do it might yet voluntarily do it out of akrasia or weakness of will: his desire to do it might prove stronger, as we say, than his knowledge-backed desire not to do it. Second, someone who knew that the action he contemplated was vicious might yet voluntarily do it simply because he wanted to do it and had no countervailing desire not to do it. In other dialogues, however, especially in the *Gorgias*, *Meno*, and *Protagoras*, Socrates seems to reject these reasons. No one ever acts out of akrasia, he argues, because the explanations of what it is to act akratically are all incoherent. And no one ever desires what he knows to be vicious, because all desire is for the good. To gauge the significance of these strange views and to determine whether or not they restore the problematic entailment that voluntary vice is impossible, we must review the arguments Socrates adduces on their behalf.

In the *Meno*, Socrates tries to show Meno that no one wants bad things, things that are bad for himself. His argument is about prudence, not, as yet, specifically about virtue or vice.

Do you think, my good man, that all men want good things?—I do not.—But some want bad things?—Yes.—Believing these bad things to be good, do you say, or knowing them to be bad, they want them anyway?—I think both.—So you think that someone, knowing that bad things are bad, can nonetheless want them?—Certainly.—In what way do you say he wants them? Wants to possess them?—That's it, to possess them.—Does he think that these bad things benefit the one who comes to possess them, or does he know that they will harm him?—There are some who think that bad things are beneficial, and some who know that they are harmful.—And do you think that those who believe that bad things benefit them know that they are bad?—Not altogether.—Clearly, then, those who do not know things to be bad do not want bad things, rather they want those things they believe to be good, but which are in fact bad. So those who are ignorant about such things and think they are good clearly want good things. Isn't that so?—It looks as though it is, at least.—Well, then, what about the others, who, as you say, want bad things, believing that bad things harm those who come to possess them: do they know they will be harmed?—Necessarily, they do.—And that those who are harmed, insofar as they are harmed, are wretched?—That, too, is necessary.—And that those who are wretched are unhappy?—I think so.—But is there anyone who wants to be unhappy?—I do not think so, Socrates.—No one, then, wants bad things, Meno, unless he wants to be such; for what else is being miserable than to want bad things and to get them?—You are probably right, Socrates, that no one wants what is bad. (77c1—78b2)

Notice that this argument does not prove that one cannot want something that is in fact bad. It is possible, Socrates allows, to want bad things believing them to be good. Nor does the argument prove that one cannot want something one knows to be bad. All it shows is that if one knows that bad things make their possessor unhappy and that X is a bad thing, then one cannot—eudaimonism granted—want to possess X. Clearly, this not a paradoxical conclusion. Indeed, "it, or some version of it, seems to be one of the most common presuppositions made in accounting for human behavior, at any rate in situations of prudential choice" (Santas 1979, 189).

So far, then, Socrates has established that no one desires to possess things he knows will make him unhappy. On the assumption that no one does something voluntarily if he does not want to do it (see *Grg.* 509e5—7), it follows that "no one voluntarily [*hekōn*] goes for bad things or things he believes to be bad" (*Prt.* 358c6—d4). This is the principle which, in the *Protagoras*, Socrates uses to show that akrasia is impossible because incoherent.[47]

The most commonly offered explanation of akratic action is that belief or knowledge about what is best to do can be "overcome by desire," resulting in a choice of something other than the best:

> The opinion of the many about knowledge is that it isn't something strong, which can control and rule a person; they don't look at it that way at all, but think that often a person who possesses knowledge is ruled not by it but by something else, in one case desire, in another pleasure, in another pain, sometimes lust, very often fear; they just look at knowledge as a slave that gets dragged around by all the others. (*Prt.* 352b3–c2)

This is the explanation Socrates targets for refutation. The many hold

(1) The good is pleasure, and evil pain. (353c3–355a5)

and

(2) Sometimes A knows or believes that X is worse than Y but, overcome by desire for the pleasures of X, chooses X. (355a5–b3)

But (1) licenses the substitution of "less pleasant" for "worse" in (2). And this yields

(3) Sometimes A knows or believes that X is less pleasant than Y but, overcome by desire for the pleasures of X, chooses X. (355d1–356a1)[48]

But (3) is absurd, because

(4) One must choose the more pleasant over the less, the less painful over the more, and of competing pains and pleasures one must choose the pleasure if it outweighs the pain and avoid the pain if it outweighs the pleasure. (356b3–c1)

Hence, the explanation of akrasia offered in (2) is unacceptable.

Now, (4) presupposes two other principles which prove to be crucially important, namely

47. See Santas (1979, 195–217); Charlton (1988, 13–33).

48. The legitimacy of this step in Socrates' argument is disputed by Taylor (1976, 180–181) and convincingly defended by Santas (1979, 319 n. 14).

(5) The strength of A's desire for X is always directly proportional to the amount of pleasure he believes X will yield.

and

(6) All desire is for pleasure and nothing else.

For without (5) a stronger desire for a smaller pleasure might overpower A's desire for a larger one. And without (6) A might fail to choose the larger pleasure out of a stronger desire for something other than pleasure.

But it is not only advocates of hedonism who have to worry about (5) and (6). This emerges vividly when we dissociate (5) and (6) from hedonism by resubstituting 'good' for 'pleasure' in them. The results are

(7) The strength of A's desire for X is always directly proportional to the amount of the good he believes X will yield (presupposed at *Prt.* 355d1−e4).

and

(8) All desire is for the good and nothing else (*Grg.* 467c5−468b4; *Ly.* 218c4−219d2).[49]

For these two principles make it impossible to explain akrasia in *any* of the ways mentioned at 352b3−c2 (above). With (7) and (8) in force, knowledge or belief about what it is best to do cannot be overcome by desire.

But if knowledge or belief about what it is best to do cannot be overcome by desire, we are thrown back on the principle that "no one voluntarily [*hekōn*] goes for bad things or things he believes to be bad." And that principle is now itself sufficient to exclude the possibility of akrasia. For akrasia essentially involves voluntarily doing things one believes to be bad (or worse than other available things).

In the *Gorgias*, Socrates uses this same principle that "no one voluntarily goes for bad things or things he believes to be bad" to show that no one "wants to do injustice, but all those who do it do it involuntarily [*akontas*]" (509e5−7). His argument is familiar from 1.8 and 3.4. Doing injustice (being vicious) is the worst thing for the one who does it, worse even than suffering injustice, because it makes him wretched and unhappy. But all that follows from this argument is that no one who

---

49. In the *Republic* (435c4−441c7), Plato rehabilitates akrasia by undermining this premise. See Reeve (1988, 131−135).

knows that injustice (vice) will make him unhappy and who knows that X is unjust (vicious) will do X voluntarily. This leaves open the possibility that he will do X voluntarily because he does not know that vice will make him unhappy.

This possibility remains open—voluntary vice remains a possibility—even though virtue is knowledge, akrasia is impossible, and no one is (in the relevant sense) voluntarily vicious. But did Socrates realize that it remained a possibility, or did he think that his arguments had closed it off altogether? Did he think, for example, that vicious actions done out of ignorance of the nature of virtue and vice were *eo ipso* involuntary? This is not a simple matter to adjudicate, as we are about to discover.

Socrates sometimes states outright that no one is voluntarily vicious:

> For I am fairly sure that no wise man believes that anyone errs voluntarily [*hekonta*] or does shameful or bad things voluntarily [*hekonta*] but knows well that all who do shameful and bad things do them involuntarily [*akontes*]. (*Prt.* 345d9−e4)

At the same time, however, he often says things which are somewhat at odds with this view. When Hippias says that those who do bad things voluntarily are worse than those who do them involuntarily, Socrates does not argue that voluntary vice is impossible; instead he argues that, if there is voluntary vice, it is better than involuntary vice (*Hp. Mi.* 371e7−376c6). In the *Apology*, he tells the jury that he has not been voluntarily vicious: "I am convinced that I am not voluntarily [*hekōn*] unjust to anyone" (37a5−6). And in the *Gorgias*, he says much the same thing: "If I do something that isn't right in my own life, know well that the error is not voluntary [*ouch hekōn*], but due to ignorance" (488a2−4). These disclaimers could be applications of the general doctrine that voluntary vice is impossible. But they do not read that way. Instead, they seem to say that Socrates in particular has not been something that he could have been, namely, voluntarily vicious. Finally, again in the *Apology*, Socrates explicitly countenances two classes of vicious acts, voluntary ones, which merit judicial punishment, and involuntary ones, which merit instruction not punishment (25d5−26a7).[50] And in other dialogues he insists that it is better for unjust people to be punished (*Grg.* 472d6−479e9).

How are we to reconcile these views, which strongly suggest that voluntary vice is possible, with the doctrine that it is impossible? Soc-

---

50. West (1979, 139−140) overlooks this passage when he concludes that Socrates is committed to the view that "all law that punishes the criminal is mis-

rates talks in the *Apology* (29b1−2) and in *Alcibiades 1* (118a4−5) about "the most blameworthy ignorance [*eponeidistos amathia*]" of thinking one knows when one does not know. He does not say outright that this ignorance is voluntary. But the word he uses to describe it, *eponeidistos*, invariably carries a very strong implication of voluntariness.[51] Moreover, Socrates suggests that vicious acts done out of such ignorance are culpable. That, it seems, is why he believes that Meletus and Anytus are doing themselves more harm than they are doing him by unjustly trying to have him put to death (30c6−d5). Socrates seems to believe, then, that though acts done out of ignorance are involuntary, they are blameworthy if the ignorance out of which they are done is blameworthy and voluntary. But are the acts themselves voluntary? Socrates is not absolutely clear. He suggests that they are; his official doctrine seems to be that they are not. However, this conflict between doctrine and dicta is not a serious one. It most likely results from the pressure we feel to call something voluntary if we think it blameworthy (*Hp. Mi.* 372a3−5, 373b6−9). But once we agree that acts done out of blameworthy ignorance are themselves blameworthy, it hardly matters whether we class them as voluntary or involuntary. So, whether or not Socrates thinks that acts done out of blameworthy ignorance are voluntary—and acts done out of ignorance about virtue would surely fall under that rubric— he certainly holds that they are blameworthy and deserving of punishment.

We turn, now, to the paradox of the inaccessibility of virtue. Here, too, Socrates' views about blameworthy ignorance help draw its sting.

The doctrine that virtue is the craft-knowledge of virtue does, indeed, entail that only those who have craft-knowledge of virtue, only those who possess the superordinate craft of politics, can be fully virtuous. This seems paradoxical because we are inclined to believe that some people are virtuous even though none possess the knowledge in question. When we think of what virtue is like according to Socrates, however, the former belief seems much less plausible: Socratic virtue,

taken." O'Brien (1967, 84−85) notices that it implies two causes of error, one ignorance and one unnamed. His conjecture that the unnamed cause is *akrasia* is very implausible.

51. "Intemperance, then, is more voluntary [*hekousion*]. Hence it is also more blameworthy [*eponeidistoteron*]" (Aristotle, *EN.* 1119a24−25). Cf. Plato, *Smp.* 184b6-c3.

like the gods, is luck-independent, incapable of making a mistake, and sufficient for happiness; the virtue we sometimes believe we possess is (alas) none of these things.

Socrates does not believe, however, that we are condemned to vice by the fact that we cannot have the craft-knowledge of virtue. By means of the elenchus, by living the examined life, we can avoid *blameworthy* vice by avoiding culpable ignorance and thereby come as close to being virtuous as is humanly possible. We can achieve *human* wisdom and with it what we might call *human* virtue. That, as we shall see in more detail in 3.10, is why Socrates believes his elenctic mission is such a boon to Athens.

3.6 HARMS AND BENEFITS

The characterization of his philosophical activities completed, Socrates begins a new line of defense. If the jury sentences him to death, they and Meletus and Anytus, who have instigated the trial, will harm themselves and Athens more than they will harm him (30c6−8). If prudence and self-interest govern their verdict, therefore, they should find him innocent. That is why he tells them that they will be "benefited by listening" to him (30c4) and that, if they listen, they will spare him (31a3).

A modern jury would be shocked to be offered an argument like this, and would rightly consider it irrelevant to its judicial task. An Athenian jury conceived of its task somewhat differently:

> The question to which our own courts address themselves is 'Has the defendant done what he is alleged to have done, or has he not?' and 'if he has done it, is it forbidden by law?' An Athenian court seems rather to have asked itself 'Given this situation, what treatment of the persons involved in it is most likely to have beneficial consequences for the community?' (Dover 1978, 39)

Thus Socrates' jury expected to hear him discuss his past service to Athens and the future service he might render if spared. And large service he thinks it is (30a5−7, 36d9−e1).

The first argument on this head (30c8−d5) concerns Meletus and Anytus, and opens with a remarkable claim:

(1) Neither Meletus nor Anytus would harm [*blapseien*] me in any way—for they would not even be able to—for I do not think that it is *themiton* for a better man to be harmed by a worse. (30c8−d1)

What does (1) mean? Literally speaking, something is *themiton* if it is in accord with *themis*, or divine law. Thus Socrates says earlier in the *Apology* that it would not be *themis* for Apollo to say something false (21b5–6). But the mere fact that something is not *themiton* does not mean that it cannot happen. Suicide is not *themiton* (*Phd.* 61c10); people kill themselves anyway. In the present passage, however, as in some other places in Plato's works (for example, *Phdr.* 256d3), *themiton* does carry the stronger implication that what is contrary to it is impossible. For Socrates thinks that because it is not *themiton* for a better man to be harmed by a worse, Meletus and Anytus "would not even be able [*oude gar an dunaito*]" to harm him (30c9). So (1) really does say that Meletus and Anytus cannot harm Socrates because it is *impossible* for a better man to be harmed by a worse.

But why should we believe this? Surely, good people are always being harmed—tortured, beaten, robbed—by less good ones. The next step in that argument partly explains why:

(2) He [Meletus] might kill or banish or disenfranchise me, which he and perhaps others believe to be great evils [*megala kaka*], but I do not believe it. (30d1–4)

One harms by inflicting evils. But the things that Meletus thinks to be evils or harms and that we have in mind when we balk at (1) are not great harms at all. (1) is a principle about serious harms, then, harms more serious than our problematic examples, harms more serious even than death.[52] The final step gives us a vital handle on what Socrates thinks these serious harms are:

(3) He [Meletus] is doing himself much more [harm], doing what he is now doing, unjustly trying to kill a man. (30d4–5)

Doing injustice is a greater harm than death, disenfranchisement, or banishment, the three most severe punishments available to the court. The implication is that the only real or serious harm that can be inflicted on someone is to make him unjust or vicious: "Shall we not say this about human beings, too, that when they are harmed they become worse in human virtue" (*R.* 335b10–11)? Moreover, we can understand why Socrates thinks this; for without virtue nothing else is unequivocally good (30b2–4). That is why only a successful attack on someone's virtue does him really serious harm.

What the crucial part of (1) amounts to, then, is

52. Cf. Vlastos (1984a, 193–194).

(4) It is not possible for a better man to be made vicious by a worse.

Now (4) is introduced to explain why Meletus and Anytus cannot harm Socrates. Hence the better man it refers to must be one who, like Socrates, avoids culpable vice by leading the elenctically examined life. Presumably, then, the worse man is someone who does not avoid culpable vice through leading such a life (we shall see below that Meletus is, indeed, a person of this sort). It follows that (4) is to be understood as

(4a) It is not possible for someone who avoids culpable vice through leading the elenctically examined life to be made *culpably* vicious by someone who is culpably vicious in part through failing to lead such a life.

And once we understand (4) as (4a), we can readily see why Socrates asserts (1) with such confidence. Drugs or torture might enable Meletus to make Socrates nonculpably vicious. But the only way to make him guilty of culpable vice would be to get him to accept and act on an immoral principle without submitting it to elenctic scrutiny. And no resolute devotee of the examined life—no good man—can be made culpably vicious in that way.

(1) looks like a contentious, even false, ethical principle. It is an unacceptable proposition. But like the other unacceptable propositions we encountered in 3.1 and 3.4, it follows from acceptable ones. And what is true of (1) is equally true of the initially shocking variant of it we encounter later on in the *Apology*:

But you, too, men of the jury, should be of good hope towards death, and you should think this one thing to be true, that there is nothing bad for a good man, whether alive or dead, and his affairs are not neglected by the gods. (41c8−d2)

Socrates is not making the outrageous claim that a good man cannot be tortured in Hades, or that there is absolutely no way—no rack efficient enough, no drug, no brain-damaging treatment—to make him nonculpably vicious. He is simply saying that someone committed to leading the elenctically examined life cannot be made culpably vicious and so cannot be seriously harmed by either man or god. This proposition poses no more threat, therefore, to Socrates' disclaimer of expert craftknowledge of virtue than (1) itself.

In the course of arguing that Meletus and Anytus cannot seriously harm him, Socrates claims that Meletus is harming himself more than he is harming Socrates:

(3) He [Meletus] is doing himself much more [harm], doing what
    he is now doing, unjustly trying to kill a man (30d4–5)

The philosophical presupposition of this claim is the unacceptable proposition that doing injustice is worse than suffering it. But the claim also
has a factual presupposition, namely, that Meletus is, indeed, "unjustly
trying to kill a man." And the latter—even leaving aside whatever problems there may be with its philosophical partner—threatens Socrates'
entire argument. For it seems that we have not been given a reason to
believe that Meletus is voluntarily, because knowingly, doing something
unjust. And that leaves open the possibility that his injustice is blame-
less, that he is not harming himself more that Socrates.

Let us suppose, then—as may well have been the case in fact—that
Meletus sincerely believes that Socrates is an impious corrupter of youth
who merits judicial execution. Does it follow that his *graphē* is non-
vicious? Not according to Socrates. For the false belief—the ignorance—
that led him to bring it is culpable. Meletus thinks he knows enough
about virtue to know who corrupts the youth and who improves them.
But his elenctic examination earlier in the trial shows us that he has
given "no thought" to virtue (25c1–4). He is, therefore, guilty of the
most blameworthy ignorance of falsely thinking that he knows about
justice and virtue. Consequently, his attempt to have Socrates executed,
even if he sincerely believes it to be just, is unjust and culpable.

It seems certain that it is because Meletus' injustice can be traced back
to this source that he harms himself more than Socrates by doing it. By
avoiding the act, through self-control (say), he could avoid becoming
unjust. By avoiding the blameworthy ignorance, through living the examined life, through submitting himself to the elenchus, he could avoid
the culpability for the unjust act (26a1–4). But by avoiding neither, he
makes himself unjust, and so seriously harms himself. Vice is the opposite of the virtue that alone makes a man's life unequivocally good for
him. Disenfranchisement, banishment, even death are small harms by
comparison.

Socrates' second argument about harms and benefits concerns the jury
and the Athenian polis they represent. It begins with a beguiling and
unforgettable piece of self-characterization.

If you kill me you will not easily find another like me, one who—
even if it is a ridiculous thing to say—is attached to this polis by the
god, as though upon a great and nobly bred horse who is rather

sluggish because of his size and needs to be awakened by some gadfly. In just this way, it seems to me, the god has fastened me to the polis; I rouse and persuade and reproach each one of you, and I do not stop lighting on you everywhere the whole day. Someone else of this sort will not easily come to be among you, gentlemen, and if you believe me, you will spare me. (30e1−31a2)

Socrates tells the jury that "if you kill me you will not easily find another like me" (30e1−2). Yet, a few pages later he appears to say the opposite:

I say, men who voted to kill me, that vengeance will come upon you immediately after my death, and a much harsher one, by god, than the sort you inflict on me by killing me. You did this in the belief that you would avoid having to examine your life, but I maintain that the opposite will happen to you. There will be many to examine you, whom I now restrain, though you haven't noticed them. And they will be harsher, since they are younger, and will vex you more. (39c3−d3)

Moreover, both statements seem to conflict, at least to some degree, with his earlier claim that many of his young followers were already aggravating their elders by imitating his elenctic examinations (23c2−d2).[53]

If these conflicts were genuine, they would be hard to explain. In fact, however, they are much more apparent than real. For Socrates makes it absolutely clear that what Athens will not easily find is someone who is like him *in being attached to the polis by the god* (30e1−3, 31a6−7), like him, that is to say, in elenctically examining in order to achieve the divinely sanctioned purpose of ridding people of their hubris and inspiring them to virtue. He is not saying that Athens will not find others to examine them or question their values and way of life, with other goals or purposes in mind, including—as in the case of his youthful imitators—that of humiliating their elders for the fun of it (23c2−5, 33c2−4). Nor is there any conflict between either of these statements and the claim that many of his young followers were already busy examining people. Restraining is not the same as preventing altogether, nor is restraining many incompatible with not restraining many more.

The next, and final, step in Socrates' argument underwrites the first and raises the important question of motivation:

53. These difficulties lead Hackforth (1933, 140−143) to the unwarranted conclusion that "23C and 39D give the true account, . . . while 31A and 33C reflect the view of Plato."

That I am someone like this, given to the polis by the god, you
might realize from the fact that it doesn't seem like human nature
that I have been careless of my own affairs and that for many years
now I have tolerated the neglect of my household, instead, always
minding your business, by going to each of you individually, as a
father or a brother might, to persuade you to care for virtue. If I got
something out of this by charging a fee, that would make some
kind of sense; but now even you see that my accusers, who accused
me so shamelessly in everything else, have not been able in their
impudence to produce a witness to say that I have ever received a
fee or asked for one. I, on the other hand, have a compelling witness that I speak the truth, my poverty. (31a7–c2)

This is a compelling argument which should be accorded proper weight;
for it does seem that only someone who believed himself engaged in a
divinely mandated mission would act as Socrates does, neglecting his
own affairs and living in poverty in order to encourage others to a
concern for virtue.

3.7 SOCRATES' PRIVATE POLITICS

The next issue Socrates engages is this:

Perhaps, though, it might seem strange that I go around saying
these things [tauta] and being meddlesome in private [idiai], but that
in public [dēmosiai] I do not dare go before the multitude [plēthos] to
advise the polis. (31c4–7)

Why, if Socrates is so concerned about the virtue of his fellows, does he
try to influence and examine individuals only? Why does he not bring
his elenchus-backed message of concern for virtue—the only possible
referent for tauta at 31c5—to the multitude?

Socrates' answer to these questions is twofold. The first is religious:

A certain voice comes, and whenever it comes, it always turns me
away from what I am about to do but never urges me to go ahead.
This is what has opposed my doing political things [ta politika
prattein]. (31d3–5).

The second is entirely secular and prudential:

Know well, men of Athens, if I had tried long ago to do political
things [prattein ta politika pragmata], I would long ago have perished,
and I would have benefited neither you nor myself. Do not be
angry with me when I speak the truth: no one will preserve his life

155

if he genuinely opposes you or any other multitude and prevents
the occurrence in the polis of many unjust and illegal things; for it
is necessary for a man who really fights for justice and who is going
to preserve his life even for a short time to lead a private but not a
public life [idiōteuein alla mē dēmosieuein]. (31d6—32a3)

Now the fact that both these texts mention "political things" is usually
taken to suggest that Socrates is saying that "anyone who 'meant to
fight for the right' must keep clear of politics" on danger of being short-
lived (Hackforth 1933, 119).[54] On this view, Socrates is claiming that he
has been *apolitical*. But is this true? We need to distinguish two cases.
First, was Socrates as a private citizen apolitical? Second, was Socrates as
an elenctic philosopher apolitical?

Socrates cites two incidents from his own life (32a4—5) to support his
claim that "it is necessary for a man who really fights for justice and
who is going to preserve his life even for a short time to lead a private
but not a public life." Here is the first:

I, men of Athens, never held any other office in the polis, but I have
been a member of the Council of Five Hundred.[55] And it happened
that our tribe, Antiochis, held the prytany when you wanted to try
the ten generals—the ones who failed to pick up the survivors from
the naval battle—as a group, which was against the law, as you
yourselves came to believe afterwards. I alone of the prytanes opposed your doing anything illegal on that occasion, and I voted
against it. And though the orators were ready to indict and arrest
me and though you were egging them on with your shouts, I
thought that I should run any risk on the side of law and justice
rather than side with you, out of fear of imprisonment or death,
when you were counseling injustice. (32a9—c3)

This makes it plain not only that Socrates has participated in politics but
that he actually held public office less than a decade before his trial—the
naval battle of Arginusae to which it refers took place in 406. It follows

54. Cf. Brickhouse and Smith (1988, 167—194); Burnet (1924, 128—129); Gomperz (1931, 2: 115—116); Kraut (1984, 196); Teloh (1986, 115); Vlastos (1983a,
500—501); West (1979, 182—183); Zeller (1962, 170).

55. Many translations suggest that Socrates held this office only once. See
Allen (1980, 53); Tredennick (1979, 64); West (1979, 38). There is nothing in the
text to support this view. See Burnet (1924, 130); 2.3.

that Socrates cannot be saying that he never participated in politics, and so cannot be trying to explain his nonparticipation.[56]

The second illustrative incident drives home this conclusion in a different way:

When the oligarchy was established, the Thirty summoned me, along with four others, to the Tholos, and they ordered us to arrest Leon of Salamis and bring him from Salamis to die. . . . But that government, strong as it was, didn't frighten me into doing anything unjust. When we went out of the Tholos, the other four went to Salamis and arrested Leon, but I departed and went home. And perhaps I would have died because of this, had not the government collapsed shortly afterwards. (32c4−d8)

Here it is not participating in politics that put Socrates at risk but his unwillingness as a private individual to obey an unjust government order. Since this incident is not even relevant to a claim about the dangers of participating in politics to a champion of justice, Socrates can hardly be using it to illustrate one.

If Socrates is not discussing the dangers of participating in politics, however, what is he discussing? The answer lies in his initial characterization of the issue at 31c4−7 (above): prudence and his *daimonion* have prevented him, not from participating in politics; but from bringing his elenchus-backed message of care for virtue and the psyche to crowds or to the polis as a whole. And the most likely explanation of why these two allies have acted in this way is that an elenchus is essentially a one-on-one affair:

I know how to produce just one witness to whatever I say, namely, the man I am having a discussion with, whoever he may be—but I ignore the many. I know how to put a question to a vote of one man, but with people en masse I do not even attempt dialogue [*tois de pollois oude dialegomai*]. (*Grg.* 474a5−b1)[57]

---

56. "To be a *bouleutēs* in his turn was not to play a part in politics, but to perform what was a citizen's duty" (Burnet 1924, 131). The implied contrast is unfounded. Why not say that it was a citizen's duty to play a part in politics when his turn came? Burnet's proposal does not help with Socrates' second illustration.

57. See Dodds (1959, 248); Kraut (1984, 201 n. 17); Robinson (1953, 15−17, 20−60).

This feature of the elenchus was sufficiently recognized by Socrates' contemporaries, indeed, to have become the stuff of comedy— Ameipsias' *Connus*, which defeated *Clouds* in 423, describes Socrates as "wisest of all where the company's small and weakest of wit where it's big" (Edmunds 1957, 1: 480–481). If Socrates disagrees with an individual on a matter of justice, the elenchus can help produce agreement (*Grg.* 474b2–5). But if he disagrees with a crowd on such a matter, the elenchus is useless, and they are likely to kill him. Socrates' two examples illustrate that fact. In each he opposes a crowd—the members of the Council of Five Hundred and the Thirty—and in each he is lucky to escape alive.

There is no evidence in these texts, then, that as a private citizen Socrates was apolitical or favoured total nonparticipation in politics. Indeed, there is conclusive proof of the opposite. Socrates did his duties as a citizen, holding office and serving in the armed forces (28d10–e4) when his turn came. And that is surely what we would expect of someone so devoted to Athens and her laws.

We turn now to the more complex issue of whether Socrates as elenctic philosopher was apolitical. Early in his speech, Socrates tells the jury that his mission left him with little leisure either for political life or private life:

> Because of this occupation, I have had no leisure worth speaking of to do any of the things concerning the polis [*tōn tēs poleōs praxai*] or any of my own private things [*tōn oikeiōn*]; instead I live in great poverty because of my service to the god. (23b7–c1).

Immediately following the verdict, he enlarges on this theme, filling out what his earlier description left vague:

> I have deliberately not led a quiet life [*en tōi biōi ouch hēsuchian ēgon*], but I have neglected what occupies the many: wealth and private affairs and generalships and being a demagogue and other types of leadership and political clubs and factions that come to be in the polis. (36b5–9)[58]

Socrates has not led a quiet (*hēsuchos*) life or a private life of making money or a typical public or political life of seeking office or being

---

58. On generalships, see Aristotle (*Ath.* 61.1–2); Carter (1986, 30–51). The demagogues are well discussed in Finley (1962). Political clubs, which played a decisive part in the oligarchic revolutions of 411 and 404/403, are discussed in Thucydides (8.54) and Calhoun (1913).

active in some political club or faction. Instead, as he puts it, he has been "meddlesome [*polupragmonō*] in private [*idiai*]" (31c4−7).

To understand this characterization and how strange it is, we must examine the terms in which it is developed: *hēsuchos*, and its close partner *apragmōn*, and their polar opposite *polupragmōn*.[59] To be *hēsuchos* or *apragmōn* was to be almost entirely apolitical. To be *polupragmōn* was to be very much engaged in everyday public political life. Thus when Socrates denies having been either *hēsuchos* or involved in conventional political life and asserts that he has been *polupragmōn*, but in private, he comes very close to saying that opposites are mixed in him, that he is neither private nor political, but somehow both at once.[60]

Now it is because he examines people that Socrates characterizes himself in this way. Because he conducts elenctic examinations, he is *polupragmōn* or political rather than *hēsuchos*, *apragmōn*, or apolitical; because such examinations are a one-on-one affair, he is political *in private*. In Socrates' view, therefore, elenctic examination must be a political activity. And in the *Gorgias* he explicitly claims not simply that it is political but that it is the only authentic form of politics:

> I am one of a few Athenians—not to say the only one—who undertake the real political craft and practice of politics, the only one among people now. (*Grg.* 521d6−8)[61]

The *Apology*, too, contains traces of this view:

> I went to each of you privately [*idiai*] conferring the greatest benefit, as I believe, by trying to persuade each of you not to care for any of his belongings before caring how he himself will be the best and wisest possible, nor to care for the belongings of the polis more than for the polis itself [*autēs tēs poleōs*], and so to care for the other things [private affairs and generalships and being a demagogue and other types of leadership and political clubs and factions] in the same way. (36c3−d1)

Socrates does not enlarge on this claim. But if, as seems likely, this text is simply an expansion of his original characterization of his mission at

---

59. The best discussion of *apragmosunē* as a political phenomenon crucial to a proper understanding of Athenian democracy is Carter (1986).

60. Cf. Carter (1986, 185); Ehrenberg (1947).

61. Cf. Xenophon, *Mem.* I.vi.15: "Would I [Socrates] play a more important role in politics, Antiphon, if I engaged in it myself alone, or if I produced as many competent politicians as possible?"

29e3−30a2, what he has in mind is clear enough. Whatever we care about (or value), whether in private or political life, our eye should be primarily on wisdom and goodness. As private citizens, we should care primarily that we (or our psyches) be the wisest and best possible. If we enter political life, whether as a general, a demagogue, or simply as a member of a political club or faction, our primary goal should be to insure that the polis itself—that is to say, its citizens (including our-selves)[62]—should be the best and wisest possible (cf. *Euthd.* 292b4−c1; *Grg.* 507d6−e1). Because elenctic examination comes as close as can be to achieving that goal, Socrates characterizes it as "the real political craft and practice of politics."

If being political is essentially a matter of being a general or a dema-gogue or a political leader of some other sort or of being an active member of a political club or faction, we have Socrates' word for it that he was apolitical. But if we follow him in thinking that elenctic exam-ination is a political activity, perhaps even the only authentic form of politics, we must accept that as an elenctic philosopher he was quintes-sentially political. It is no simple matter, then, as it is in the case of Socrates the private citizen, to decide whether as an elenctic philosopher Socrates is political or apolitical. At stake is the very nature of politics itself. Perhaps, therefore, we should not strive to do better than Socrates in this regard, but should rest content with his own description of himself as being *polupragmonō . . . idiai*—political in private.

3.8 TEACHING

Socrates confronts individuals, not crowds, reproaching them about their lack of care for virtue and their psyches, examining those who protest that they do care. It seems natural to say that he teaches the people he examines, natural to describe him, as many writers do, as an ethical teacher.[63] Yet, in the somewhat shocking series of disclaimers which signals his return to the question of whether he corrupts the youth, Socrates seems to reject this commonplace characterization out-right:

62. "In every case, the Polis was identical to the totality of its citizens. There-fore, the name of the State was taken from the citizens, not from the town or territory" (Ehrenberg 1968, 709).

63. "The greatest teacher in European history" (Jaeger 1939, 2: 27). "We can hardly avoid speaking of him as a teacher, though he himself disclaimed the appellation" (Grote 1888, 7: 87).

But throughout all my life, if I was ever active in public [*dēmosiai*], it was plain that I was the sort, and in private [*idiai*] the same, who never agreed to anything contrary to justice with any of those who my slanderers assert to be my students, nor with anyone else. I have never become anyone's teacher [*didaskalos*]. But if anyone ever wanted to hear me speaking and doing my own things, whether he was younger or older, I have never begrudged it to him. And I do not converse only when I receive money. I offer myself to be questioned by rich and poor alike, and if anyone is willing to answer my questions, he may hear what I say. And whether any of these becomes a good man or not, it would not be just to make me responsible, since I promised knowledge [*mathēma*] to no one and taught [*edidaxa*] none. If someone asserts that he ever learned anything from me or heard privately what everyone else did not, know well that he does not speak the truth. (33a1−b8)

There is an apparent inconsistency to be resolved, therefore, between our natural inclination to describe Socrates as an ethical teacher and his own rejection of that description.

One obvious suggestion, which many scholars have made, is that Socrates is using the verb 'teach' (*didaskō*) in a special or technical sense.[64] And a candidate sense of this sort is not, in fact, far to seek. Socrates disclaims expert craft-knowledge of virtue. Elsewhere he ties knowledge and teaching very closely together (*Prt.* 356e2−361b7). Perhaps, then, he also distinguishes—if only implicitly or in practice—*craft-teaching*, or the teaching of craft-knowledge, from ordinary teaching, disclaiming the one in the present passage and not the other.

This is an attractive resolution of the inconsistency. But it cannot be right. Witness what Socrates says to the jurors just before they bring in their verdict:

Therefore, we should not accustom you to perjure yourselves, nor should you make a habit of it. That would be impious conduct for both of us. So do not think, men of Athens, that I should act before you in ways that I do not believe to be fine nor just nor pious, especially, by god, when I am being prosecuted by Meletus here for impiety. Clearly, if I persuaded you and forced you by begging, after you had sworn the [juror's] oath, I would be teaching [*didaskoimi*] you not to believe that there are gods, and in defending

64. See Bluck (1964, 196−197); Crombie (1962, 222); Devereux (1978); Vlastos (1987b, 86−87). Kraut (1984, 294−304) is critical.

myself I would be accusing myself of not believing in gods. (35c5−d5)

If he gained acquittal by swaying the jurors through an appeal to their emotions, Socrates thinks that he would be getting them to break their juror's oath to render judgement according to the law, and so would be guilty of Meletus' charge of teaching them not to believe in the gods by whom they swore that oath. But appealing to the emotions of the jury is not offering them craft-instruction or anything like it. It follows that the teaching he disclaims, which must certainly include the corrupting teaching with which he is charged by Meletus (26b2−7), cannot be craft-teaching.

What, then, is he disclaiming? There is a general reason to think that it cannot be anything out of the ordinary. Socrates must be aware that the jury will understand him to be using *didaskō* in its ordinary sense unless explicitly instructed to do otherwise. If he were relying on a special sense of *didaskō* when he denies that he teaches, therefore, we would expect him to make this plain—as he does, for example, in his disclaimer of knowledge by distinguishing human wisdom from expert craft-knowledge. Since no explanatory glosses are in fact forthcoming, there is good reason to think that none are needed.

Now one ordinary sense of the verb *didaskō*, as of its equivalent 'teach', is 'to impart or convey knowledge or information'. And a survey of Socrates' use of *didaskō* in the *Apology* suggests that this is what he means by it. At 19c1, the knowledge or information concerns science and rhetoric; at 19d2, it concerns whether Socrates talks about science or rhetoric to any extent; at 20b8 (20c1) it concerns virtue; at 21b1−2 it concerns the origin of the ancient slanders; at 23d3, it concerns what Socrates teaches to corrupt the youth; at 26a3 and 26a5, it concerns what Socrates might be doing involuntarily, because unknowingly, to corrupt them; at 26b4, 26b6, 26c2, and 26c6, it concerns the gods or the gods of the polis; at 27c5, it concerns daimons; at 33b5−6, it is knowledge or information generally (*mathēma*); at 35c2, it is knowledge of the facts of a legal case; finally, at 35d4, it is knowledge which would influence the jurors' emotions.

When Socrates disclaims teaching, then, he is not disclaiming craft-teaching or some other as yet unexplored, nonstandard kind of teaching, but ordinary teaching, the imparting or conveying of knowledge or information.

This does not rule out the possibility, however, that Socrates' disclaimer of teaching is to be understood as restricted in some way. Socrates begins by saying that he is the same just man in private as he is in the agora (33a1−5), that he has never agreed to any injustice with his so-called students. He ends by saying that no one "ever learned anything from me or heard privately what everyone else did not" (33b6−8). This suggests that he may not be disclaiming teaching (or the imparting of knowledge or information) in general, but only *private* or *secret* teaching. Moreover, he specifically mentions the fact that he does not accept any money for what he does (33a8−b1), and he speaks of not having "become anyone's teacher" (33a5−6). This suggests that he may be denying only that he has entered into formal, paid, teacher-student relations with anyone and that he has taught anyone (private) things in that capacity.

Both these suggestions have some truth in them. Socrates *is* denying that he teaches anything in private and that he has entered into paid, formal, teacher-student relations with anyone. But the suggestions come to wrack because he is also denying much more. For he says that whether any of those nonpaying, informal students who listened to him in public become good men or not, he cannot be held responsible, because he "promised knowledge to no one, and taught none" (33a5−b6). And that entails that his disclaimer of teaching must cover its public and private, its formal and informal, its paid as well as its unpaid varieties.

One restriction, however, is in operation: Socrates' disclaimer of teaching applies only to the elenctic situation. This is established by two facts. First, he describes what he is doing in court as teaching: "I do not think it is just to beg the jury nor to be acquitted through begging, but to teach [*didaskein*] and to persuade" (35b9−c2). "I am going to teach you [*didaxein*]," he tells the jury at 21b1−2, "where the slander against me has come from." So it is hardly likely that he is disclaiming all teaching. Second, his disclaimer is itself focused entirely on elenctic examination. What he is denying is that in doing his own things, in asking his questions of young and old, rich and poor, out there in full view in the agora, he is teaching.

But if that is what Socrates' disclaimer amounts to, if he is simply denying that *elegchein* is *didaskein*, that to examine is to teach, are we any further ahead with the inconsistency we are trying to resolve? Because of the special nature of the Socratic elenchus, we are. Socrates' opening move is a reproach in the form of a question, "Are you not ashamed . . . ?" It is followed up by an elenctic examination only if the examinee claims that he already cares for virtue more than for wealth or honour. It seems reasonable to conclude that so far Socrates has not imparted or conveyed any knowledge or information to the examinee, that, in the relevant sense, he has not taught him anything. Then, the elenchus proper begins. But, as we saw in 1.8, it draws entirely on the sincerely held beliefs of the examinee, who must never agree to anything in it contrary to his own opinion, in order to reach conclusions that, on Socrates' view, he already (implicitly) believes. Hence it is reasonable for Socrates to hold that the beliefs involved in an elenchus are—like the beliefs of the slave-boy in the *Meno*—in the examinee all along, either explicitly or by entailment.[65] But, then, of course, it is also reasonable for him to hold that he does not impart or convey any new knowledge or information to those he examines.

If this is in fact what Socrates means when he claims that he does not teach, his disclaimer of teaching—like his disclaimer of expert craft-knowledge of virtue, to which it is intimately related—is completely sincere and completely intelligible. Socrates does not believe that elenctic examination is teaching, because he does not believe that such examination conveys or imparts any knowledge or information that the examinee did not already possess. The information or knowledge Socrates draws out of the examinee is—to revert to a famous simile—no more his own than the baby she delivers is the midwife's (*Tht.* 149a1–151d3). Because of this, because he has "promised knowledge to no one and taught none," Socrates disclaims responsibility for how some of those who have listened to him have turned out.

Yet despite the fact that these disclaimers are intelligible when deciphered in this way, they are still troublesome. We may agree that the beliefs involved in an elenchus are the examinee's, that he is responsible for them and their consequences, not Socrates. But it still seems to be true—and true even if we agree that teaching must involve conveying or imparting knowledge or information—that Socrates teaches in the elenctic situation and that he must be aware that he does. He knows that the rich young men who follow him around learn to construct elenctic arguments, by watching him. He must be aware, then, that he teaches them such arguments—as surely, at any rate, as he would teach the jury not to believe in the gods if he appealed to their emotions. Why, then, does he not think of this, if only to exclude it as irrelevant, when he claims that elenctic examination is not teaching?

Before attempting an answer, it is well to have some sense of the scope of the question. Socrates advocates the examined life. His own consists almost entirely of elenctic examination of himself and others. Yet we never find him reflecting on elenctic examination in particular or asking whether it is the best or only way to lead the examined life. He uses the elenchus to disabuse people of hubris, of the false conceit of knowledge, yet he nowhere reflects on the question of whether it achieves this aim or

65. This important point is made by Nehamas (1985, 19). Cf. Stokes (1986, 19–20).

whether it makes people better or worse. When he is confuting the
ancient caricature, it does not occur to him that the elenchus might be a
technique capable of making the weaker argument the stronger. When
dealing with the issue of whether he has corrupted the youth, he dis-
cusses only his message of care for virtue and the psyche, not the elenctic skills his young followers bootleg from him. So it is not just in the
present context that Socrates ignores the elenchus, implicitly excluding
it from the ambit of his teaching. He characteristically ignores it; it is the
unexamined part of his so thoroughly examined life: "The 'What is F?'
question which Socrates pursues elenctically about other things, he
never poses about the elenchus, leaving us only his practice of it as our
guide when we try to answer it ourselves" (Vlastos 1983b, 28).

There is a large question here, then, not just one about teaching. Once
we factor out its two components, however, it is a reasonably tractable
question. The components are these: Why did Socrates take the elenchus
as a technique of rational inquiry on trust? Why did he take it on trust
in every other way as well? The answer to the first question is reasonably obvious. Looked at simply as a technique of rational inquiry,
the elenchus—the practice of refuting propositions by showing them to
have entailments inconsistent with obvious truths—seems to be self-
justifying.[66] And therein, surely, lies at least part of the answer to the
second question, for use of the elenchus in just this sense led Socrates to
believe that the gods and their commands were supremely wise and
virtuous. How could the elenchus be anything other than completely
trustworthy, then; how could it be anything other than the greatest good
that had come to Athens (30a5−7), when Apollo himself had commanded its near-indiscriminate employment?

Socrates' trust in the elenchus is not, however, to be laid entirely at
Delphi's door, for having disclaimed teaching, Socrates turns to another
argument bearing on the charge that he has corrupted the youth:

> Now, if I corrupt some of the youth and have already corrupted
> others, then surely some of them, who have grown older and who

66. It took the genius of Plato to discover that the elenchus, even as a technique of rational inquiry, is not self-justifying. What Plato noticed is that acceptable propositions may seem obvious to us not because they are true, but because
as a result of socialization we find them obvious. The problem of ideology and
false consciousness thus raised puts the deliverances of intuition and with them
the reliability of acceptable propositions in jeopardy. This problem and Plato's
ingenious solution to it are explored in Reeve (1988, 5−42, 101−109, 235−250).
The point remains, however, that the elenchus has the look of innocence and
obviousness. "Where is justification to end," a recent writer on ethics asks, "but
in truisms?" (Pincoffs 1986, 54).

realize that I gave them bad advice when they were young, should have come forward themselves to accuse me and get their revenge. Or, if they were unwilling to do so themselves, then some of their families, their fathers or brothers or other relations, should have remembered and taken their revenge, if their family had been harmed by me. I see many of them present here. . . . And I could mention many others, some of whom Meletus should surely have called as witness in his own speech. If he forgot to do so, then—I yield time to him—let him do it now. You will find, gentlemen, that it is wholly the opposite, that everyone is ready to come to my aid, the corrupter, the man who has harmed their families, as Meletus and Anytus claim. Now, those who were corrupted might well have reason to help, but the uncorrupted ones, their relatives, who are older men, what reason to help me could they have other than the right and just one, that they know Meletus is speaking falsely and that I am telling the truth? (33c8–34b5)

Sober inspection of his young followers, then, which showed Socrates to be no corrupter of the youth, underwrites the elenchus itself, confirming what Apollo had already rendered so certain.

Turning back, now, to the narrower problem of why Socrates implicitly excludes the elenchus from the ambit of his teaching, we can see our way to a plausible solution. Socrates confronts the question of teaching in the context of the charge of corruption. The issue is what he could have taught the youth that might have the potential to corrupt them. Naturally enough, his primary focus is on things in the elenctic situation which might have that potential. Could the elenchus itself be among them? For all the reasons just canvassed, it seems likely that Socrates did not even consider the possibility.

The elenchus as an apparently self-justifying form of rational inquiry led Socrates to trust the gods; the gods and observation led him to total faith in the elenchus. Was his faith well placed? Some of his contemporaries did not think so. They believed that learning the elenchus tended to corrupt the young.[67] And, as we shall see, their suspicions cannot simply be dismissed out of hand.

Aristophanes is often characterized as attacking, not Socrates in particular, but the genus intellectual or sophist. And this may in fact be the

---

67. A belief not shared or much discussed by more recent writers. Grote (1888, 7: 168) describes the elenchus as "a process of eternal value and universal application." Vlastos, (1971, 20) places it "among the great achievements of humanity." Burnyeat (1980) and Nussbaum (1980, 43–97) are more skeptical.

best way to understand him. But there is some suggestion in *Clouds* that he may have understood enough about elenctic philosophizing to have aimed his major criticisms at the narrower target.[68] The competition between just and unjust logic, for example, which is the centerpiece of the play, looks something like an elenchus of the former by the latter. Unjust logic argues from things conceded by his opponent (942), in order to refute his opponent (943, 1037, 1314, 1040), he puts forward few substantive views of his own. To be sure, Socrates is not presented as being the partisan of unjust logic (or of just logic, for that matter). But it is fair to say that he is shown as being in favour of something like elenctic debate itself. It is up to Strepsiades to decide which logic his son will learn (937–938, 1105–1106). Socrates does not tell him. Nonetheless, it is by watching that competition and seeing who comes out ahead that Socrates expects Strepsiades to reach his decision. In fact, as we saw, Pheidippides learns both logics and can "argue down justice" (887–888, 1339) with either one (1336–1337). The implication is that, whether it is Socrates' aim to teach it to them for this purpose or not, his young followers learn a skill from watching elenctic arguments which, like the unjust logic, enables them to make the weaker argument the stronger. And this, the play insists, results in their becoming moral or religious skeptics and corrupt opportunists.

This critical view of the elenchus seems to have been shared by many relatively ordinary Athenians—Meletus, Anytus, and Lycon, for example, and all the others, "ambitious, violent, and numerous" (23d9–e1), whom they represent. On Socrates' own account of the matter, these people were all opposed to him *because of the elenchus*. Of course, he does not believe that their opposition stemmed from concern about the effects of the elenchus on the youth, but from concern about its deflationary effects, in young hands, on their own reputations for wisdom (23c2–24b2). Perhaps there is some truth in what he says. But it is also possible that this aetiology was itself in part the product of Socrates' faith in the innocence of the elenchus. Implicitly, at least, this seems to be the judgement of history. For it is almost universally accepted that the real reason Meletus' *graphē* was brought, the real reason it gained a conviction, was that Socrates was believed to have been the teacher of Critias and Alcibiades. And if this is indeed true, it is surely likely that genuine concern for the youth played a larger role in the general suspi-

---

68. Nussbaum (1980, 67–79) gives a detailed defense of this view. The issue is complicated by the similarities between the Socratic elenchus and methods of argument used by many of the sophists. See Kerferd (1981, 30–34, 59–67); n. 69 below.

cion of the elenchus than Socrates allows. Who would not be concerned, indeed, with these men as supposed examples of the effects of Socratic teaching?

Aristophanes may not have understood Socrates terribly well and may not have liked him. Meletus, Anytus, and the rest probably understood him less and liked him less. That weakens their testimony, such as it is, about the effects of the elenchus. But the next witness—Plato—is unimpeachable on both counts. Yet his condemnation of the elenchus is, if anything, even stronger than theirs:

> We hold from childhood certain convictions about what is just and fine, we grow up with them as with our parents; we follow them and honour them. . . . However, there are other ways of living opposite to those, which give pleasure, which pander to the psyche and attract it to themselves, but which do not convince decent men who continue to honour and follow the ways of their fathers. . . . And, then, I said, a questioner comes along and asks a man of this kind, "What is the fine [*ti esti to kalon*]?" And when he answers what he has heard from the traditional lawgiver, the argument refutes him [*exelegchēi ho logos*] and by refuting [*elegchōn*] him often and in many places shakes his conviction and makes him believe that these things are no more fine than shameful, and the same with just and good things and the things he honoured most.[69] What do you think his attitude will be then to honouring and following his earlier convictions?—Of necessity, he [Glaucon] said, he will not honour and follow them in the same way.—Then, I said, when he no longer honours and follows those convictions and cannot discover the true ones, will he be likely to adopt any other way of life than that which panders to his desires? . . . And so from being a man of conviction he becomes lawless and unprincipled. (*R.* 538c6–539a3)[70]

With friend and foe alike so united, it would be unwise to treat the evidence of either cavalierly.

---

69. It is significant that, in *Clouds* 1019–1021, just logic accuses unjust logic of producing precisely this effect in his victims: "You will be persuaded to believe everything shameful [*aischron*] to be fine [*kalon*], and the fine shameful [*to kalon d' aischron*]."

70. See Grote (1865, 3: 239); Nussbaum (1980, 88); Reeve (1988, 5–9, 107–110).

Moreover, this is not Plato's only explicit criticism of the elenchus in the *Republic*. He also questions its efficacy in combating hubris:

> Adeimantus said: No one would be able to contradict what you've said, Socrates. But this is how those who hear what you now say are affected on each occasion. They think because of their inexperience in the game of question and answer, they are at every question led astray a little bit by the argument and that, when these little bits are added together at the end of the discussion, a big false step appears which is the opposite of what they said at the outset . . . yet [their view about] what is the truth of the matter is not affected by this outcome. (487b1−c4)

If Plato is right, instead of disabusing people of their false conceit of knowledge, Socrates merely confirmed them in their dogmatism and gained a reputation for sophistry into the bargain.

None of these attacks on the elenchus is decisive, of course; they rely on controversial claims about its effects. But, decisive or not, they raise deep questions about Socrates and about the success of his service to Apollo; questions which—largely ignorant ourselves about the effects of the elenchus—we are not in a position to answer with authority.

3.9 THE COUNTERPENALTY

After the Peroration (34b6−35d8), which marks the conclusion of Socrates' formal defense and in which he explains why he has not brought "his children and many of his friends and family into court to arouse as much pity as he could" (34c3−5), why he has not made "the customary appeal *ad misericordiam*" (Burnet 1924, 144), 280 jurors return a verdict of guilty, 220 a verdict of not guilty. Thus, by a narrow margin, Socrates is convicted.

Because he was charged by means of a *graphē asebeias*, however, his trial was an *agōn timētos*. No penalty was fixed by law. Instead, the jury had to choose between the penalty (*timēsis*) demanded by the prosecution and a counterpenalty (*antitimēsis*) proposed by the defendant.[71] The verdict having been reached, it fell to Socrates, therefore, to propose an alternative to the death penalty demanded by Meletus.

What does he propose? Everyone agrees that there are two contenders:

---

71. See Harrison (1968, 2: 80−82)

Meals in the prytaneum (36e1–37a1)[72]

and

A fine of one mina of silver (38b4–5), increased at the urging of his friends Plato, Crito, Critoboulos, and Apollodorus, who agree to stand surety for the difference, to thirty minae (38b6–9).

Almost everyone agrees, too, that Socrates' first proposes meals in the prytaneum and then changes his proposal to a fine. But there agreement ends. Some claim that Socrates does not seriously propose any counterpenalty at all: "The Platonic *antitimēsis* . . . is wholly ironical" (Riddell 1877, xix). Some claim that he cannot consistently propose one:

To propose any penalty whatever would amount to admitting guilt, and Socrates has already told the court that he regards himself as a minister of God for good to his countrymen. Hence he cannot in consistency propose any treatment for himself but that of a distinguished public benefactor (*sitēsis en prutaneiōi*). (Taylor 1952, 166)

Some claim that Socrates could propose a genuine counterpenalty but that he opts for meals in the prytaneum in order to provoke the jury to put him to death:

The demand to be fed in the Prytaneum would necessarily produce the effect of mockery or of such an underlining of all that the indictment attacked, that those members of the court who are not wholly on his side could hardly reply otherwise than with the severest verdict. And it would be false affectation to say that Socrates could not speak otherwise. He could very well without compromising himself in the least. . . . But there seems to be in Socrates a conviction that a mission such as his ought not to be fulfilled peacefully, but must work itself out through ruin. That is why he provokes his own death. (Guardini 1962, 58–61)[73]

Some claim that Socrates must propose a genuine counterpenalty and that he does propose one:

Only this alternative [the fine] will satisfy each of Socrates' moral commitments; if he pays the fine, he will thereby obey the law by

72. The prytaneum was the common hearth of the polis. The custom of providing free meals there to victors in the Olympic games was "a survival of the time when kings invited honoured guests to share their board" (Burnet 1924, 155). Cf. West (1979, 211–212).

73. Cf. Knox (1964, 58); Stone (1988, 230).

offering a recognizable counter-penalty, he will in no substantial way harm himself or anyone else, and he will be free immediately to return to the streets of Athens to do the god's bidding. (Brickhouse and Smith 1988, 225)

With so much disagreement on such an apparently straightforward matter, there is little for it but to start over.

Does Socrates initially propose meals in the prytaneum? Here is what he says:

> What, then, do I deserve to suffer for being such a man [an elenctic philosopher]? Something good, men of Athens, if you give me what I deserve according to my true worth, and a good of a sort that would befit me. What, then, is fitting for a poor man, a benefactor, who needs leisure to exhort you? There is nothing more fitting, men of Athens, for such a man than to be given his meals in the prytaneum, much more so for him than for anyone of you who has won a victory at Olympia with a pair or a team of horses: for he makes you seem to be happy, while I make you be it; and he is not in need of upkeep, but I am. So if I must propose what I justly deserve, I propose that I be given meals in the prytaneum. (36d1–37a1)

The key sentence is:

(1) If [*ei*] I must propose what I justly deserve, I propose that I be given meals in the prytaneum. (36e1–3; cf. 36d2–4)

(1) is a conditional whose consequent is a proposal of meals in the prytaneum. The question, therefore, of whether Socrates actually does unconditionally propose meals in the prytaneum hinges on whether the antecedent of (1) is true. Now, (1) is equivalent to

(2) If I do not propose that I be given free meals in the prytaneum, it is not true that I must propose what I justly deserve.

But the antecedent of (2) is true, for Socrates proposes a fine. Consequently, the antecedent of (1) is not true, and (1) cannot be an unconditional proposal of anything at all. It follows that Socrates does not—even temporarily—propose meals in the prytaneum as a counterpenalty.[74]

Nonetheless, Socrates does claim that what he really deserves is free meals in the prytaneum, and he was aware that to those with little sympathy or understanding of his mission this would seem like rank

---

74. Cf. Brickhouse and Smith (1988, 219–221).

arrogance (37a2–4): how could a mere philosopher dare to compare his worth to that of an Olympic victor or a great public benefactor? But it is arrogance only if the claim is unwarranted. And Socrates believed—and believed that, given more time, he could persuade the jury—that it was not unwarranted but rather the simple truth (37a5–b2; 3.10).

The fact remains, however, that Socrates has not been able to persuade the jury. And it is this that explains why, even though he deserves meals in the prytaneum, he cannot propose that he be given them. Socrates has tried to persuade the court that he is innocent of Meletus' charges; he has failed. Hence Persuade or Obey requires him to abide by the court's decision (cf. 19a6–7; 3.2). He must, as it were, adopt the role of a man found legally guilty of impiety. That is why he cannot propose what he justly deserves. The court's decision subjects him to the law requiring him to propose a counterpenalty. Since he accepts Persuade or Obey, he must either obey that law, or, if obedience would be unjust, he must disobey it and defend himself if he is charged with violating it. What would constitute obedience? The obvious answer is surely the right one. Socrates must propose something that is *a genuine legal penalty*. If he proposes that he be awarded something that is a great public honour, he will not have obeyed.[75]

Because he accepts Persuade or Obey, Socrates must propose a genuine legal counterpenalty. Because he believes that he has committed no voluntary injustice, he believes that he cannot propose something bad for himself:

> Being convinced, then, that I do not do injustice to anyone, I am far from doing an injustice to myself and from saying against myself that I am worthy of something bad [*kakou*] and from proposing this sort of thing as what I deserve. (37b2–5)

The task Socrates faces, then, is to try to find a counterpenalty which satisfies two conditions: it must be a genuine legal penalty; it cannot be something he believes to be bad for him.[76] And it is to this task that most of this part of the *Apology* is in fact devoted.

75. It may not, however, have been *illegal* to propose a frivolous penalty. MacDowell (1978, 254), though he relies on the claim that Socrates unconditionally proposes meals in the prytaneum, suggests that there were no legal limits on what a defendant could propose. Nonetheless, for Socrates to suggest anything other than a genuine penalty would be to oppose the spirit of the law in an obvious way and make a mockery of the court and its verdict.

76. Penalties must be bad things. We think that someone has been punished (although not necessarily adequately punished) if something bad has been im-

Socrates rejects both imprisonment and imprisonment pending the payment of a fine as acceptable counterpenalties, because he knows that each of them is bad (37b7−8). But he does not know whether death is good or bad (37b6−7). He knows, too, that banishment would also be bad (37c4−38a6). If he continued to examine people elsewhere, he would eventually be driven out—by the elders if he lets the young men listen to him, at the urging of the young if he refuses.[77] On the other hand, if he abandoned the elenchus for a quiet life, he would both disobey the god and lose the greatest good for a man.

Socrates believes, however, that there is a counterpenalty which is both a genuine legal penalty and not a bad thing, namely, a fine. Hence he proposes that he pay a fine of thirty minae. Now, no one disputes that this counterpenalty is not a bad thing for Socrates. But there has been considerable dispute about whether or not it is a genuine legal penalty. Much of this dispute has focused on the amount of Socrates' own contribution. Some argue that one mina is a ridiculously small amount in the circumstances.[78] Others disagree. Even one mina, "the equivalent of one hundred days' wages," was not a trifling sum (Brickhouse and Smith 1988, 227). But the amount of Socrates' contribution to the fine is beside the point. For Socrates is explicit that he would pay the largest fine he could afford (which just happens to be one mina of silver):

I am not in the habit of thinking myself to deserve something bad.
If I had money, I would have proposed as much money as I could

posed on him. But when something bad is not believed to be bad by the person on whom it is to be imposed, our intuitions lose their cut-and-dried quality. Thus someone might reasonably believe that only something bad could be a genuine penalty. But it would be equally reasonable to believe, as Socrates does, that as long as something is generally held to be bad and is the sort of thing commonly imposed by a court as a penalty, then it is a genuine penalty.

77. "Since Socrates' present predicament showed that even in democratic Athens his mission was not tolerated, he could be quite confident that its practice would be prohibited elsewhere" (Brickhouse and Smith 1988, 222). The problem is that the Athenians allowed Socrates to philosophize for almost thirty years. If other places were only one half as tolerant, that would still leave him a few years of service to Apollo elsewhere. A few years is a long time for someone already seventy. The real reason Socrates is unwilling to propose exile—strongly suggested by 37c5−d6—is that even the *possibility* of being hounded from polis to polis in old age makes banishment sufficiently bad that he cannot choose it over death.

78. See Burnet (1914, 182); Friedländer (1964, 2: 170; Grube (1975, 40 n. 12); Taylor (1952, 166).

pay, for that would not harm me. But I do not have any, unless you wish me to propose as much money as I am able pay. Perhaps, I would be able to pay you about a mina of silver. So I propose that much. (38a8–b5)[79]

There can be no doubt, therefore, that one mina was *for Socrates* a very substantial fine.

What then of the actual fine of thirty minae Socrates proposes? Thirty minae was a large sum, "the equivalent of approximately eight-and-one-half years' wages," according to one recent estimate (Brickhouse and Smith 1988, 227); enough to buy a library of three thousand philosophy books, if the price of Anaxagoras' book is any guide (26d6–e2). And that is what we would expect, for it is hard to believe that Socrates' wealthy friends would propose an inappropriately small fine when his life was at stake (see *Cri.* 44b5–c5). As far as amount goes, then, there is every reason to believe that a fine of thirty minae satisfies both of the requirements Socrates imposes on a viable counterpenalty: it is a genuine legal penalty, but it is not a bad thing for himself.

But is this fine a genuine penalty in other respects? Some argue that it is not:

> [Socrates'] counter-proposal is half-hearted. His first idea—that he deserves free meals in the Prytaneum (*Ap.* 36d4–37a1)—assures the jury that he is entirely unrepentant; so the court knows, when he supercedes his first proposal with another, that even if Socrates pays a hefty fine, he is nonetheless going to be back in the marketplace committing philosophical acts once again. And surely, in that case, he would be tried and convicted a second time. In effect, by first proposing free meals, Socrates sabotages the attempt made by his friends to extend his life a bit longer. That is why thirty minae, whatever its value in the Athenian economy, represents a half-hearted counter-proposal. (Kraut 1984, 89–90 n. 49)

Leaving aside the fact that Socrates does not propose free meals in the prytaneum, the crucial presupposition of this argument is that no proposal Socrates could make would be whole-hearted unless it reassured the jurors that he repents having philosophized and would cease phi-

---

79. Xenophon (*Oec.* ii.2–4) has Socrates' estimate his total worth at five times the figure mentioned here: "I expect that if I found a good buyer, everything, including my house, would bring five minae." If Xenophon's figure is correct, we may infer either that Socrates' total worth declined or that he was not willing to beggar his family in order to save his life.

losophizing if released. But this sets the conditions for whole-heartedness far too high; such an agreement would violate Socrates' deeply held conviction that he must continue to philosophize even at the cost of his life. The most we can reasonably expect as a condition of whole-heartedness, therefore, is that Socrates will go as far towards satisfying his legal obligation to propose a genuine counterpenalty as his fundamental ethical principles allow. And, in proposing a fine of thirty minae, that seems to be precisely what he does.[80]

A final issue bearing on the counterpenalty, somewhat different in kind, relates to the evidence we have about how it was received by the jurors. Socrates makes one speech to those who found him guilty and a separate speech to those who voted for the death penalty (cf. 38c7−d2, 39c1−2). This suggests that these two groups were not identical. The fact that he describes those who voted to acquit him as "you whom I would rightly and finely call jurors" (40a2−3) suggests that there was no overlap between this group and the group who voted for death. For Socrates would hardly be likely to refer to the latter in such flattering terms. It follows that *fewer* jurors voted for the death penalty than voted guilty. This contradicts the claim made by Diogenes Laertius (2.42) some five centuries later that there were eighty more votes for the sentence of death than for the verdict of guilty. But it is surely what we would expect: jurors who believed Socrates to be innocent would hardly vote to put him to death; some of those who did find him guilty are likely to have recoiled at the death penalty.

Writers who credit Diogenes Laertius argue that the eighty changed their votes because they were irrationally angry at what Socrates said, between verdict and sentence, about deserving free meals in the pry-taneum.[81] But this is almost certainly a case of using a prejudice to explain a nonfact. Only uncritical reliance on contemporary comedy (especially the plays of Aristophanes) and other sources biased against democracy makes it any more reasonable to believe that so many Athenian jurors would behave in this disreputable way than to believe the same thing about a jury of our own peers.[82] For more than one reason, therefore, it is better to accept the evidence of the *Apology* and to be skeptical of Diogenes Laertius.

80. Cf. Gomperz (1931, 2: 101−102).

81. See Burnet (1924, 161); Phillipson (1928, 376); Taylor (1933, 119); Zeller (1885, 201).

82. See Forrest (1966, 21−34); Grote (1888, 7: 9−17); Ste. Croix (1981, 362, 370−371).

Socrates does not propose meals in the prytaneum, then. Instead, he proposes a genuine legal penalty, and he does so wholeheartedly. But because he does not want to compromise either his principles or his innocence, the penalty he proposes cannot be something he considers bad. A fine of thirty minae fits this double bill. No doubt the fact that he emphasizes that the fine is not something he considers bad and insists he will return to philosophy if released pretty well guaranteed that most of the jurors who found him guilty would choose the death penalty instead of the fine. But there is no good reason to believe that any of those who found him innocent were sufficiently provoked by his counterproposal to send him to his death. Nor is there any reason to believe that in proposing a fine—rather than, say, banishment—Socrates was courting death by purposely inciting the jury. A death wish is one thing; willingness to die for one's deepest principles is another.

3.10 THE REAL OLYMPIAN

Throughout the *Apology*, but nowhere more so than in the sections which follow the verdict, Socrates makes a series of extraordinary claims about the elenchus which it will be well to collect :

I think that no greater good [*meizon agathon*] has come to be in the polis than my service to the god. (30a5−7)

I went to each of you privately conferring the greatest benefit [*tēn megistēn euergesian*], as I believe, by trying to persuade each of you not to care for any of his belongings before caring how he himself will be the best and wisest possible [*hōs beltistos kai phronimōtatos*], nor to care for the belongings of the polis more than for the polis itself, and to care for other things in the same way. (36c3−d1)

He [the Olympic victor] makes you seem to be happy [*poiei eudaimonas dokein einai*], while I make you be it [*egō de einai*]. (36d9−e1)

It is the greatest good [*megiston agathon*] for a human being to discuss virtue every day and the other things about which you hear me conversing and examining both myself and others, for the unexamined life is not worth living for a human being. (38a2−6)

If you suppose that by killing people you will escape being reproached for not living the right way, you do not think finely, for to be let off is neither possible nor fine, but it is both finest and easiest, not to restrain others, but to equip oneself to be the best possible [hōs beltistos]. (39d3−8)

But certainly the greatest thing [megiston] is that I could pass my time testing and examining people there [in the next world], just like those here, as to who among them is wise, and who thinks he is, but is not. . . . To talk with, associate with, and examine them would be inconceivable happiness [amēchanon . . . eudaimonias]. Surely they do not kill one on this account, for they are happier there in other respects than those here, and they are deathless for the rest of time, if indeed what we are told is true. (41b5−c7)

How are we to understand these claims? What justifies Socrates in making them?

An answer implicit in many accounts of Socrates is this: (1) Socrates believes that knowledge of virtue is identical to or necessary and sufficient for virtue. (2) The aim of the elenchus is to discover accounts of the virtues which embody this knowledge. (3) Therefore, a completely successful elenchus results both in knowledge and in virtue. (4) Virtue makes its possessor (very) happy. (5) Therefore, a successful elenchus makes its subject happy.[83]

On this view, 36d9−e1 entails that the Athenians possess craft-knowledge of virtue. It also entails that Socrates himself possesses this knowledge. Yet he denies that he possesses any craft-knowledge of virtue and denies that he teaches virtue. Indeed, he makes the majority of his defense hinge on the truth of those denials. Hence, if we adopt this view, we have to find a plausible explanation for these denials and for their use in court.

Irony of some sort is the favourite candidate explanation. Socrates knows the answers to his own questions. But he ironically disclaims this knowledge, "engaging would-be learners in elenctic argument to make them aware of their own ignorance and give them the opportunity to discover for themselves the truth the teacher had held back" (Vlastos 1987b, 87). But this explanation is difficult to accept. First, Socrates knows things about virtue, including some accounts of what it is. But none of this knowledge is at once explanatory, teachable, luck-independent, elenchus-proof, and certain; none of it is the superordinate craft of politics. Socrates does not possess this craft; neither does any other human being. This is compelling reason to take Socrates' dis-

---

83. The best defense of this sort of account of Socrates is Vlastos (1983), (1985), (1987b).

claimer of craft-knowledge and its inculcation at face value. Second, the function assigned to irony in an elenchus does not carry over in a plausible way to the courtroom situation. Socrates is not examining the jurors, after all. His aim, as we have seen, is to prove his innocence, not to awaken in the jurors a sense of their own ignorance. Finally, this account of Socrates misrepresents the value of the elenchus. What is really valuable, according to the account, is the knowledge, virtue, and happiness to which a successful elenchus leads. The elenchus is valuable only as a means to them. When they are reached, it loses much of its value.[84] But this is not Socrates' view of the matter. As we have seen, he denies that the elenchus achieves the goal of craft-knowledge of virtue, and he repeatedly portrays the elenchus itself as the greatest good. He claims, indeed, that unending elenctic examination after death would be inconceivable happiness. This would not be so—unending elenctic examination would not be inconceivable happiness—if happiness lay only at the end of an elenctic examination successfully completed.

The present account of Socrates' extravagant claims about the benefits of the elenchus is problematic, then. What are we to put in its place?

Examining someone on a regular basis gets him to see that acceptable propositions he is unwilling to deny or abandon entail such unacceptable propositions as that it is better to suffer injustice than to do it, that "virtue makes wealth and everything else good for a man," and that the conventionally distinguished virtues are identical to the superordinate craft of politics. Someone who really and sincerely believes these propositions will—on Socrates' view—care more for virtue than for anything else. So far, so good. The problem is that these propositions might be *false*. They are tied down by arguments of iron and adamant. But those bonds might yet be undone in future elenctic argument. How, then, can Socrates claim that, by getting people to believe them and to reshape their values and lives accordingly, he is "conferring the greatest benefit"? How can he claim that he makes the Athenians happy? Surely, he bene-

84. Irwin (1977, 97) is one of the few to see this clearly: "Since Socrates is no moral expert, the Socratic dialogues never threaten the elenchos with obsolescence; but if moral inquiry and knowledge are valued for their results, the value of the elenchos must be strictly limited." The *Apology* does not merely leave the elenchus unthreatened with obsolescence, however; it explicitly states that the elenchus (or the life of elenctic examination) is the greatest human good. The craft-knowledge of virtue cannot, then, be something Socrates envisaged as a possible *human* possession (cf. 23a5−b4). By the same token, he cannot have valued the elenchus because it helps to gain that possession for us. The source of its value must, therefore, lie somewhere else altogether.

fits and makes them happy only if the propositions he persuades his interlocutors to believe are in fact *true*.

Examining someone gets him to believe, for example, that virtue just by itself produces happiness. Repeated examination, living the examined life, helps save him from the hubris of thinking that any of his ethical convictions amount to expert craft-knowledge. He believes that virtue by itself produces happiness, because that belief is tethered by arguments of iron and adamant. But he recognizes that at best—that is to say, if it is in fact true—his belief amounts to nonexpert knowledge, neither explanatory, nor teachable, nor luck-independent, nor elenchus-proof, nor certain. And because he recognizes that his belief has this status, the need to reexamine it constantly, to resubmit it to elenctic scrutiny, is also recognized. Even if it is false that virtue by itself produces happiness, then, someone who believes it in this way avoids both "the most blameworthy ignorance" of thinking he has expert craft-knowledge of virtue when he does not (29b1−2) and the blameworthy vice to which such ignorance often gives rise. That is why frequent elenctic examination helps someone to become as good or wise or virtuous as it is possible for a human being to be. That is why elenctically discussing virtue every day is the greatest good *for a human being*. That is why Socrates confers "the greatest benefit" on the Athenians and makes them really happy (or as close to being really happy as possible). Without the craft-knowledge of virtue, the closest we can come to virtue (which is identical to that craft-knowledge) and happiness (which virtue alone produces) is to avoid blameworthy ignorance and blameworthy vice. If we manage this, however, if we achieve human wisdom, we also achieve human virtue, for if wisdom is virtue, *human* wisdom is, surely, *human* virtue.

The temptation to hubris and blameworthy ignorance, moreover, is perennial—even in the next life it continues to plague us (40e4−41b7). That is why the elenchus never loses its value. It is always our only guard against culpable ignorance and vice: "How could you think," Socrates asks Critias, "that I would refute you for any reason other than the one for which I would refute myself, fearing lest I might inadvertently think I know something when I don't know it?" (*Chrm.* 166c7−d2). The examined life is the best human life, no matter how long it lasts. Prolonged without end, it would bring us the greatest happiness of which we are capable—inconceivable happiness.

We can now understand why Socrates rates his elenctic mission so highly and why he is convinced that, if he got what he justly deserved, he would sup in the prytaneum, not drink the hemlock.

Socrates' attitude to death and his behaviour in the face of it have inspired many.

> The picture of the dying Socrates must have afforded to his pupils, in the highest degree, what it now after centuries affords to us—a simple testimony to the greatness of the human mind, to the power of philosophy, and to the victory of a spirit pious and pure, resting on clear conviction. (Zeller 1885, 236)

But what was the conviction in question? What was it that enabled Socrates to face death with such exemplary calm? Part of the answer is in the Digression itself. We do not know whether death is good or bad. Hence to choose vicious action out of fear of it is to be guilty of "that most blameworthy ignorance of thinking that one knows when one does not know" (29b1−2). Another part of the answer is contained in the Epilogue (34b6−35d8). We do not become immortal by avoiding death on a particular occasion; death must be faced at some time:

> Now, if those of you who are considered surpassing, whether in wisdom or courage or some other virtue, were to act in this way [arousing the pity of the jury], it would be shameful. Yet I have often seen such people do this sort of thing when standing trial, men who are believed to be something, doing amazing things, as though they believed that they would suffer something terrible if they died and would be immortal if you did not kill them. (35a1−7)

In the closing address (38c1−42a5), however, it emerges that Socrates' confidence in the face of death eventually finds a source in something else as well, something beyond his lack of "adequate knowledge of things in Hades" (29b5), beyond the fact that "death, a necessary end, will come when it will come" (*Julius Caesar*, II.ii.15−20).

After a few largely reiterative remarks, first, to those who have condemned him to death (38c7−39b8) and then to those who have found him guilty (39c1−d9), Socrates addresses the following argument to the jurors who voted to acquit him (I have numbered its premises and conclusion for ease of subsequent reference):

> To you, as to friends, I want to show the meaning of what has happened to me. An amazing thing has occurred, jurors—you whom I would rightly and finely call jurors. [1] The usual sign from my *daimonion* was always very frequent in all of the time before this

and held me back even on small matters, if I was about to do something that was not right. [2] But now, as you can see for yourselves, that I was faced with what someone might think to be the greatest of evils, the sign of the god [*to tou theou sēmeinon*] did not hold me back, neither when I left my house this morning, nor when I came here to the court, nor anywhere in the speech when I was about to say something. Yet in other talks it often held me back in the middle of speaking. But now, concerning this business, it has opposed no word nor deed of mine. What, then, do I take to be the explanation of this? I shall tell you. [3] It looks as though what has happened to me is a good thing, and there is no way that we are right if we suppose death to be bad. For me a great proof of this has happened: [4] There is no way that the usual sign would not have opposed me, if I were not about to do something good. (39e5–40c3)

It is a remarkable argument for two reasons. First, Socrates supports his conclusions about death entirely on the silent, elenchus-certified authority of his *daimonion*. In this respect, its closest parallel in the *Apology* is Socrates' oracle-inspired elenctic mission itself. Second, as we shall see, that authority makes those conclusions not just probable, but certain.

Initially, Socrates might seem to be arguing as follows:

(1a) The *daimonion* always opposes Socrates when he is about to do something wrong.

(2a) But in this case, the *daimonion* did not oppose him.

(4a) Therefore, Socrates is about to do something good.[85]

But there are three reasons that this cannot be what he has in mind. First, (1a) is much stronger than anything he actually says in the text. Second, (4a) does not follow from (1a) and (2a). All that follows is the weaker proposition that Socrates is not about to do something bad. Finally, (4a) is not in fact what Socrates concludes.

Socrates' does not say that the *daimonion* always opposed him if he was about to do something wrong. His thought—as (1) and (2) make clear—is that, because the *daimonion* very frequently opposed him even in small matters if he was about to do something that was not right, it would

---

85. Brickhouse and Smith (1986) defend this analysis of Socrates' argument but later (1988, 237–257; cf. 106) they reject it in favour of one closer to that defended below.

certainly have opposed him if, in drinking the hemlock, he was about to inflict on himself *the greatest of evils*. As he puts it: "There is no way that the usual sign would not have opposed me, if I were not about to do something good."

Leaving (3) aside for a moment, let us turn to (4). If (4) implies that death is always a good thing or is a good thing absolutely speaking, it no more follows from (1) and (2) than (4a) does from (1a) and (2a). But (4) does not imply this. At 41d3–6, Socrates restates his conclusion as follows: "It is certain that it is now better for me to be dead and to leave my troubles behind. Because of this, the sign did not hold me back." In other words, death is better than continued life in his present circumstances (the other available option). Therefore, in comparison to life in such circumstances, death is a good thing. Since the *daimonion* would certainly have opposed him if this were not so, Socrates concludes that it is certain that he is about to do something good.[86] It follows that (3) there is no way we are right if we suppose that death is always a bad thing or that it is a bad thing absolutely speaking.

Socrates' second argument is an independent secular argument for a weaker conclusion about death:

> Let us also reflect in this way how much hope there is that it [death] is a good thing, for being dead is either of two things: either it is nothing and the dead have no awareness of anything, or, as we are told, it is some kind of change and migration of the psyche from here to another place. And if there is no awareness, but it is like sleep in which the sleeper has no dream, death would be a wonderful gain. . . . All time would appear to be nothing more than one night. But again, if death is something like a journey and if the things that are said are true, what greater good could there be than this, men of the jury? (40c4–e7)

Death is either a dreamless sleep, or— "if the things that are said are true"—it is transportation to a place where endless elenctic examination brings "inconceivable happiness" (41c3–4). But the things that are said may not be true. Death may be, as Homer suggests (*Od.* 11.488–491), transportation to a much more unpleasant place. That is why there is only "hope [*elpis*]" that death is a good thing rather than the certainty there would be if the possibilities Socrates mentions were the only ones.

Hope is the mortal predicament. When Prometheus is asked how he alleviated mortal misery, he replies: "I planted blind hope [*elpidas*] in

---

86. Cf. Brickhouse and Smith (1988, 256–257), who argue that Socrates has no legitimate route from (1) to (4).

them" (Aeschylus, *PV* 250). But the god, who "is really wise" (23a5–6), has no need of hope; he has certainty: "Now it is time to go, I to die and you to live. Which of us goes to a better thing is uncertain [*adēlon*] to everyone except the god" (42a2–5). However, the god shares his certainty on some matters with some privileged mortals: "It is certain [*dēlon*]," Socrates says, "that it is now better for me to be dead and to leave my troubles behind. Because of this, the sign did not hold me back" (41d3–6).[87] No wonder he goes to his death with such equanimity.

87. *Dēlon* literally means 'clear', 'plain', or 'manifest'. See Liddell and Scott (1966, s.v. *dēlos*). But the suggestion of certainty or of the most secure kind of knowledge is never far away. Note that Socrates' certainty that death is a better thing *for him* than life is quite consistent with his uncertainty, and that of all other mortals, on the question of whether death is always a better thing than life or whether death is a better thing for him than life will be *for the jurors* he is addressing.

CONCLUSION

Socrates . . . was a sacrifice to the anger of the fathers at his "corruption of
the youth."   —NIETZSCHE

Most portraits represent Socrates as the great ironist of philosophy. He
knows but ironically denies that he knows. He teaches but ironically
denies that he teaches. He claims that knowledge is identical to virtue,
ironically disclaiming the one yet implying that he possesses the other.
Even when he is on trial for his life, he is what he says he is not and is
not what he says he is. He is perpetually masked in order to stir up in
those he examines a fertile and productive search for virtue.

Now, sustained and unrelenting irony of this sort, irony which
characterizes a whole life, is incompatible with sincere self-disclosure,
with unmasking. But it is equally incompatible with explanation: the
unremitting ironist does not engage in diagnosis of how it is that he
acquired his reputation. Yet this is what Socrates must be seen as doing
in the *Apology* by anyone who believes him to be always ironical. He
denies that he possesses the craft-knowledge of virtue and carefully
explains how he nonetheless acquired a false reputation for it, a reputation which casts his denial in an ironical light. On seeing him refute
others, people inferred that he possessed the very craft-knowledge he
showed others to lack.

Socrates denies that he teaches. But his denial is not that of a self-
aware ironist, consciously distinguishing one kind of teaching from
another and setting provocative interpretative puzzles to his perplexed
hearers in hopes of spurring them on to discovery. Instead, it is a denial
based, on the one hand, in beliefs about the elenchus and, on the other,
in a common conception of teaching.

Socrates denies that he has expert craft-knowledge of virtue. But he
nowhere claims to possess virtue itself. All he claims is that he possesses
nonexpert knowledge of virtue and that he has avoided hubris and voluntary vice through leading the examined life.

There is, therefore, no fundamental irony in Socrates. Rather he is—
like Cassandra, that other misunderstood servant of Apollo—someone it
has proved very difficult to take at his word.

Many portraits of Socrates represent him, too, as a searcher after the very knowledge he lacks. But the *Apology* subordinates this characterization to another. For Socrates presents his elenctic mission as rooted not simply in the search for knowledge of virtue, but also in the desire to serve Apollo by disabusing people of hubris. The goal of his philosophic mission—the goal of the examined life as Socrates lives it—is not to discover the craft-knowledge of virtue (which is all but impossible for humans) but to produce in himself and those he examines the amalgam of epistemic modesty and overriding concern for virtue and the psyche that is human wisdom, and—wisdom and virtue being one—human virtue.

But for all that his mission originates in Apollonian injunctions, Socrates is not primarily a man of faith. His mission is based in religion, but his religion is based in elenctic philosophy: "Not now for the first time, but always, I am the sort of man who is persuaded by nothing in me except the argument that when I reason seems to me to be the best" (*Cri.* 46b4−6). And it is as a philosopher, albeit a religious one, that we must understand him if we are to make sense of his life as he describes it. If Socrates had not been a philosopher, Chaerephon's oracle from Delphi could not have had the effect it did. But if, having deciphered that oracle, he had not trusted in the divine command he found in it, there would not have been an elenctic mission.

On trial for his life, Socrates neither argues fallaciously nor evades the real charges or their real basis nor intentionally provokes the jury. His response to the formal charges may not be the best one he could have made. That is an open question. But it is part of a reasonable and intelligible defense compatible with his deepest principles, and it establishes his innocence. His broader defense establishes, too, that the ancient prejudicial caricature of him as a scientist, orator, and sophist teacher of virtue is based on a misunderstanding of his own vividly portrayed human wisdom. If the jury relied on the ancient caricature, then, and found him guilty at least in part to save Athens from the dangers posed by such advanced thinkers, they were doubly at fault—they unjustly convicted an innocent man, and they did so for the wrong reasons. If, on the other hand, it was Socrates' association with Alcibiades and Critias and his supposed antidemocracy that told against him with the jury, then the verdict was not only unjust because irrelevant to the charges he faced, it was also, because of the Amnesty of 403, in violation of Athenian law.

Partly as a result of his elenchus-based faith in Apollo, however, Socrates does not deal in a forthright way with what—for some of his contemporaries at least—seems to have been a major cause of worry about him, namely, that his young followers learned the elenchus by watching him and had a tendency to become ethical skeptics as a result. This worry may have been justified, or it may not have been. Without more knowledge, we simply cannot say.

Neither can we say how successful Socrates' mission was in its own terms. Did it disabuse many of their hubris and persuade them to lead the examined life? Or did being refuted simply leave most people as dogmatic as it found them? The temptation to turn away from these questions as somehow irrelevant and to take up instead the fact of Socrates' extraordinary philosophical influence is a sign of both how much we are—and how much we are not—his heirs.

When Socrates looks for comparisons to himself, he finds them in the great warrior heroes, Achilles and Ajax (28b9–d4, 41a8–b4). These are not the comparisons we expect, and yet they are curiously appropriate. The unwillingness to yield even in the face of death, the seemingly extravagant sense of confidence and worth that would be arrogance in lesser men, the capacity to succeed in unending competition, whether brazen or elenctic, mark all three as possessors of "the heroic temper" (Knox 1964, 58). Achilles and Ajax are tragic figures, of course, heroes of tragedies. But this, too, is something they have in common with the philosopher who invokes their names.

BIBLIOGRAPHY

Adam, J. 1963. *The Republic of Plato.* 2d ed. Vols. 1–2. Cambridge: Cambridge University Press.

Adkins, A. W. H. 1960. *Merit and Responsibility: A Study in Greek Values.* Oxford: Clarendon Press.

Allen, R. E. 1980. *Socrates and Legal Obligation.* Minneapolis: University of Minnesota Press.

———. 1984. *The Dialogues of Plato.* Vol. 1. New Haven: Yale University Press.

Baldry, H. C. 1937. "Plato's 'Technical Terms'." *Classical Quarterly* 31: 141–150.

Beck, F. A. G. 1964. *Greek Education 450–350 B.C.* London: Methuen.

Beckman, J. 1979. *The Religious Dimension of Socrates' Thought.* Waterloo, Ontario: Wilfred Laurier University Press.

Bluck, R. S. 1964. *Plato's Meno.* Cambridge: Cambridge University Press.

Blumenthal, H. 1973. "Meletus the Accuser of Andocides and Meletus the Accuser of Socrates: One Man or Two?" *Philologus* 117: 169–178.

Bonner, R. J., and Smith, G. 1938. *The Administration of Justice from Homer to Aristotle.* Vols. 1–2. Chicago: University of Chicago Press.

Brandwood, L. 1976. *A Word Index to Plato.* Leeds: W. S. Maney & Son.

Brickhouse, T. C., and Smith, N. D. 1984. "Vlastos on the Elenchus." *Oxford Studies in Ancient Philosophy* 2 (1984): 185–195.

———. 1986. " 'The Divine Sign Did Not Oppose Me: A Problem in Plato's *Apology.*" *The Canadian Journal of Philosophy* 16: 511–526.

———. 1987. "Socrates on Goods, Virtue, and Happiness." *Oxford Studies in Ancient Philosophy* 5: 1–27.

———. 1988. *Socrates on Trial.* Oxford: Clarendon Press.

Burkert, W. 1985. *Greek Religion.* Cambridge, Mass.: Harvard University Press.

Burnet, J. 1900. *Platonis Opera.* Vols. 1–5. Oxford: Clarendon Press, 1900–1907.

———. 1914. *Greek Philosophy: Thales to Plato.* London: Macmillan.

———. 1924. *Plato's Euthyphro, Apology of Socrates, and Crito.* Oxford: Clarendon Press.

Burnyeat, M. F. 1971. "Virtues in Action." In *The Philosophy of Socrates,* edited by G. Vlastos, 209–234. Garden City, N.Y.: Anchor Books.

———. 1980. "Aristotle on Learning to Be Good." In *Essays on Aristotle's Ethics,* edited by A. O. Rorty, 69–92. Berkeley: University of California Press.

———. 1987. "Platonism and Mathematics: A Prelude to Discussion." In *Mathematics and Metaphysics in Aristotle,* edited by A. Graeser, 213–240. Berne and Stuttgart: Paul Haupt.

———. 1988. "Review of *The Trial of Socrates,* by I. F. Stone." *New York Review of Books* 35: 12–18.

Calhoun, G. M. 1913. *Athenian Clubs in Politics and Litigation.* Reprint. New York: Burt Franklin, 1970.

Carter, L. B. 1986. *The Quiet Athenian.* Oxford: Clarendon Press.

Charlton, W. 1988. *Weakness of Will: A Philosophical Introduction.* Oxford: Basil Blackwell.

Clark, P. M. 1955. "The *Greater Alcibiades.*" *Classical Quarterly* 5: 231–240.

Cohen, S. M. 1971. "Socrates on the Definition of Piety: *Euthyphro* 10A–11B." In *The Philosophy of Socrates*, edited by G. Vlastos, 158–176. Garden City, N.Y.: Anchor Books.

Cooper, J. M. 1982. "The *Gorgias* and Irwin's Socrates." *Review of Metaphysics* 35: 577–587.

Cornford, F. M. 1939. *Plato and Parmenides.* London: Routledge and Kegan Paul.

Coulter, J. A. 1964. "The Relation of the *Apology of Socrates* to Gorgias' *Defense of Palamedes* and Plato's Critique of Gorgianic Rhetoric." *Harvard Studies in Classical Philology*: 269–303.

Crombie, I. M. 1962. *An Examination of Plato's Doctrines.* Vol. 1. London: Routledge and Kegan Paul.

Davies, J. K. 1971. *Athenian Propertied Families: 600–300 B.C.* Oxford: Clarendon Press.

Denniston, J. D. 1987. *The Greek Particles.* 2d ed. Oxford: Clarendon Press.

Derenne, E. 1930. *Les Procès d'impiété intentés aux philosophes a Athènes au Vme au IVme siecles avant J.-C.* Reprint. New York: Arno Press, 1976.

Devereux, D. 1978. "Nature and Teaching in Plato's *Meno.*" *Phronesis* 23: 118–126.

Diels, H., and Kranz, W. 1952. *Die Fragmente der Vorsokratiker.* 5th ed. Vols. 1–3. Berlin: Weidmann.

Dittmar, H. 1912. *Aischines von Sphettos.* Reprint. New York: Arno Press, 1976.

Dodds, E. R. 1951. *The Greeks and the Irrational.* Berkeley and Los Angeles: University of California Press.

———. 1959. *Plato: Gorgias.* Text and Commentary. Oxford: Clarendon Press.

Dover, K. J. 1968. *Lysias and the Corpus Lysiacum.* Berkeley and Los Angeles: University of California Press.

———. 1971. "Socrates in the *Clouds.*" In *The Philosophy of Socrates*, edited by G. Vlastos, 50–77. Garden City, N.Y.: Anchor Books.

———. 1972. *Aristophanic Comedy.* Berkeley and Los Angeles: University of California Press.

———. 1974. *Greek Popular Morality in the Time of Plato and Aristotle.* Berkeley and Los Angeles: University of California Press.

———. 1976. "The Freedom of the Intellectual in Greek Society." *Talanta* 7: 24–54.

———. 1978. *Greek Homosexuality.* Cambridge, Mass.: Harvard University Press.

Edmunds, J. M. 1957. *The Fragments of Attic Comedy.* Vols. 1–3. Leiden: E. J. Brill.

Ehrenberg, V. 1947. "Polypragmosyne: A Study in Greek Politics." *Journal of Hellenic Studies* 67: 46–67.

————. 1968. "Polis." In *The Oxford Classical Dictionary*, 709. Oxford: Clarendon Press.

————. 1973. *From Solon to Socrates*. 2d ed. London: Methuen.

Engberg-Pedersen, T. 1983. *Aristotle's Theory of Moral Insight*. Oxford: Clarendon Press.

Ferguson, J. 1970. *Socrates: A Source Book*. London: Macmillan.

Finley, M. I. 1962. "Athenian Demagogues." *Past and Present* 21: 3–24.

Fontenrose, J. 1981. *The Delphic Oracle: Its Responses and Operations with a Catalogue of Responses*. Berkeley and Los Angeles: University of California Press.

Forrest, W. G. 1966. *The Emergence of Greek Democracy*. New York: McGraw-Hill.

Frede, M. 1987. *Essays in Ancient Philosophy*. Minneapolis: University of Minnesota Press.

Freeman, K. 1977. *Ancilla to the Pre-Socratic Philosophers*. Cambridge, Mass.: Harvard University Press.

Frey, R. G. 1978. "Did Socrates Commit Suicide?" *Philosophy* 53: 106–108.

Friedländer, P. 1964. *Plato*. Vol. 2. Translated by H. Meyerhoff. New York: Bollingen Foundation.

Furley, D. 1987. *The Greek Cosmologists*. Vol. 1. Cambridge: Cambridge University Press.

Geach, P. T. 1972. "Plato's *Euthyphro*: An Analysis and Commentary." In *Logic Matters*, 31–44. Oxford: Basil Blackwell.

Gill, C. 1973. "The Death of Socrates." *Classical Quarterly* 23: 25–28.

Gillespie, C. M. 1912. "The Use of *Eidos* and *Idea* in Hippocrates." *Classical Quarterly* 6: 179–203.

Gould, J. 1980. "Law, Custom and Myth: Aspects of the Social Seclusion of Women in Classical Athens." *Journal of Hellenic Studies* 100: 38–59.

Gomperz, T. 1931. *Greek Thinkers*. Vols. 1–4. Translated by G. G. Berry. London: John Murray.

Griffin, J. 1980. *Homer on Life and Death*. Oxford: Clarendon Press.

Griffith, G. T. 1966. "Isegoria in the Assembly at Athens." In *Ancient Society and Institutions: Studies Presented to Victor Ehrenberg*, 115–138. Oxford: Clarendon Press.

Grote, G. 1865. *Plato and the Other Companions of Socrates*. Vols. 1–3. London: John Murray.

————. 1888. *A History of Greece*. Vols. 1–10. London: John Murray.

Grube, G. M. A. 1975. *The Trial and Death of Socrates*. Indianapolis: Hackett.

Guardini, R. 1962. *The Death of Socrates: An Interpretation of the Platonic Dialogues: Euthyphro, Apology, Crito, and Phaedo*. Translated by B. Wrighton. New York: Meridian Books.

Gulley, N. 1968. *The Philosophy of Socrates*. London: Macmillan.

Guthrie, W. K. C. 1955. *The Greeks and Their Gods*. Boston: Beacon Press, 1955.

————. 1968. "Delphic Oracle." In *The Oxford Classical Dictionary*, 261–262. Oxford: Clarendon Press.

————. 1971a. *Socrates*. Cambridge: Cambridge University Press.

———. 1971b. *The Sophists*. Cambridge: Cambridge University Press.

———. 1975. *History of Greek Philosophy*. Vol. 4. Cambridge: Cambridge University Press.

Hackforth, R. 1933. *The Composition of Plato's Apology*. Cambridge: Cambridge University Press.

Hammond, N. G. L. 1959. *A History of Greece*. Oxford: Clarendon Press.

Harrison, A. R. W. 1968. *The Law of Athens*. Vols. 1–2. Oxford: Clarendon Press, 1968–1971.

Henderson, J. 1975. *The Maculate Muse: Obscene Language in Attic Comedy*. New Haven: Yale University Press.

Irwin, T. H. 1977. *Plato's Moral Theory: The Early and Middle Dialogues*. Oxford: Clarendon Press.

———. 1979. *Plato: Gorgias*. Oxford: Clarendon Press.

———. 1986a. "Socrates the Epicurean?" *Illinois Classical Studies* 11: 85–112.

———. 1986b. "Socratic Inquiry and Politics." *Ethics* 96: 400–415.

———. 1986c. "Coercion and Objectivity in Plato's Dialectic." *Revue Internationale de Philosophie* 40: 49–74.

———. 1989. "Socrates and Athenian Democracy." *Philosophy and Public Affairs* 18: 184–205.

Jaeger, W. 1939. *Paideia*. Vols. 1–3. Translated by G. Highet. New York: Oxford University Press, 1939–1944.

Jones, A. H. M. 1960. *Athenian Democracy*. Oxford: Basil Blackwell.

Kahn, C. H. 1981. "Did Plato Write Socratic Dialogues?" *Classical Quarterly* 31: 305–320.

Kerferd, G. B. 1981. *The Sophistic Movement*. Cambridge: Cambridge University Press.

Kierkegaard, S. 1965. *The Concept of Irony: With Constant Reference to Socrates*. Translated by L. M. Capel. Bloomington: Indiana University Press.

Kirk, G. S., Raven, J. E., and Schofield, M. 1983. *The Presocratic Philosophers*. 2d ed. Cambridge: Cambridge University Press.

Knox, B. M. W. 1964. *The Heroic Temper*. Berkeley: The University of California Press.

Kraut, R. 1979. "Two Conceptions of Happiness." *Philosophical Review* 78: 167–197.

———. 1981. "Plato's *Apology* and *Crito*: Two Recent Studies." *Ethics* 91: 651–664.

———. 1983. "Comments on Vlastos." *Oxford Studies in Ancient Philosophy* 1: 59–70.

———. 1984. *Socrates and the State*. Princeton: Princeton University Press.

Krentz, P. 1982. *The Thirty at Athens*. Ithaca: Cornell University Press.

Lacey, A. R. 1971. "Our Knowledge of Socrates." In *The Philosophy of Socrates*, edited by G. Vlastos, 22–49. Garden City, N.Y.: Anchor Books.

Lesher, J. H. 1987. "Socrates' Disavowal of Knowledge." *Journal of the History of Philosophy* 25: 275–288.

Lesser, H. 1980. "Suicide and Self-Murder." *Philosophy* 55: 255–257.

Liddell, G. H., and Scott, R. 1966. *A Greek-English Lexicon*. 9th ed. Oxford: Clarendon Press.

Lloyd-Jones, H. 1971. *The Justice of Zeus*. Berkeley: University of California Press.

Lyons, J. 1963. *Structural Semantics: An Analysis of Part of the Vocabulary of Plato*. Oxford: Basil Blackwell.

MacDowell, D. M. 1962. *Andokides: On the Mysteries*. Oxford: Clarendon Press.

———. 1978. *The Law in Classical Athens*. Ithaca: Cornell University Press.

McPherran, M. L. 1985. "Socratic Piety in the *Euthyphro*." *Journal of the History of Philosophy* 23: 283–309.

———. 1986. "Socrates and the Duty to Philosophize." *Southern Journal of Philosophy* 24: 541–560.

Mansfeld, J. 1980. "The Chronology of Anaxagoras' Athenian Period and the Date of His Trial." *Mnemosyne* 33: 17–95.

Mikalson, J. D. 1983. *Athenian Popular Religion*. Chapel Hill: University of North Carolina Press.

Momigliano, A. 1973a. "Freedom of Speech in Antiquity." In *Dictionary of the History of Ideas*, Vol. 2, edited by P. Wiener, 252–263. New York: Scribner's.

———. 1973b. "Impiety in the Classical World." In *Dictionary of the History of Ideas*, Vol. 2, edited by P. Wiener, 565–566. New York: Scribner's.

Montuori, M. 1981. *Socrates: Physiology of a Myth*. Amsterdam: J. C. Gieben.

Murdoch, I. 1986. *Acastos: Two Platonic Dialogues*. London: Chatto & Windus.

Nagel, T. 1979. "Death." In *Mortal Questions*, 1–10. Cambridge: Cambridge University Press.

Nehamas, A. 1985. "Meno's Paradox and Socrates as a Teacher." *Oxford Studies in Ancient Philosophy* 3: 1–30.

———. 1987. "Socratic Intellectualism." In *Proceedings of the Boston Area Colloquium in Ancient Philosophy*, Vol. 2, edited by J. Cleary, 275–316. Lanham, Md.: University Press of America.

Nilsson, M. P. 1948. *Greek Piety*. Translated by H. J. Rose. Oxford: Clarendon Press.

Nussbaum, M. C. 1980. "Aristophanes and Socrates on Learning Practical Wisdom." *Yale Classical Studies* 26: 43–97.

———. 1986. *The Fragility of Goodness; Luck and Ethics in Greek Tragedy and Philosophy*. Cambridge: Cambridge University Press.

O'Brien, M. J. 1967. *The Socratic Paradoxes and the Greek Mind*. Chapel Hill: University of North Carolina Press.

Parke, H. W. 1961. "Chaerephon's Inquiry about Socrates." *Classical Philology*: 249–250.

———. 1967. *Greek Oracles*. London: Hutchinson.

———. 1977. *Festivals of the Athenians*. Ithaca: Cornell University Press.

———, and Wormell, D. E. W. 1956. *The Delphic Oracle*. Vols. 1–2. Oxford: Basil Blackwell.

Parker, R. 1983. *Miasma*. Oxford: Clarendon Press.

Penner, T. M. I. 1971. "Thought and Desire in Plato." In *Plato: A Collection of Critical Essays*, Vol. 2, edited by G. Vlastos, 96–118. Garden City, N.Y.: Anchor Books.

———. 1973. "The Unity of Virtue." *Philosophical Review* 82: 35–68.

Phillipson, C. 1928. *The Trial of Socrates*. London: Stevens and Sons.

Pincoffs, E. L. 1986. *Quandries and Virtues: Against Reductivism in Ethics*. Lawrence: University Press of Kansas.

Polansky, R. M. 1985. "Professor Vlastos's Analysis of the Elenchus." *Oxford Studies in Ancient Philosophy* 3: 247–259.

Reeve, C. D. C. 1981. "Anaxagorean Panspermism." *Ancient Philosophy* 1: 89–108.

———. 1985. "Socrates Meets Thrasymachus." *Archiv für Geschichte der Philosophie* 67: 246–265.

———. 1988. *Philosopher-Kings: The Argument of Plato's Republic*. Princeton: Princeton University Press.

Rhodes, P. J. 1972. *The Athenian Boule*. Oxford: Clarendon Press.

Riddell, J. 1877. *The Apology of Plato*. Reprint. New York: Arno Press, 1973.

Robinson, R. 1953. *Plato's Earlier Dialectic*. Oxford: Clarendon Press.

Romilly, J. de. 1975. *Magic and Rhetoric in Ancient Greece*. Cambridge, Mass.: Harvard University Press.

Ryle, G. 1966. *Plato's Progress*. Cambridge: Cambridge University Press.

Ste. Croix, G. E. M. de. 1972. *The Origins of the Peloponnesian War*. Ithaca Cornell University Press.

Santas, G. X. 1979. *Socrates: Philosophy in Plato's Early Dialogues*. London: Routledge and Kegan Paul.

Schaerer, R. 1930. *Epistêmê et Technê: étude sur les notions de connaissance et d'art d'Homère a Platon*. Macon: Protat Freurs.

Sharvy, R. 1972. "*Euthyphro* 9d–11b: Analysis and Definition in Plato and Others." *Noûs* 6: 119–137.

Shorey, P. 1933. *What Plato Said*. Chicago: University of Chicago Press.

Stokes, M. C. 1986. *Plato's Socratic Conversations: Drama and Dialectic in Three Dialogues*. Baltimore: Johns Hopkins University Press.

Stone, I. F. 1988. *The Trial of Socrates*. New York: Little, Brown.

Strycker, E. de. 1975. "The Oracle Given to Chaerephon about Socrates." In *Kephalaion: Studies in Greek Philosophy and Its Continuation Offered to Professor C. J. de Vogel*, 39–49. Assen: Van Gorcum.

Tate, J. 1936. "Greek for 'Atheism'." *Classical Review* 50: 3–5.

———. 1937. "More Greek for 'Atheism'." *Classical Review* 51: 3–6.

Taylor, A. E. 1911. *Varia Socratica*. Reprint. New York: Garland, 1987.

———. 1933. *Socrates*. Reprint. New York: Anchor Books, 1952.

———. 1952. *Plato: The Man and His Work*. 6th ed. Reprint. New York: Meridian Books, 1956.

Taylor, C. C. W. 1976. *Plato: Protagoras*. Oxford: Clarendon Press.

Teloh, H. 1986. *Socratic Education in Plato's Early Dialogues*. Notre Dame: University of Notre Dame Press.

Tredennick, H. 1979. *The Last Days of Socrates*. Harmondsworth, England: Penguin Books.

Vlastos, G. 1967. "Was Polus Refuted?" *American Journal of Philology* 88: 454–460.

———. 1971. "The Paradox of Socrates." In *The Philosophy of Socrates*, edited by G. Vlastos, 1–21. Garden City, N.Y.: Anchor Books.

———. 1975. "Ethics and Physics in Democritus." In *Studies in Presocratic Philosophy*, Vol. 2, edited by R. E. Allen and D. J. Furley, 381–408. London: Routledge and Kegan Paul.

———. 1978. "The Virtuous and the Happy." *Times Literary Supplement* 24 February: 230–231.

———. 1983a. "The Historical Socrates and Athenian Democracy." *Political Theory* 11: 495–516.

———. 1983b. "The Socratic Elenchus." *Oxford Studies in Ancient Philosophy* 1: 27–58.

———. 1983c. "Afterthoughts on the Socratic Elenchus." *Oxford Studies in Ancient Philosophy* 1: 71–74.

———. 1984a. "Happiness and Virtue in Socrates' Moral Theory." *Proceedings of the Cambridge Philological Society* NS 30: 181–213.

———. 1984b. "Reasons for Dissidence." *Times Literary Supplement* 24 August: 931–932.

———. 1985. "Socrates' Disavowal of Knowledge." *Philosophical Quarterly* 35: 1–31.

———. 1987a. " 'Separation' in Plato." *Oxford Studies in Ancient Philosophy* 5: 187–196.

———. 1987b. "Socratic Irony." *Classical Quarterly* 37: 79–96.

———. 1988. "Elenchus and Mathematics: A Turning-Point in Plato's Philosophical Development." *American Journal of Philology* 109: 362–396.

———. "The Paradox of Socratic Piety." (Unpublished.)

Vogel, C. J. de. 1955. "The Present State of the Socratic Problem." *Phronesis* 1: 26–35.

Wakefield, J. 1987. "Why Justice and Holiness Are Similar: *Protagoras* 330–331." *Phronesis* 32: 267–276.

West, T. G. 1979. *Plato's Apology of Socrates*. Ithaca: Cornell University Press.

Wood, E. M., and Wood, N. 1978. *Class Ideology and Ancient Political Theory: Socrates, Plato, and Aristotle in Social Context*. New York: Oxford University Press.

Woodhead, A. G. 1967. "*Isēgoria* and the Council of 500." *Historia* 16: 129–140.

Woodruff, P. 1982. *Plato: Hippias Major*. Indianapolis: Hackett.

Woozley, A. D. 1979. *Law and Obedience: The Argument of Plato's Crito*. Chapel Hill: University of North Carolina Press.

Zeller, E. 1885. *Socrates and the Socratic Schools*. Translated by O. J. Reichel. New York: Russell and Russell, 1962.

Zeyl, D. J. 1980. "Socrates and Hedonism: *Protagoras* 351b–358d." *Phronesis* 25: 250–269.

———. 1982. "Socratic Virtue and Happiness." *Archiv für Geschichte der Philosophie* 64: 225–238.

GENERAL INDEX

INDEX LOCORUM

PLATO: DISPUTED OR SPURIOUS WORKS

C. D. C. Reeve, Professor of Philosophy and the Humanities at Reed College, is the author of *Philosopher-Kings: The Argument of Plato's Republic* (Princeton, 1988.)

Socrates in the Apology
by
C. D. C. Reeve
was set in
Bembo
by
Andresen Typographics

Bembo
was cut by
Francesco Griffo
for the Venetian printer
Aldus Manutius
and was first used in
De Aetna
a book by
Cardinal Bembo
in 1495